T0130116

Finish the Journey

A Man's Guide Through Divorce

Joe Florentino

iUniverse, Inc.
New York Bloomington

Finish the Journey
A Man's Guide Through Divorce

iUniverse books may be ordered through booksellers or by contacting:

iUniverse
1663 Liberty Drive
Bloomington, IN 47403
www.iuniverse.com
1-800-Authors (1-800-288-4677)

ISBN: 9781440172045 (sc)
ISBN: 9781440172021 (dj)
ISBN: 9781440172038 (ebk)

Library of Congress Control Number: 2009936529

Printed in the United States of America

iUniverse rev. date: 10/21/2009

To Dr. Dana Fillmore
(San Diego, CA)

Your expertise, guidance and patience is one of the essential reasons
I was able to turn tragedy into triumph.

I can never thank you enough…

"Tomorrow is the most important thing in life. Comes into us at midnight very clean. It's perfect when it arrives and it puts itself in our hands. It hopes we've learned something from yesterday."

—John Wayne, 1981
(You Gotta Love "The Duke!")

"While we'd like to think that time heals all wounds, the fact is time doesn't heal—time passes. Insight heals. We can't get better until we understand what happened."

—Daphne Rose-Kingma, 2000

CONTENTS

Finish the Journey—Introduction

Welcome to Divorce

The day is forever etched into my memory; just as a stone mason chisels letters permanently into a piece of granite. I was awoken that morning by the bright summer sunlight breaking through the mini-blinds of my spare bedroom. The sickening feeling perched in the deepest fathoms of my gut was still with me, just as it had been for over a month. Guess this wasn't a bad dream after all...

It had been about a month since my wife told me she wanted a divorce. We'd been living cordially in separate rooms while I looked for a place. As with most divorces cost was a factor, so I was limited to finding a small place—a divorce crash pad. (is this starting to sound familiar???)

I actually found a decent little place; a small granny-style house located in the backyard of another larger house. It was only a one-bedroom, but had been recently refurbished and was pretty nice inside. That Sunday morning it took me all of two trips in my ex's SUV to move what little things I had:

-My clothes
-A used twin bed with a basic metal frame
-A 19" TV/VCR combo that had been mounted in my garage
-Some cheap dishes from Walmart
-A few little odds-and-ends

I began around 9am and was done by 10:30am. And just my luck, that weekend was a true Southern California August heat wave and my new place didn't have A/C.

My seven-year-old son was excited about our new "Man House," so he stayed with me and wanted to spend the night. I actually enjoyed his company; he kept me from collapsing into a big bumbling mess of useless tears on my new living room floor. By 11:00am, I'd put away my few meager possessions and turned on the TV for my little guy.

We then lay together on my mattress that I'd simply thrown on the living room floor. I was emotionally drained and had zero energy, so I did the bad parenting thing of using my TV as a babysitter.

But then, by about 12-noon, it was 114 degrees inside my new little "Home Sweet Home." My son and I were soaking ourselves in wet towels as we lay on the bare mattress trying to watch a kid movie on video. (I didn't yet have Cable T V)

Continuing to get worse, by 1:00pm it was 117 degrees inside (I'm not exaggerating, it really was), and we just had to get out. We drove to the mall to watch the latest kid movie on the air conditioned big screen. But of course, everything was sold out from the masses of people also trying to escape the apparent "Hole in the Ozone."

Left with no other choice, we went back to our new bachelor pad and slept all night with my one and only fan and some wet towels. My son actually chose to stay with me despite the heat. Again, it was great to have the company of "My Little Buddy…"

I tell this story to begin by sharing just one of my many difficult divorce experiences. As I write this book, I find myself trying to put into words the pain and challenges that divorce has meant for me.

If you're reading this book, it goes without saying that you're looking for answers to a million different questions…

- When's it going to get better?
- When will I stop feeling sick?
- When will I feel like me again?
- Who will I actually be when I'm "the new me?"
- How do I begin to rebuild?
- How do I parent my children as a divorced dad?
- How will I pay my bills?

- Am I financially ruined?

It's a wonder any of us make it through this crazy challenge to our health and sanity. I promise I'll do my best to get you answers to all these questions, and many more.

But the good news; men do make it through and you're not alone. In fact, depending on which expert you quote, as many as 50% of all first marriages in the United States (and nearly 70% of second marriages) end in divorce.

According to "Divorce Rate" (www.divorcerate.org):

First marriage divorce rates:	50%
Second marriage divorce rates:	67%
Third marriage divorce rates:	75%

According to "Enrichment Journal" (http://enrichmentjournal.ag.org/) divorce rates are:

First marriage divorce rates:	41%
Second marriage divorce rates:	60%
Third marriage divorce rates:	73%

"Divorce Rate" further breaks down divorce statistics:

Age	Women	Men
Under 20 years old	27.6%	11.7%
20 to 24 years old	36.6%	38.8%
25 to 29 years old	16.4%	22.3%
30 to 34 years old	8.5%	11.6%
35 to 39 years old	5.1%	6.5%

So whichever statistical data you believe, none dispute the fact that a lot of people get divorced. This means there're millions of guys just like you who made it through to see the light of a better life. Approximately 1,000,000 couples divorce each and every year in the United States. Many of these people have experienced their pain evolve into a far better life than they ever imagined during their unhealthy marriage. The challenge is, how do you get there?

And don't kid yourself, boys, there's no quick fix. I can't say anything that will make this all go away in one fell swoop. Most experts agree that, divorce is generally ranked as the second most stressful event a person can face in their entire lifetime. On average, only the death of one's child or spouse ranks higher than divorce as an emotionally traumatizing event.

I was actually surprised to learn that, not even going to war is rated by the experts at the same stress level as divorce. I've personally spoken about this topic with combat veterans who are also divorced. Although these men certainly echo similar comments about the tragedy of war, they all agree divorce is often much, much worse.

These veterans have generally told me that, in war they had one mission—stay alive and keep their buddies alive. One 27-year-old Iraq War veteran even told me:

> *"In war, when they're shooting at you, you get to shoot back and call in artillery and air strikes. You get to fight back! But when you're getting divorced, you just feel like a one-legged-man in an ass-kicking contest! You can't do anything about it."*

I was shocked to hear these words spoken by a young man who'd seen the very worst of humanity. But now, having lived through my own divorce, I can identify with many of his frustrations.

As far as I can figure (based on my own divorce and extensive research), divorce is so bad because it's the ultimate threat to the very things we hold most dear—our family, our dreams, our finances, our homes, our children's emotional stability, joint family holidays, etc, etc, etc, etc…

Also, one of the most difficult aspects of divorce is that it's a "Zero Score Game." No one wins in a divorce when we approach it as a competition—or even worse, a battle. Divorce is not a competition between you and your ex. Divorce is a solo game of you against yourself. It's truly the farthest you'll ever get from a team sport.

Even though you may have great coaches (meaning supportive friends and family), in the end you're alone in the ring fighting your own demons, your own fears, and your own emotions. Although extensive court battling lies ahead for some of you, divorce is more importantly about the time you spend going toe-to-toe with your own thoughts and feelings.

I hope I can help you find the place where you feel you've won for you, and for you alone. This experience is all about you; how you will improve your life; how you will grow; how you will parent your children better…

It shouldn't matter how she comes out of the divorce, and don't take it personally if she does well afterwards. If you're at all like most men, you'll probably want her to get struck by a falling meteor and vaporize in a slow and painful death.

But trust me; I speak from experience when I say that, this level of hostility will lessen as you gain emotional distance from the relationship. Remember that phrase for later, "Emotional Distance." It will be critical in moving through this process.

Trust me, no one was more hurt by their divorce than me. For months I could have never imagined me ever wishing my ex well. But I eventually did arrive at that place, and today I wish for stability and happiness in her life. (that's not some book writing bullshit. I really do and I'll elaborate later…)

However, in the beginning it would drive me nuts when my mom told me story after story of people who actually ended up friends with their ex-wife and her new boyfriend/husband. I thought, "*Friends, with my ex and some guy she may be with!!! No way! Not now! Not ever!*"

But oddly enough, here I am over a year later with no ill feelings toward my ex and anyone she may ever choose to date. That's her business and hope for the best in her life.

That level of acceptance certainly didn't happen overnight. It took me quite a while to arrive at a place where I'm extremely thankful for my divorce. I'm not saying there's no place for anger. This process has several stages and "anger" is a very important step in the journey. You certainly have the right to stand up for yourself and assert how she wronged you in the relationship.

In fact, understanding what you both did wrong is a critical part of the healing and learning process. I just spent far too many long nights being angry and it truly got me nowhere.

This is one of the main reasons you will find no "ex bashing" in this book. If you were hoping for pages and pages of reasons to hate your ex, you've come to the wrong place. There are many other resources that can help you drive out the demons of your ex through anger and childish rituals.

While researching divorce, I found many-a-book detailing ways to put a "voodoo curse" on your ex. (Don't laugh. I really found shit exactly like that) I even found books on how to conduct "exorcisms" on the memories of your ex. Some books are also filled with chapters on getting revenge and silly rituals like burning your ex's clothes, etc.

I've read so many crazy divorce resources to help steer you, my readers, toward what I believe to be the proper information that will move you toward true emotional freedom and personal success. This book is about serious self-reflection, personal growth, and trying to realistically function and maintain during the dark days of divorce. If you're new in your divorce process, please don't feel pressured to immediately dump all of the anger and hostility. Just know that should be your ultimate goal.

I also want to clearly state that I'm not a physiologist, psychiatrist, or a marriage and family therapist. I relied on people much smarter and better trained than me to develop this book.

I am simply an average guy who became obsessed with learning all I could from my divorce; mainly because I wanted to grow beyond the pain and do things better in the future. As I put what I learned to paper (and began sharing select bits-and-pieces with several divorcing friends) I saw the real need to make this information available for all divorcing men.

And all of these concepts don't just apply to guys who got dumped; divorce can be just as difficult an experience for men initiating the process. I've found most men getting divorced generally fit into one of three categories:

1) <u>The Dumpee:</u>
   These are the guys who obviously don't want the divorce, but their ex is proceeding anyway. Actually, about 75%

of divorces are filed by women. But the most important fact about dumpees is that, just because you're getting dumped shouldn't automatically infer you were happily married. Be careful not to lie to yourself just because she initiated the divorce. If you weren't happy, either, you need to acknowledge that within yourself. Dumpees also have a large tendency to play the victim. Trust me, I was a dumpee. I know this first hand.

2) The Dumper:
Being the person who initiates the divorce has its own set of emotional trials and complications that can be just as debilitating as the other way around. That's because, although you initiated the divorce process, you may not have necessarily wanted it. Maybe your wife had an affair and you just can't forgive the betrayal—you're still devastated and heartbroken. Or, maybe you were simply the one who had the courage to leave a mutually bad situation. No matter what the circumstances, it doesn't necessarily make things much easier just because you were the one who started the divorce. Also, a dumper often feels much more guilt; subsequently causing a lot of men to just say, *"Fuck it! This is all my fault. She can have everything!"* I'm not saying you need to be a dick and fight for everything, just don't be a guy who allows guilt and regret to cause you to damage your life further by walking away with absolutely nothing. Dumpers also must often deal with a lot of people (even their own parents) being really angry at them for ending the marriage. In some ways, I think being a dumper can be a lot more difficult than the other way around.

3) The "I'm Just Worried About the Money" Guys:
If this is you, you can be in serious danger of repeating the same mistakes. My experience shows me that, this category of men often spend very little time learning

> from their failed marriage. They generally feel pretty good emotionally, so they give very little thought to what went wrong and how they can grow. They are tortured by the financial woes of divorce. These men still must stop to ask: *"Why'd I choose that type of woman to marry and how I can do things better next time; what were my contributions to the failure of my marriage?"* If it's mainly the money eating at you, don't forget the little thing called "personal growth" that must come with every divorce. Consider yourself warned. Don't get over confident and think you've got it all figured out just because the primary thing concerning you is the money.

No matter where you fit, mostly everything in this book related to growth should apply. And remember, your ultimate goal in this lengthy and complicated process must be to arrive at a place where you accept the divorce as a positive event in your life. You should want to learn from the experience. To become emotionally, mentally, physically, financially, and even spiritually, better off than you were during your unhealthy marriage.

But tragically, during my divorce, I found very few quality resources available to support "regular guys" during this critical process. Most of the books I saw for men detailed two main ideas: how to protect your financial assets, and how to go out and "screw chicks." Although neither is a bad idea to read about (and I touch on both in this book), I was desperately searching for something written specifically for men detailing the entire divorce experience, from initial separation to the legal finalization.

Most divorce books also have a tendency to be very clinical and dry—something that's not good when you're already emotionally drained and can fall asleep from exhaustion at any moment. Reading pages of sterile (and often belittling) materials are enough to make a man forfeit his quest for answers and support.

Although I did find a lot of self-help literature, if you've ever read self-help books you know they can be a bit "out there." One can only read, "think happy, happy thoughts" so many times before you want to puke or fall asleep. Self-help books can certainly assist in many aspects of your divorce, I'm simply speaking of the shear masses of information that are often difficult to navigate within the confines of the average man's thought process.

I'm not saying men are dumb, because we're not! It's just that we're generally much more simple-minded and straight forward. So, when referring you to self-help resources, I'll do my best to ensure positive materials that we as guys can easily follow.

There's certainly a very spiritual side of divorce, but in the beginning I was simply trying to make it through the day. The benefits from reading self-help literature came after the painful part of my divorce had passed and I began to move beyond hate, anger, and pain—toward true personal growth.

Further complicating things, it's no secret that guys generally don't talk about our emotions—especially in public and especially with other guys. We pretend; we ignore; we put up a front that everything is fine and we're tough enough to handle everything.

But men are emotional, men are sensitive, and men are affected by divorce in ways that are so traumatic to our very heart, mind, and soul. Sorry if I sound like a pussy, but it's true and you know it's true because you're reading this book. (Pussy! Sorry, I couldn't resist)

Divorce changes us, yet we try and rush through it like we do everything else in our busy lives. We attempt to schedule our pain, limit our hurt, and control our emotions. Yet, when we disregard our pain, we generally learn nothing and are often doomed to repeat the same mistakes in future relationships.

Just imagine, fellas, another failed marriage and having to live through this divorce hell all over again. *"Not me,"* you insist? Well tragically, too many men ignore the learning part of divorce to go out and marry the same kind of woman as before; and/or we remain the same jerk we were while married and never take advantage of this opportunity for self-improvement.

For those of you who don't know, one definition of "insanity" is doing the same thing repeatedly and expecting different results. Get the picture? You must grow during this process in order for true success to be part of your future.

Even though I knew the divorce stats (and had many friends and family who'd gone before me), I found very few guys who really wanted to talk about their experiences. Getting a man to open up and share their deepest pains is literally like pulling teeth.

And when I turned to the experts for help I was equally discouraged with the aforementioned self-help mantra, *"Just think happy, happy, happy,"* and it will soon be all better. Well this ain't the fuckin' *Wizard of Oz*, and clicking my heels together saying, *"There's no place like home. There's no place like home,"* didn't bring me back from Over the Rainbow!

In the end, I just longed for a book that spoke directly to men. A book for the average middle class fella who was all messed up about his divorce. But when I couldn't find one, all I could do was to keep telling myself that time would heal my pain as I muddled through life a bumbling blob of emotional goo.

I would have given my left nut to turn off the 24/7 obsessive divorce thoughts running through my head. Not to mention, my four month stomachache that made the flu seem like a small gas pain that I could have simply passed with a brief game of "Pull My Finger" played while sitting in the garage with a good buddy. (What? This is a guy book after all. You're telling me you never played pull my finger—yah right!)

I was bombarded by the emotional guilt about what I'd done wrong. Thoughts of what this divorce would mean to my son brought hysterical bouts of tears to my eyes. And let's not forget the money problems and the worries that came with that. You see fellas, I had it bad. I took my divorce really, really hard.

I guess I was looking for a Cliff Notes version of the things a man will face throughout the journey of divorce. I wanted a book I could keep with me that contained quick reference chapters to almost everything I'd have to confront.

I hope this book will be that guide for you. Something you can refer to when you need a pep-talk; a reminder that things will get better and you're truly not alone. I'd be quite happy if, at the end of your journey through divorce, you were forced to throw away this book because you had referred to it so much it simply fell apart. I hope you'll keep this book in your glove box, your lunch pail, or your brief case, so you can turn to it when you need words of encouragement.

I also pray this book will bring some stability to a relatively unstable time in your life. One of the most frustrating things was the way my emotions would shift from day to day, hour to hour, even minute to minute. One moment I'd be feeling fine (maybe even a little excited about my future), but the very next minute something subtle would send me back into an obsessive bout of anxious depression.

But as we already know, most divorce books and resources are not formatted to fit with the average guy's thought process. It makes sense that the majority of books on any given topic are written by professional authors—with divorce books being no exception. Not to take away from their expertise, but I'm a regular guy who wants clear advice from someone who thinks, talks, and writes just like me; a middle class working schmuck with whom I can relate. But nothing like that was available. (and trust me, I looked)

Another big problem is that divorce also brings a unique physical turmoil to one's body. I have never felt as sick as when I was right in the middle of my divorce. In fact, prior to getting divorced, I never understood how stress could truly prevent a person from eating. (or cause over eating) Well, after not being able to eat a good meal for four months, I quickly understood the power of stress.

On several occasions I remember feeling so bad mentally and physically that, I really wouldn't have cared if I had gotten hit by a bus. Although I never contemplated killing myself, I'd have been fine if fate had ended it all for me. That was just how sick and depressed I felt at my lowest points. There were times it just seemed too much to deal with, and I wanted a plane to fall on me so I wouldn't have to feel anymore pain.

This is why you'll find an entire chapter dealing with your body's physical responses to stress, along with detailed descriptions of mental and emotional problems such as Panic Attacks, Anxiety, Depression, PTSD, etc. I also cover medications that can help, along with finding a good therapist so you can use counseling as a tool for real growth. Yes, I'm going to push you toward therapy, but don't freak out. I'll explain later.

As for the book title, Finish the Journey, it has a special meaning for me. One day, when I was right in the middle of the most painful part of my divorce, I was speaking with my friend's older brother, Carlos.

(who himself had lived through a very painful divorce several years before me)

Carlos is the perfect big brother; he has the ability to put things in the simplest words to clarify almost any issue. Whereas my friends and I will contemplate something for an hour or two and still not have an answer, Carlos throws out a one liner that is so poignant it demands no further discussion.

On this particular day, I was discussing with Carlos the possibility of trying to convince my wife to get back together—to give us another shot.

Carlos then softly replied, *"You can't, you have to finish the journey."*

I asked him to elaborate and he replied, *"You're swimming across a lake and you're halfway to the other side and you want to turn around and go back, but happiness is on the other side. You must finish the journey."*

After those comments our conversation promptly ended with me in amazement at the simplicity of his words.

I also knew this would be the title of my book, Finish the Journey: A Man's Guide Through Divorce. I found no other words that sum up the process of divorce better than those uttered by Big Brother Carlos.

Another very important idea contained in the title is that divorce is "A Journey," and a journey has a beginning and an ending. I can promise you first hand that things will get better; you'll finish this journey and the process of divorce will come to an end.

Unfortunately, I cannot guarantee just how well you'll be doing at the end of your divorce. This is something only you can decide. Each man must take charge of his own post divorce destiny. I know you may not want to hear this while smack dab in the middle of your own personal hell, but it's so true. This is a time for you, about you, and critical for you for the sake of the rest of your life.

I actually wrote much of this book as I experienced the process of my divorce. These are the words of my journey through the most challenging time of my life. Those of you currently in the thick of divorce may, or may not agree, but often (especially in the beginning) I'd have given anything if the "Fairy Fucking Godmother" would have told me I could slide back into my marriage. Even though I was not happy, it was familiar and secure—I knew what to expect.

I now know what battered women must feel. (although to a much greater degree) We have all heard the stories of women who are continuously beaten and battered, yet they stay with the asshole for years. As a police officer, I've personally responded to hundreds of 911 calls made by distraught wives being abused by their husbands.

However, on more than one occasion, the very woman who called for our help has literally jumped on my back as soon as we slapped the cuffs on her man. During one incident, I even had a wife try and pull my gun from the holster, and I had to kick her away from me over a coffee table.

Now of course this is not a book about battered women, but I tell you this for a reason—love and divorce/separation literally make people do things that others in their right mind would view as crazy. The kind of emotional suffering sparked by divorce can drive you mad and tear your guts out.

In the end, it takes an amazing amount of courage to face your divorce. Even when you feel like shit and think you may be going nowhere, it still takes courage. I admire all men who have made it through divorce for having an amazing inner strength that so often goes unnoticed. Divorce has just become so common that, as a society, we long ago forgot the triumph that should come from living through this experience.

In her book, The Courage to be Rich, Suze Orman writes:

> *"It takes courage to live with financial hardship, and, unbelievable as it may seem, it takes courage to be rich. Why? Because choosing wealth as a goal requires facing everything about your money bravely, honestly, with courage—which is a very, very hard thing for most of us to do, but it can be done."*

Divorce is exactly the same way. It took more courage than I ever imagined I could muster to face my divorce honestly and openly—to look in the mirror and admit my faults while embracing my future. And just like the day I moved out, the darkest times of my divorce have become the fire that fuels my new life.

Even now, years later, one of the many painful memories will suddenly enter my mind and I'll sometimes feel a brief reminder of the hurt. But these experiences have become some of the most solid building blocks of my very soul. They're part of what measures me as a man; a testament to strength I never knew I had deep within me.

And you have my word that, each and every story you'll read is true. The names have been changed to protect the privacy of those men brave enough to share their personal stories knowing I was writing this book. Even my own personal stories have been disguised to respect the privacy of my ex-wife. But again, I can't stress enough that nothing in this book is embellished. It's all true with the exception of the names and specific information that could aid in revealing the identity of those involved.

So now, I truly implore you to feel the hurt, live the process, experience the journey, and your divorce may become one of the deepest and most profound periods of growth in your entire life. God knows it was for me…

CHAPTER 1

FACE IT, YOU'RE GONNA BE A BASTARD

You may be wondering why I go on and on about growth in the Introduction, yet I titled the first chapter, "Face it, You're Gonna be a Bastard." That's because the best place to begin real growth is from the very bottom; it's essential to understand your failed marriage from its rawest point. I can't think of anything more honest than to look at yourself and accept that you were probably not Romeo, Prince Charming, or Sir Shrek. (Hey, Shrek may have been a big green Ogre, but he still rescued the princess, right?)

"Face it, You're Gonna be a Bastard" is a chapter title that best captivates the true meaning of owning up and reconciling with yourself. The title also perfectly describes how many people will view you—whether deserving or not.

An apples-and-oranges comparison would be to look at an alcoholic. Alcoholics can't get help until they first admit:

- They drink too much
- Understand the reasons they drank
- And seek to understand what harm they did to others while drinking

I know it's not the best analogy, but I'm confident you'll see point. Before we can do anything else, we must first accept responsibility to gain understanding. We must understand all of the reasons why our marriage failed.

I simply cannot stress enough how failing to take responsibility really damages personal growth. For example, I once interviewed a woman named Erica. She was in her mid-thirties and divorcing after nearly ten years of marriage. Erica only had one child—a three-year-old girl. I spoke with Erica about fourteen months following her separation. Erica was extremely distraught because her ex-husband continued being difficult and confrontational; this constantly extended their divorce proceedings.

About a month before the court date to finalize their divorce, Erica's ex decided he was not going to cooperate with one single aspect of the divorce. He insisted she could only obtain a divorce through "Default." This term is used in California to describe a divorce in which one party wants nothing to do with it, to be a completely inactive part of the process. Erica's ex would not provide any income verification or other necessary documentation. Erica's attorney was forced to subpoena everything—which increased costs and delayed the process.

It was clear Erica's ex didn't want the divorce, but it had been fourteen months. At some point one needs to let go, accept responsibility, and move on. Erica's ex continued blaming her for every single aspect of their failed marriage. Never once did he even suggest he had any culpability in the divorce.

This chapter is the basis of admitting (at least to yourself) your responsibility in the divorce. But "Face it, You're Gonna be a Bastard" is not at all about beating yourself up. Quite the contrary; it's about freeing yourself. It takes a very elevated level of acceptance to understand the reality of your marriage and the mistakes you made, and to then forgive yourself.

This will be the time when you truly begin a period of fundamental emotional separation. If you retain anger and denial, you're still connected to your ex. Separating emotionally is a process that has distinct steps; it doesn't happen from one day to the next. Letting go provides for freedom, but you can't be truly free until you've evolved to a level of total and complete truth.

I'm in no way insinuating that your divorce is completely your fault. There is no need to throw yourself on a grenade because you're a piece of shit and your ex is a saint. I have known many men who took the concept responsibility to the extreme and accepted blame for everything. That's going way too far in the other direction.

For example, I interviewed a guy named Steve who began his divorce with exactly this attitude; Steve blamed himself for every single thing that ever went wrong. It took me and another friend to help Steve see the light.

Steve had been married for about twenty years when his wife caught him cheating. She went off the deep end and allegedly came after him with a knife during an argument just after she found "the evidence." Steve had no choice but to call the cops. He felt so bad that he lost over ten pounds the week following the incident.

In the beginning, everyone was mad at Steve and hated him—her family, their kids, their friends, everyone! Of course, Steve needs to claim some real responsibility since he was the one who cheated; however, he was not the sole reason his marriage collapsed. Even though everyone wanted it to be totally his fault, many things were done on her part that contributed to the culminating events of the affair. And let's not forget the fact that she attacked him with a knife. Maybe that indicates a little instability on her part?

I share this story because it describes how "Face it, You're Gonna be a Bastard" means you must become comfortable with the instability and downright hostility you may get from many people as a result of your divorce. It's a given that your ex may probably have some pretty hostile feelings toward you (maybe even flat out hatred), but there will also be many others.

I must also admit that even though I hate drama, I made the big mistake by causing a lot of my own. I was one of those guys who spent each day fumbling around like a bumbling emotional mess sharing way too much information with far too many people. I would talk about my divorce with anyone and everyone who listened.

I guess it was only natural since it was on my mind 24/7 for over four months. Although talking about your situation with the right people is essential, my experience shows me that talking about it with anyone and everyone (even the homeless dude begging at the corner) is going way too far.

One reason I talked about my divorce with so many people was that I was looking for comfort. In the beginning, I wanted to hear I wasn't such a bad guy. I wanted to feel okay about the divorce. But now I see how I was somewhat of a bastard. I wasn't a peach to be married to, and I did some downright shitty things in my marriage. I was not the dream man I should have been to my wife, and I often made her feel bad and regularly disappointed her.

Now, looking back at the first few months of my divorce, I wish I'd spent more time and energy trying to accept my status as a crappy husband rather than running my mouth with far too many people. In short, I now realize I spent way too much time playing "The Blame Game" with her rather than simply accepting responsibility for my own actions.

But let me clarify; I never beat my ex, I was never unemployed, never made my kid go hungry, never prostituted my ex on the streets of the inner city, etc. I was simply not the best partner to my wife. Of course there're a lot of reasons for this (which I'll detail throughout this book), but the bottom line is it was not all her fault the marriage failed, and I was not the poor victim angel.

In short, I was often a bastard of a husband. Had I just accepted this fact sooner rather than later, it could have saved me a lot of stress. Even though this concept was tough and made my stomach crawl, it was a fact I needed to embrace in order to move toward real growth.

A divorced man named Mitch once told me, *"When I finally begin to accept responsibility, I was able to start understanding why I'd done some of the shitty things in my marriage. I began to look at my ex in a different light and see the cause and effect of things we had both done to each other."*

I'm confident the road to emotional recovery begins with accepting that you're not going to be seen as the same wonderful man she told her friends and family about in the beginning. In fact, you just might end up being a complete son-of-a-bitch. Honestly ask yourself, are you ready for this inevitable fate of your reputation—that you will be viewed in a negative light by more than one person?

For example, let's take the topic of affairs. Quite often I found that if it was the guy who had the affair, he is labeled an insensitive son-of-a-bitch who is just another typical man. All he cares about is being a womanizer, and it's all his fault the marriage is over.

However, if the woman cheated on the man, it's often still his fault because he created a situation that forced her to cheat. He was emotionally unavailable and a workaholic; he didn't help enough around the house; she wanted a man who could take care of her emotionally and he couldn't; etc. Trust me, I've interviewed hundreds of divorced men and women, and this is a very common theme.

So again I stress to you, you're going to be viewed as a bastard by more than one person as a result of your divorce. Maybe your ex is going to hate you, and maybe your former mother-in-law, and what about the nosy neighbors who may side with her? Your entire life is going to change, not everyone will like you, and there is nothing you can do about it.

I actually find it strange that so many men have trouble with the concept of "Face it, You're Gonna be a Bastard." After all, many guys maintain stressful jobs in which they would never survive without being able to confront others with difficult issues on a daily basis. Yet we often come home and cannot exude the same strength within our personal lives.

Another tough aspect will be the splitting up of friends. I've found that it's very rare for a divorced couple to maintain a close relationship with many of the same friends they had before their split. It's inevitable that most friends will eventually gravitate toward one of the divorced parties.

Even if some of your friends want to maintain a relationship with both you and your ex, one or both of you will make it almost impossible for them to do so. History shows that either you or your ex (or both) may inundate your friends with so much bullshit about your divorce that the friends simply pull away from one of you to gravitate toward the other.

Believe it or not, I've actually become very comfortable with being a bastard. As I learned to love myself outside of my former marriage, being a bastard has come to symbolize I have the courage to stand up for myself. I've developed the intestinal fortitude to not settle in any relationship and to be proud of who I am.

Becoming a bastard is also extremely critical to understand before you enter another serious relationship. Based on my research, a major contribution to the failure of many marriages is that men so often don't stand up for themselves. Too many men seem content to just let their wife or girlfriend run their daily lives. Much of this is laziness. Admit it; we men are often great at being lazy and letting our women do everything. You know that's true for a lot of men!

Remember, women are nurturers by their very nature. If shit is not getting done, women often just do it. However, they subsequently (and often justifiably) develop resentment for our lazy asses. On the other hand, women can often be controlling and bossy, and sometimes it's just a lot easier to let them play "mom" rather than for us to put our foot down and stand for what we want. So, no matter what the specific dynamics of your failed relationship, accepting your part in the divorce should lead you to see things you can do better.

As for me, I won't make this mistake in a new relationship. I'm now very comfortable being a bastard when need be. This may sound contradictory, but standing up for myself has actually helped the quality and success of my post-marriage relationships.

You must take the time to really learn who you are and respectfully take a stand from the very beginning of a new relationship. If a new girl leaves because you're being properly assertive, then be thankful because it wasn't meant to be.

Now, if you date 10 or 15 different women and they all leave because you've gone beyond bastard and become a flat out dickhead, you may want to adjust your tactics. But I'm sure you get my point. Also, if you were a lazy guy, like me, recognize it and correct the behavior. "Relationships take effort" is truly one of the most underrated (yet overly used) sayings that ever was.

Another way you can take this bastard thing too far involves your kids. If you have kids, you *cannot* badmouth your ex in front of the little ones. Remember, you're an adult going through this crap, but they're losing their mom and dad as a family. I don't care if your ex is the whore of the century and would win "Best Tramp" at the annual Porn Star Academy Awards, these are your babies and you must not become a bastard around them.

I know this is much easier said than done. A divorced man named Sully once told me, *"I would have loved to sit my four-year-old down and tell her all about her mother! But as bad as she was, that's still her mom..."*

Sully went through a particularly ugly divorce, but I cannot commend him enough for being able to maintain focus while protecting his little girl. Just listen to how stupid it sounds—actually say out loud, *"My four-year-old is gonna hear the truth about her mother!"*

And compounding the issue, what if you're so upset that you simply trash your ex to the kids by saying things that are mostly untrue? This was the case with Alfonso as he explained, *"As time progressed from my relationship, I really saw how my ex was a good person and a great mom, and it was just a bad marriage. Any negative I would have said to my kids would have been untrue, and I would have looked like a real asshole and really hurt my children!"*

Remember, when you're in the middle of divorce, it's just like any other seriously threatening situation—it's almost a given that you'll develop tunnel vision. Maybe you've experienced this phenomenon before. If you're a combat veteran, you know exactly what I mean. During times of severe stress, people can get so engrossed in the threat that they only see what's directly in front of them. Nothing to either side is taken into consideration.

In the case of divorce, your kids often become peripheral issues standing off to the side that you can easily lose sight of. And remember, once you say something to your kids, you can never take it back. Even if you later apologize to your kids and admit you were wrong about what you said, they'll always remember what you said. I've learned kids have amazing memories.

This also goes back to the idea of sharing too much with too many people. Trashing your ex to the kids when you're just rambling with unstable emotions is only going to hurt the little ones—the truly innocent victims of divorce.

I spent many long nights sobbing to friends and family about my ex and how messed up I thought things were in my life. But when it came to my son, I said his mother was the most beautiful woman and I would always love her. I told him we would always be a family, just a different kind of family. Don't gag at the sound of these words. You really need to get there for your kids!

Unfortunately, I'm sure we can all think of kids we know who've been negatively affected by mom and dad acting like complete asses in front of them. You may have even been a product of this yourself when your own parents divorced. I personally admit that keeping my mouth shut around my son was not always an easy thing to do, but I knew it was the one and only off limits area.

If you've been tempted to trash your ex around the kids, I'll touch on strategies for faking it around the children in later chapters. For now, just know this is something that must not be done. If you've already been trashing mom with the kids in earshot, just STOP. Don't make it worse.

Perhaps even sit your kids down (if they're old enough) and explain why you said such mean things about their mother. (and no, you can't tell them the truth: that you're divorcing because their mother is a tramp) If your ex's infidelity is what broke up your marriage, those negative qualities that caused her adulterous behavior will surface soon enough on their own. Basically, if she has bad traits, let your kids figure it out on their own.

It's also understandable (and almost expected) that you must take some time to act like a sissy and mope around with friends and family. But in front of your kids you better show some cool and man-up. As I said, taking care of your kids is the one non-negotiable absolute during a divorce.

Luckily for me, I have only one son and he was seven at the time of our split. He didn't care that we ate fast food for four months. (Actually, he ate it. I felt too much like shit.) He also didn't mind that we lived in a small "Man House" with limited furniture and nothing on the walls. In fact, for a boy, it was like a camping trip. But what did matter was that I took care of his emotions.

My son never really had a hard time with the divorce because his mother and I did what was best for him and always shielded him from our disagreements and tirades of mutually slung insults. Tragically, I recognize many of you don't have it that easy when it comes to your ex saying appropriate things around your kids.

I have about four friends whose ex-wives said horrible things about them to their kids. This kind of behavior is something that truly breaks my heart. As I'll repeat throughout this book, the kids are innocent victims and they must be spared as much as possible.

Each of my four buddies chose restraint as the better part of valor. When their kids were younger (and on through their pre-teen years) each of my friends chose to keep his mouth shut about the ex's derogatory comments to their kids.

In each of these cases, the kids would come over and share with their dads the downright sinful comments their moms had said about them. However, each man continuously replied with something similar to, *"Well, your mom is entitled to her own opinion."*

Quite often, the kids would ask dad why mom would say such mean things while dad had nothing bad to say. These guys simply continued to say something positive about their ex and reaffirm that she's entitled to her own opinion.

Surprisingly, each of these men told me that saying nice things about their ex in spite of the mean comments was actually pretty easy. That's because these men never forgot that their children were deserving of more than immature responses to such ignorant statements.

Of course there were times when things got to my buddies and their human side wanted to take over. For some very brief moments, they all said they'd have loved to fire back when their kids started relaying shitty comments made by the ex. But each of these men restrained himself.

As each of their kids became teenagers and realized what had been occurring for years with their mothers' comments, they became closer to their dads. The time and effort of these men to protect their children paid off in the end.

There's also a very important difference between how a parent responds to "bashing" as opposed to "brainwashing." My experience leads me to believe that most unhealthy divorced parents tend to simply say bad things about their ex in front of the kids—this is what we call bashing.

Things like, *"Your dad is a lazy bastard; He doesn't pay his child support; He's selfish,"* etc. are just a few examples. You can usually counter bashing statements with simple discussion and proper behavior modeling. Actions speak louder than words. Show your kids you're not lazy, that you provide great support, and that you're not selfish, etc.

Things get far more serious, however, if your ex actually attempts to brainwash the kids against you. In Chapter 5, "Going Into Battle; The Ex Wars," I delineate the difference between bashing and brainwashing and provide resources to help. Whether you've already experienced this, or if you even suspect your ex is the slightest bit capable of brainwashing your kids against you in the future, pay extra special attention to this topic.

How your kids fare through the divorce is going to be completely up to you. In most cases I've seen where one parent successfully brainwashed the children against the other, there was almost always something the man could have done to counter the problem and prevent the alienation. Tragically, many men often think they're doing everything right by staying quiet, yet they miss the warning signs and never see it coming.

I challenge you to ask yourself, *"How will I be when it comes to my kids?"* You alone hold the key to this question. And remember, if you screw this one up, your ex may be the one who takes care of your children's emotions.

You could just as easily be the one who is dramatic and says stupid shit in front of your children, and she could be the mature parent doing what's right. In the process of protecting both yourself and your children, you'll almost certainly end up being a bastard in someone's eyes.

In fact, you and your ex may even get along fine, but what about your ex mother-in-law? Any of you have one of those who hate your guts? I've known guys who've actually been friendly and cordial with their ex-wives, but the ex in-laws were flat out assholes. It really sucks when the ex in-laws are the ones saying crappy shit to your kids about you.

Making things even tougher, in-laws and grandparents often think they have certain rights to help raise their grandchildren. Many grandparents feel a downright sense of entitlement. *"I'm older and wiser and I know what's good for my grandkids!"* My response to anyone who thinks that—Piss Bullshit Granny!

If jerky grandparents like this were truly stable and mature adults, they'd be a source of emotional stability for their grandkids. This is especially true if grandma and grandpa are still married and could serve as an example of a healthy long-term relationship for the children.

And let's not ignore that it's quite possible your parents could be the dramatic people while your ex in-laws remain the mature ones who help protect your kids from the divorce. Oh yes. It could just as easily be your mom or dad who says stupid shit about your ex in front of the kids, and you'll be forced to intervene and confront your very own parents. It's absolutely essential that you protect your kids from anyone who would say anything bad about their mother, no matter who they are.

Again, I remind you that you're not going to escape divorce without being a bastard to more than one person. Just accept it. Get comfortable with it. Don't fight it. It's just the way it has to be if you want to take care of your children and yourself.

And here's another thing that drives me crazy—the new girlfriend drama. I've known guys who've had great relationships with their exes and whose kids are doing fine following the divorce. But then some new girlfriend comes along and screws up everything by trying to make the guy feel bad for being friendly with his ex. I'm sure you've seen this at least once in your life.

This may seem simple, but it's not for a lot of guys. Don't get blinded by "new love." Your kids come first. I personally won't date a woman who'd try to put me before her kids, or who'd ask me to put her before my son. It's simple to me; a woman who puts her kids first has her priorities straight. She may not always be able to hang out at a moment's notice; however, this is just the way it has to be when you have kids.

And speaking of dating, there may even be people who get mad at you because they've got a friend they want you to date, but you're not interested. I know every guy has heard at least once, *"Oh, have I got the perfect girl for you! You just have to meet her."* God I hate hearing that line! This exact thing actually happened to me shortly after my divorce.

During my divorce, a family member wanted to set me up with a girl. She was nice and cute, but she just didn't do it for me. So, I never really pursued anything. But then, about five or six months later when I got a new girlfriend on my own, this family member started being cold to me. I knew the reason for her bad mood, but what was I going to do? I couldn't go out with a girl just to please someone else. So, there I was, trying to do what was right for me and getting crap for it.

Here's one final example of "You're Gonna be a Bastard." It comes from Greg. About eight months into Greg's separation/divorce, he began dating a great girl, Pam, who had a three-year-old daughter. Greg himself had a two-year-old girl. Based on our conversations, I honestly believe Greg and Pam did everything right. They took things slow; they didn't introduce their kids for several months to make sure it was a relationship that had serious potential; and they made sure they maintained separate interests and didn't get stupid with new love.

Unfortunately, Pam's only sister-in-law, Barbara, became a total bitch when she learned of their relationship. Barbara insisted that because Pam was also in the process of a divorce, it was way too soon for her to be dating anyone. Barbara demanded that Pam not date until her divorce was final because she was technically still married. Barbara also said Greg and Pam caused serious physiological problems to Pam's young daughter. (even though the little girl loved Greg right away and constantly asked to spend time with him and his daughter)

In short, Barbara became such a downright bitch that she refused any contact with Pam. Making things worst, Barbara's husband was too much of a wimp to put his wife in check—it was obvious she wore the pants. Tragically, Pam lost this part of her family as a result of dating against the wishes of someone else.

Even though Greg and Pam went out of their way to protect their kids and extended families from any new relationship shock, Greg and Pam quickly became "bastards" in Barbara's eyes. I honestly got the feeling Greg would have no problem admitting it if he and Pam had done something wrong with blending their two families.

However, in this case, Greg and Pam put aside their new love (and lust) and strictly followed the advice of respected authors and therapists about the healthiest ways of blending families. So you see, there's just no avoiding it. You'll be a bastard to someone as a result of your divorce.

I certainly can't close this chapter without reminding you how important it is to accept responsibility for your contributions to the failure of your marriage. However, don't get caught up in The Blame Game. I personally spent the first few months of my separation searching for some way to understand what happened, and I was consumed with The Blame Game.

I repeatedly asked myself things like, *"Were we each 50/50 responsible for the failure of our marriage; was it more her than me; was I really the bad guy who screwed it all up?"* The questions flowed through my mind like a gushing water main break.

Once I simply embraced my responsibility in the divorce, a very big burden was lifted from my shoulders and I really began to grow. It may sound contradictory, but the idea of "Face it, You're Gonna be a Bastard" really brought me some much-needed comfort.

So go forth. Be a shiny new bastard. As crazy as it sounds, it just might make you feel better…

CHAPTER 2

PICK YOURSELF UP, YOU BIG BUMBLING IDIOT (THE MAN UP CHAPTER)

For many of you, this will be a very tough chapter to read. I know this because it was very tough to write. In fact, I wasn't even able to write this segment of the book until I was through the hardest part of my divorce and had a clear head. Much of this chapter is actually based on things my close friends and family told me that I really needed to hear—you know, the tough "man up" comments.

And be forewarned; this chapter is not just for the guys who got dumped. All of these concepts are just as applicable if you're the one initiating the divorce as "the dumper." A dumper can just as easily be a "Big Bumbling Idiot." It may just manifest itself in other ways. So no matter whether you're a dumpee or a dumper, open your mind and pay very close attention.

First off, let's define what I mean by the term Big Bumbling Idiot. This is when you're fumbling though life, dwelling on your divorce, and generally not moving forward. The title of this chapter is not to insult you or infer that, by having normal emotions you're a Big Bumbling Idiot.

On the contrary, you'd be hard pressed to find any relationship expert who'd chastise you for having a tough time with divorce. We're all expected to struggle over things like divorce, serious illness, financial troubles, employment issues, etc. But there's a clear difference between the normal grieving process and being a self-destructive Big Bumbling Idiot.

Notice I use the words "self destructive." It's essential you don't damage your life, your reputation, or your dignity by being stupid during your divorce. Grief is part of the process, but there can be no growth without humility.

So ask yourself these questions:

- Am I a Bumbling Idiot?
- Am I healing properly?
- Do I have a plan?

When handled wrong, grief doesn't always lead down the road of healing. I'm sure you've known people who seem trapped within the grief process, as if they've been condemned to remain in the past without the ability and/or motivation to positively embrace the future.

One of the best writings about healthy grieving comes from the author Elisabeth Kubler-Ross in her 1969 book, On Death and Dying. I first learned of this book while taking a college class about ten years prior to my divorce. Never would I have imagined I'd be applying these principles to ease the emotional trauma of my own divorce.

Kubler-Ross writes of grief as a normal process that must be accepted and understood. I learned the tough way that fighting the natural grief process only prolongs emotional suffering. There's just no easy way to speed through the pain of divorce while doing things right.

Consider the following analogy when speaking about proper healing:

> When one receives a long and deep cut, it must be properly cared for. First, the wound must be thoroughly scrubbed clean of bacteria. (that really sucks!) Anyone who's ever had this done knows how excruciatingly painful the cleaning can be. Then, and only then, can the wound be properly sutured and nicely dressed. If you were to skip the cleaning and suturing process and just cover the wound with clean dressings, it may initially look okay from the outside of the nice new bandage. But as time progresses, infection would almost certainly develop, and the injury would begin to seep

> puss and ooze blood. The unhealthy fluids would flow through the dressings and the wound would become much, much worse.

I'm sure you get my drift. You must care for emotional healing the same way you care for a physical injury. The entire healing process cannot be ignored, skipped, or rushed. After all, our minds and our emotions are not much different from our physical bodies—they're essentially one in the same. Therefore, since we must follow certain steps to heal a broken bone, what makes anyone think they can rush emotional healing?

So, let's talk about what must be done to create a healthy grieving and healing process. In her model, Kubler-Ross describes five distinct stages by which people deal with grief and tragedy:

Denial:	"It can't be happening."
Anger:	"Why me? It's not fair."
Bargaining:	"Just let me have one more chance and I know I'll do it right."
Depression:	"I'm so sad, why bother with anything?"
Acceptance:	"It's going to be OK."

It's important to understand that these stages don't always manifest themselves in a predictable order. In fact, you could easily experience any one of these stages in a random order at reoccurring times throughout the grief process.

For example, a guy may be so miserable in his marriage that he experiences acceptance during the first several weeks following his initial separation. He may go about his life relaxed and relieved because the day-to-day fighting is over. The real tragedy of the divorce may not set in for several months, at which time he may finally feel denial, anger, and depression—but again, not necessarily in an organized fashion.

This was a big problem for me. I went crazy because I never knew what emotion I'd be feeling. In one single day, I could go through each and every one of the five stages. Sometimes I'd be so tired from my brain and emotions running on overload, I'd simply sit down on the couch and nearly pass out in the middle of the day.

It's also important to understand these individual stages may not manifest themselves in ways that clinically follow the traditional definitions of each word. For example, take stage #1, denial. When I think of denial, I picture a person who is openly saying, "This is not happening. I can't believe I'm getting divorced."

A divorcing man named Wayne told me:

> *"I never really said anything to myself that denied my divorce. Hell, I knew I was getting divorced. My ex reminded me of it every time we saw each other and she was so happy, happy, happy, and super excited about it. My denial manifested itself in another way; I would pick fights with my ex. Without even recognizing I was in denial, my feelings surfaced by me confronting my ex and forcing her into frequent arguments. Although I may have consciously been trying to see if there was anyway of convincing her to get back together, my subconscious was really in denial."*

Wayne's story demonstrates how divorce is such a unique experience and we must accept it will affect us each in very different ways. It's also important to note that Wayne said he only came to this conclusion after going to therapy and working through his actions and emotions. Again, this is just another example/reminder to think seriously about therapy during your divorce.

It's also critical to think outside the box regarding the term "Bumbling Idiot." For most of us, the very term Bumbling Idiot conjures images of some guy with his shoulders slouched forward and his chin dragging as he stares at the ground in front of his shuffling feet. But being a self-destructive person can manifest itself in so many different ways. Here's an unorthodox example of what I mean.

I once worked with a guy we'll call "Jimmy." Jimmy was a good guy and fun to work with. We all knew he was a bit over opinionated, but then again so are most men, so it wasn't that big of a problem. Anyway, Jimmy was married for a few years when they had their first kid. Child #2 quickly followed about two years later. From the outside looking in, Jimmy seemed like he had the perfect American family.

Things slowly started leaking out that all was not as it seemed. Jimmy began dropping hints that he was having less and less sex, while his wife started telling Jimmy he was becoming an overbearing asshole. But rather than keeping things between him and his wife, Jimmy began sending email after email to all their friends, both male and female.

That's right; Jimmy actually sent emails to other people about his marriage troubles. Jimmy would ramble about how messed up his wife was and how he couldn't understand it. Some of these people began confronting Jimmy's wife about the emails and why she was ruining their marriage. Talk about unhealthy drama!

As you can imagine, this behavior didn't do much in the way of encouraging Jimmy's wife to fall madly back in love with him. Jimmy's antics actually continued for several years while his marriage spiraled downward.

Jimmy also couldn't eat and lost an amazing amount of weight because of stress. His marriage was all he talked about. It got so bad that Jimmy's wife began asking him to leave. She repeatedly told him that she didn't love him and needed a break. However, Jimmy remained adamant it was only a phase. I personally have never heard of a phase lasting several years, but that's beside the point.

Jimmy's bumbling behavior continued escalating until his emails to others became confrontational and he started making accusatory phone calls. Each time Jimmy heard something new about his wife not wanting to be with him (for one reason or another), he'd go on the warpath trying to find out more details. Jimmy never quite understood just how foolish he looked to everyone. I personally had to stop talking to Jimmy because he became such a jerk.

There's so much to Jimmy's story it could consume its own detailed chapter, but I'll stop here. It's just sad that Jimmy never saw what an idiot he'd become. And toward the end, he began trying to blame others for his failed marriage.

A mutual friend once shared one of Jimmy's confrontational emails. An excerpt read:

> *"...I'm working my ass off to keep my family together and it seems like anyone associated with you and (so-and-so) is fucking with me and my family. I don't get it..."*

Jimmy sent that email after his wife confronted him with something negative she had heard about him. Jimmy didn't take it well, so he went on the hunt trying to discover who had said something to his wife. The truth was Jimmy's wife had been getting information from a lot of different people. But by that time, Jimmy had gone off his rocker and was simply tongue lashing at people. He also began snapping at people at work and making some real enemies. More and more people just got tired of Jimmy being a dickhead.

Furthermore, I never once heard Jimmy say anything about what he had done wrong. Everything was about his messed up wife and how she'd lost her mind. Jimmy once complained to me about how his wife had changed over the years of their marriage. He said, *"Man, I just want my 23-year-old wife back."* Wow! What an unhealthy statement.

In the end, Jimmy just made it too difficult for me to maintain a friendship with him. I'm cordial if we run into each other at a mutual social gathering, but it's just better if I keep my distance until he pulls himself together.

Jimmy's situation also brings up another important point. You can't live your life totally stressed out and expect to maintain your cool. It's important to think of stress as being rated on a scale of one to ten. The number one represents no stress at all, as if you were meditating. The number ten represents being so stressed out that you're completely out of control; your emotions have taken over and you're borderline violent. During your divorce, if you operate at a daily stress level of more than five, you're in real danger of snapping in response to relatively simple issues.

I remember another guy I worked with, Chandler, who lived through his entire divorce period (over a year) at about an eight on the stress scale. If anyone looked at him wrong, he'd jump down their throat. Everyone eventually just stopped talking to Chandler, and it really affected his career. Needless to say, he was a real Bumbling Idiot.

Another very common Bumbling Idiot thing I've seen occurs when guys want to "have their cake and eat it, too." These are the guys who "half-ass dump" their wives so they can "have some space," yet they keep their wives straggling along while they go back and forth between home and their girlfriend(s). Here's an example to help clarify.

I was once friends with a guy who was happily married for many years. Let's call him Sam. As Sam approached his mid-thirties, he began telling people how he was *"getting confused."* Sam and I talked a lot about how he struggled with his job and his family life because he just wasn't happy, yet he claimed to not know why. (Hell, that sounds like just about every guy I've met in their mid-thirties…)

Sam would praise his wife as a good woman who was clearly faithful and took great care of him. Yet Sam would constantly mumble about not being able to remain faithful. It was as if he acted like a scared and confused victim so he could have an excuse for his lack of responsibility. Sam used to go on and on about how he knew admittedly that he was *"fucked up"* and needed to get his shit together, yet he never went to therapy or did anything to help himself grow.

Sam used to tell me, *"I'm just not ready to go to therapy. I'm not ready to deal with my issues yet."* Now that's some immature crap—to know you have issues but to refuse to seek the help and guidance to resolve them and grow.

Sam continued with this behavior for several years. Sam and his wife struggled through continuous cycles of him moving in and out of the family home for several months at a time. Everyone knew Sam had many girlfriends, yet his wife still waited for him. Each time Sam left, his wife endured her own turmoil and hoped that someday he'd get his shit together.

Sam's young son would also act out and have problems each time Sam moved in or out. I lost contact with Sam and his wife some time ago. But, as far as I knew, they were still dealing with his back and forth crap.

Many of you have personally experienced how separations and divorces are not always simple and definitive. Couples often do that back and forth thing for years before finally divorcing. Although I'm not a big fan of the back and forth cycles, I'm more concerned with how you handle things.

Are you acting like a Bumbling Idiot as you force this process upon your wife and family? Remember, there's no dishonor in having problems. The shame comes from handling things improperly and acting like a stupid moron during the process.

If you're not sure whether you're being a Bumbling Idiot, I recommend taking a good, hard look at yourself. Don't be afraid to do regular self-assessments. Pretend you're not you; pretend you're one of your friends looking at you from the outside. What would your trusted friends say about how you're handling things?

But, on the other hand, I must once again strongly caution you to be very careful about the people you lean on and ask for advice. This was personally one of my biggest problems and can be summed up in the very old saying, "Misery loves company." When you're going through a serious personal tragedy, people who "just really want to help" often seem to come out of the woodwork.

You must really examine any newfound rescuers and question their motives. Are they helping you because they really want to see you get better, or are they suffering emotionally themselves but too scared and/ or weak to address their own issues? Remember, a true friend who really wants you to heal does not always tell you what you want to hear. A good friend will push you to get better, even if it hurts.

For example, I once knew a divorced woman, Jessie, who mostly dated either married men (I'm not kidding), or guys who were just out of a relationship/marriage. It seemed very strange as I observed her behavior for many years.

It was obvious Jessie was a good person, but she was plagued by a whole host of her own relationship issues preventing her from dating men that were emotionally healthy. Jessie would spend hours with these men listening to their problems and holding their hand—becoming a true crutch for them to lean on.

I'm only speculating, but it seems that by dating men more screwed up than her, Jessie never had to address her own emotional baggage. Jessie would often become somewhat serious with these men. But things always fizzled as the guys grew beyond there own pain. They no longer needed Jessie as they got better.

If you're experiencing severe emotional trauma over a divorce, it's very easy to remain around people who will coddle and baby you rather than pushing you through the proper healing process. We all know people who need to be the savior, who must come to everyone's rescue. They love to play the healer, the mentor, and the amateur shrink. Although this type of support can provide a temporary form of relief, I'm a firm believer it's a true "Band-Aid approach" to treating the wounds of divorce.

Here's another analogy. (those of you who are parents can really relate to this) When your kids don't want to do something because they're scared, you love and support their right of hesitation. But at some point you must take off the training wheels, remove the arm floaties, make them confront the bully, and force them to sleep in their own room despite "The Closet Monster."

You may remember the cartoon with the baby vulture who didn't want to fly from the nest. (it was one of my favorites) The momma vulture had an Italian accent and would say to her son, *"Now-a jou go out and-a jou get-a me a rabbit!"*

The young vulture would always reply, *"Nope! Nope! I'm not gonna do it ma! Nope! Nope!"* But the momma would simply kick his ass right out of the nest and force him to fly.

It's exactly the same thing when we talk about the supportive process for emotional trauma. We need friends and family that can be our momma vulture and kick us out from the nest of emotional coddling. Unfortunately, it's often very tough to find friends who know exactly when to push.

I remember one morning I called my childhood best friend, Justin, spewed my daily sea of whining bullshit about my sad state of affairs. Until this point, Justin always listened and coddled me as one would expect from a good friend, but that was not the case on this particular morning. Using a harsh and abrupt tone, Justin quickly replied, *"Dude, I just can't help you anymore. It's time you man up and move on! I'm super busy. I gotta go."* He then abruptly hung up the phone.

I got off the phone thinking, *"What a dick!"* I was in the middle of the biggest emotional crisis of my life, and my best friend since childhood just blew me off. So what did I do? I quickly called one of the other people on the self-created "Joey Support Network" and complained about Justin. How dare he say something so harsh to me in my time of need!

Well, can you guess the response I got from this second friend? (who just happened to be female) Yup, you're right, she said she was sorry, but Justin was right and there was not much else my friends could do for me.

My stomach dropped! I was overcome by two emotions. First, I immediately felt like the world's biggest pussy! Up until then, I was a self-created victim. But now I felt embarrassed that I'd forced two of my closest friends to tell me what a wimp I'd become. After all, I'd always felt like a tough guy. I'm a cop and had spent five years on a SWAT team; I was no pussy! But guess what? I'd become one big, fat pussy and a real "Bumbling Idiot!"

Secondly, I got really scared because that was the first moment I felt really alone. At the time, I was about four months into my separation. Up until that point, I had people coddling me almost daily. But this was the first time I truly felt the pressure that I was essentially alone—that no one else could complete my journey for me.

I tell you this story because maybe you've built up your very own support network of friends/family who will tell you what you want to hear, not what you need to hear. Just know a time should come when you must "man up," start living your life, and move forward.

Here's another way to look at the emotional support network provided by friends. Think of a person who suffered a major knee injury. He/she goes through surgeries and various levels of physical therapy. However, at some point the person must stand alone and fight the pain. The knee will never heal properly without working through the pain and pushing the injury to heal "properly."

Proper grieving is by no means being a "Bumbling Idiot." Live your divorce, feel the pain, experience the growth, spoon with the cat, watch sappy Lifetime chick movies, cry in your car when you're alone, etc, etc, etc… Just remember, when your divorce is over, you'll eventually return to your right mind and have to answer to yourself and others if you completely got lost during your divorce.

Divorce Author Mel Krantzler writes, *"Freedom means taking personal responsibility for one's own behavior, which is the difficult but necessary demand that divorce imposes on every man or woman who separates from a spouse."*

I can think of no better words to close the topic of "Pick Yourself Up, You Big Bumbling Idiot."

CHAPTER 3

FAKE IT 'TIL YOU MAKE IT

Since the beginning of your divorce, I'm sure you've heard family and friends repeatedly say things like, "There's a much better life awaiting you," and, "You just have to let time heal and you'll get there."

Hearing a certain amount of encouraging words is crucial during your divorce, but I often found many of these limited gestures to be superficial and somewhat belittling. I remember thinking, *"No shit it'll get better someday, but what about right now? I feel like I'm gonna puke out a lung. I'm not worried about the future; I'm just trying to make it through today! Just today! Right now I'm simply worried about the next eight hours."*

I was longing for the right advice to carry me from one moment to the next, to just make it through until tomorrow, to actually sleep through the night without waking up in a cold sweat and short of breath at 2:00 a.m. while starting to cry. The stress, the worry, the stomachaches, and the headaches all took a heavy toll on every aspect of my life. I searched high-and-low for something to help me live through the daily process of divorce, but I always came up empty handed.

In her book Coming Apart: Why Relationships End and How to Live Through the End of Yours, Daphine Rose Kingma writes:

> *"Ending a relationship is so painful and makes us feel so awful—bad, hopeless, inadequate, desperate, lost, lonely and worthless—that most of us are afraid we won't live through it. We feel bad about what our families will think, we're afraid of what the neighbors will think, we feel*

> *terrible about our children, we worry about leaving our houses, and we're anxious about our financial futures. But worst of all, we feel badly about ourselves. Not only are we losing context, history, and the familiar choreographies of our lives, but we are also losing a sense of who we really are and we get shaken to the core about our own self worth."*

Living day-to-day through divorce truly tests the fabric of your very soul. "Fake it 'Til You Make it" reflects a mindset and strategy I hope you'll be able to develop. There should be a method to existing through the dark days of divorce, and it often means playing a little make-believe with yourself. You'll need to create a system by which you protect your mind, body, and soul from excessive suffering. You still need to live through the process of divorce, but you don't need to experience unreasonable trauma.

Kingma also writes:

> *"We all seem to be the experts at falling in love. We even have a number of commonly agreed upon rituals for courting. But we don't know much about what goes on inside of a relationship, and we know even less about how to end one. Survivors of ended relationships haven't left us much of a trail as to how they made it through this painful rite of passage. We know that there are some survivors, that hardly anyone dies or ends up in an insane asylum because of having ended a relationship. Indeed, among the 'survivors,' we know many examples of transformed men and women, people who are happier after their break-ups and divorces. But we don't know how they made it through the terrible experience."*

Here's an analogy. We all know it's great to save money for a rainy day and to invest for retirement. But you must first live for today (pay for your house, food, car, clothing, etc) in order to survive to retirement. Divorce is the very same way.

You can't just spend all your time learning and planning for the future while ignoring the present. And unfortunately, 99.999...% of us aren't Hollywood movie stars able to live in seclusion while feeding off the millions made from our last box office blockbuster. We still have to go to work, take care of the kids, mow the lawn, clean the house, fix the leaky roof, repair the car, etc.

But please don't misunderstand me. "Fake it 'Til You Make it" is in no way inferring you should just "play happy" and ignore the severity of your divorce. I certainly don't want you shaving your head, buying a pair of leather sandals, and becoming a Buddhist monk just so you can ponder the meaning of the cosmos while relaxing all day in metaphysical bliss. My goal in this chapter is to hopefully make your divorce just a little less painful of an experience.

So how does one "fake it?" How do you hide the pain from your kids, your boss, your co-workers, and the entire world? A close friend, James, said something to me during my divorce that really hit hard. I was right in the middle of another worrisome day filled with obsessive thoughts about how shitty my life was because of my divorce. James challenged me by saying, *"You'll eventually feel better and move past your marriage, but I don't want you to be left with nothing because you fucked up every other aspect of your life along the way."*

James was referring to my job, my relationships with family and friends, and my relationship with my son. His comments were a true wake up call that helped me see how bad I'd become. (Remember the last chapter about being a Bumbling Idiot?)

James stressed the importance of managing my everyday life better. If not, I may eventually be happily divorced but possibly unemployed with few friends and a son who'd always remember what a pussy I was. James made some great points, and it became painfully clear I needed to learn to "Fake it 'Til I Make it!"

This discussion also prompted me to take note of the good things I had going for me at that very moment. For the first time since my separation, I thought about what I stood to lose. After all, I had a great son with whom I enjoyed an awesome relationship, I had a good job and some great friends and family who were really supportive, and I was still relatively young. (in my early thirties) In short, my conversation with James momentarily smacked me out of my over-analyzing depressive funk.

James' comments also got me a little scared. I really didn't want to lose my job or have my kid live with memories of seeing his dad as a big sobbing mess. I wanted to do things better. For the first time in several months, I felt a momentary boost of energy and motivation.

Later that night, I did something I never thought I'd do—I made a list. I know, I know, most guys hate doing shit like making lists. But it actually helped me a lot, and this is where I hope you'll begin your process of faking it. Just follow me for a minute with an open mind…

I sat down with a single piece of paper and made three columns.

The Good Things Now	What I Want in the Future	Why I'm Getting Divorced

Under column #1, "The Good Things Now," I listed all the good things I had going for me at that time. Surprisingly, I was able to list quite a few things. I say surprisingly because, up to that point, I'd been obsessing over the bad things associated with my divorce. I was playing the victim and feeling sorry for myself. Remember, I was a dumpee, and playing the victim is very common for us.

In column #2, "What I Want in the Future," I listed all the things I was looking forward to. This really gave me a lot of hope. The excitement continued to grow as I fantasized about my future dreams. I momentarily forgot about my immediate reality. I indulged myself in a bit of happy thoughts and it felt great. Column #3, "Why I'm Getting Divorced," was great to look at when I got lost from reality, like when I had unreasonable thoughts about wanting to try to convince my ex to reconcile.

I religiously carried this piece of paper in my pocket everyday. I looked at it over and over. It became a constant reminder of my reality. It actually became a pretty good friend, too. I know it also gave my friends and family a nice break from my constant phone calls when I needed to be cheered up. Rather than dialing a friend, I'd often refer to my list for the momentary boost I needed.

This also added momentum to my growing personal pride. I was increasingly handling my emotions on my own. I was taking care of business without always whining to others. Amazing how something so simple can make such a big contribution to growth.

I looked at my list so much that, about a month later, it was practically falling apart. So, I just sat down and made a new list. However, I didn't simply recopy the first list verbatim. My second list was completed based on my evolving emotions and where I stood a month after making the first. I repeated this ritual of re-creating a new list about every four to six weeks, for a total of about six months.

With each new rendition, Column #1 (the good things) was growing longer, while Column #2 (my future hopes) was getting shorter. That was because, as I progressed further into my divorce, I began living the life I had wished for when my divorce first started.

By about the third re-write, I was also able to completely drop column #3. (why I'm getting divorced) I simply no longer needed the reminder. My thought process had evolved to a place where stupid and unhealthy thoughts about my ex had faded away. This was actually a really cool moment!

I still have each of these lists, and I refer to them occasionally. It's great to see how my life has changed and to remember where I've been and how far I've come.

Divorce is a series of relatively small successes and simple milestones. If you don't pay close attention to these little moments, they just might pass you by and you'll miss the opportunity to recognize important points of excitement and triumph.

I know many of you may be thinking, "Joey, you son-of-a-bitch! I thought I was gonna get through this divorce shit without doing any crap like making lists and meditating!" Hey, I'm simply offering suggestions. It's completely your choice how you handle things. I'm just sharing what worked (and didn't work) for me.

And don't worry, I'll never ask you to do anything too weird, like meditate. Don't laugh, but I actually tried that shit once. I even took a Yoga class, too. (Hey, stop laughing, there were A LOT of hot chicks at Yoga) Both the meditation class and the Yoga session were an hour each.

Well, I only lasted about seven minutes in the meditation class, and a whopping nine minutes in Yoga. I'm just way too ADD (Attention Deficit Disorder) to meditate. But don't take my word for it. I recommend trying everything for yourself. Just because I'm a real man doesn't mean your girly ass won't like sissy stuff like meditation and Yoga. (Ha! Just kidding!)

But in all seriousness, one of the most debilitating problems with divorce is the constant lack of mental and emotional clarity. I never knew from moment-to-moment which emotion was going to kick me in the balls next. The roller coaster of emotions was literally enough to often make me feel like I was going nuts.

But my lists were always there when I needed a clear reminder of what was important. Now these lists in no way ever took away all of the pain. Instead, my lists offered just the right amount of help during the really tough moments.

I consider these lists to be my light at the end of the dark tunnel of divorce. In the very beginning of my divorce, I couldn't even see the light. I knew deep down that my life would someday get better, but I was stumbling through the pitch black tunnel and couldn't see a single glimmer of hope. When I read my lists during the really dark times, they became that beacon of faint light calling me to continue in the right direction.

And if making lists is seriously just not your thing, that's really quite alright. I just strongly advise you to develop some type of ritual that helps you maintain some focus about the good things you still have, and what you stand to loose, if you go off the deep end. Just make sure whatever you develop helps you track those small divorce milestones, too.

Reviewing my lists often gave me that little jolt of energy I needed to drag myself out of the house. One of the worst things you can do during your divorce is to become a hermit. Of course there're definitely times for a night home alone and/or a sick day from work with old movies and some rum and Coke. (in moderation, of course) But this should by no means become your norm.

And trust me, getting out was actually really difficult for me. Because I'm not a big fan of bars, I had to think about what I would want to do if I were happy. I'm not kidding. I really asked myself, "If I weren't so fucked up emotionally, what would I feel like doing?" I know it's playing word games, but it worked for me.

During the first few months of my divorce, if I had a weekend day free without my son I would literally have physical anxiety trying to think of what I wanted to do—especially since my body was screaming that all it wanted to do was sleep!

So, I just played a word game. Rather than asking "What do I want to do this Saturday?" I asked myself, "What would I like to do if my divorce was over and I was in a healthy place emotionally?" Well shoot, then it became really easy. I was able to write down about 15 different things I'd like to do if I felt good. All I had to do was play a little mind game with myself and I instantly had my answer. It sounds strange that something so simple worked, but it did.

I remember one of the things I wrote down was that I wanted to try taking a rowing class. I've always enjoyed the outdoors (camping, hiking, dirt bike riding, kayaking, etc.), and most of the things on my list had to do with this kind of stuff. One Saturday morning I signed up for a beginners rowing class.

I had to wake up at "O-Dark-Thirty" to make it to the class by 6:00 a.m. On a side note, I never understood why outdoor people need to do everything so early in the morning. It drives me nuts. But anyway, on with the story…

The night before, I just knew I'd want to puss out in the morning and not get out of bed. To help, I made sure I set several alarms and psyched myself up for the morning. I think I may have even slept in my clothes. Although it was literally all I could do to drag myself out of bed, I made it after hitting the snooze bar about a zillion times.

It was a really sunny and crisp October morning in San Diego, and I arrived feeling like I was going to throw up. (in fact, I may have actually puked. I can't remember for sure) But I am sure I remember running to the bathroom a few minutes before start time because I felt an onset of that nervous kind of bad diarrhea. (don't worry, I'll spare you the details)

I remember being really out of it as the instructor began explaining the boats and how to paddle them. It was just like reading a book but realizing after a few pages that you didn't process anything you just read; your eyes were simply scanning the words but the content never made it to your brain. Has this ever happened to you?

That's exactly what I felt like as I watched the instructor talk about paddling the boats. I just stood there with my mind going a mile-a-minute about how shitty I felt—both emotionally and physically. I didn't process a single word he said.

After about 45 minutes of this guy rambling about something related to paddling the boat in unison as a group, we put the thing in the water. It was a 10-person boat inside of which we sat in single file. On a cool side note, there were actually two cute chicks in the group. Although I was way too screwed up to even talk with them, they were still nice to look at.

We began paddling and it was actually kind of fun. Everyone soon started laughing as our paddles continuously hit each other. We were all beginners and couldn't keep the same stroke. Each of us became the victim of some unintentional splashing as our paddles hit the water out of sequence in a true unorganized fashion.

We paddled for about two hours, and toward the end I actually relaxed somewhat. I still felt like puking, just not as bad. (remember to savor the little moments) When we finished and were packing up, I actually got the feeling I could have engaged the two cute chicks in further conversation and maybe even got their numbers. Although in the end I was too much of a chicken to do it, it was still a great little ego boost to complete a fun morning.

Of course this experience didn't by any means end the pain of my divorce, but it did give me a brief sense of relief. I remember taking some time after that to drive along the coast, grab a cup of coffee, and feel a momentary break from my despair.

The rowing class was just one of the things I wrote on my list. Being able to cross it off gave me a silly (but real) sense of accomplishment. Even though it meant nothing in the grand scheme of the world, it did mean something to me.

Another thing that helped me was finding a few places my son and I could just "pop in" without notice and even spend the night. My mom's, my sister's, my aunt's, and a few other places all became accepted locations where we could stop by and make ourselves at home.

This was actually pretty cool because my son had a lot of fun and it kept me out of my tiny little divorce house. For several months, I simply kept an overnight bag in my car with enough clothes and toiletries for me and my son. We'd just make a few calls and head to one of our random "crash pads."

I remember this also really helping my son more than I could have ever imagined. Although it was okay with him when we stayed home together, he had the energy of a seven-year-old while I felt like a burned-out light bulb. He wanted to jump on the furniture, and I wanted to play "The Bear Game." You know the game; where you lay down and ooze into a year-long hibernation. By spending time at my mom's, my aunt's, my sister's, etc, there were always things for him to do and kids to play with. It also allowed me to drift into my usual mental fog without having to worry about my son.

He thought it was cool because we coined ourselves "The Party Crashing Bachelors." I'd pick up my boy and the first thing he'd excitedly say was, *"Where we going tonight, Dad?"* I actually think this was one of the main reasons my son made it through the divorce with so few problems. I was able to keep his little mind so busy and entertained that he simply had way too much fun to worry about mom and dad's problems.

It also gave me peace of mind to know I was helping to protect him from the divorce process. As I mentioned, one of my biggest problems was the emotional guilt I felt over letting my son down and forcing him to deal with a broken home. By working hard to ensure he stayed busy, it took a lot of pressure off me.

I remember one night, just several weeks after my split, my son and I joined a buddy and his son for a "daddy/son night." My friend was also in the beginning of a separation, and his boy was just a year older than my son. The kids thought it was a blast that we were having "guy time."

We went to a Mexican restaurant, had a bite (and some BIG margaritas), and then went "Cosmic Bowling." It felt good to get out, have a few drinks, and hang out with my buddy and the kids. My friend also knew I was more messed up at that point than he was, so he drove so I could get, well, more messed up.

By the time we got to the bowling alley, the boys were bouncing off the walls with excitement. I enjoyed the bowling, but about 30 minutes into it I began to feel really depressed. (Remember what I said about emotions changing at the drop of a hat!) I could barely keep from crying right in front of my son.

But the good news is, I was quickly able to improvise and turn the situation around while continuing to protect my son. I told my boy he could bowl my turns because he was having so much fun. With the biggest smile on his face, he gave me a huge hug and said, *"Thanks Dad! You're the best!"*

I was then free to wander a few lanes away as my crying faucets began flowing—which of course I didn't want my son to see. And even though I felt like shit, it was a relief to know that I took care of my son that night. I ensured he was protected, which in turn allowed me to feel good about something on a night when I would have otherwise been spooning with the cat while lying in bed pissing myself. (Okay, so I never pissed myself, but on with the lesson…)

Now don't laugh, but my son and I also became "Resort Pool Crashers." This is actually something I used to do with my friends when we were teenagers. We'd scrounge just enough gas money to make it downtown in my buddy's junk car. We'd then sneak into one of the various resorts and spend the entire day swimming in their lavish pools. I know it's against the law, but we were kids with not a lot of money. At least were weren't taking drugs and stealing cars!

And don't tell anyone, but during my divorce I introduced "Pool Crashing" to my son and he loved it! We'd grab our swimsuits, park a block away from a nice downtown resort, and walk in the back gate and mingle with the guests around the pool. He thought it was the greatest thing to swim in such extravagance.

Obviously, my divorce budget didn't allow for us to actually stay at one of these hotels, nor did we have a pool at home. But pool crashing was one of the most fun things we did during my divorce.

On a side note, when I later began dating, I even took a chick pool crashing a few times. It felt just like being crazy teenagers all over again—it was a blast!

Another time, my son and I went to a really cool outdoor movie theater. My sister was a hair dresser at a high-end salon in a ritzy part of town. The owner of the place was a great guy. I would stop by to visit my sister (and see all the hot chicks who worked there and came for their $200 haircuts—whatever!) and I got to know the guy pretty well.

As a hobby and side-business, the owner built an unbelievable outdoor movie theater directly next to the salon. I kid you not; this was a real honest to God movie theater that seated about 50 people. It had a huge screen and stage surrounded by amazing metal framing, decorative lighting, bubble machines, fountains, thick foliage, a VIP box, a snack bar, and a bunch of other cool stuff. But the best part was the seating. He had installed these amazing reclining "anti-gravity chairs."

The guy ran a movie season from mid-spring to mid-fall. He would show the same old movie four nights a week and then switch to another movie the following week. I took my son to watch *The Princess Bride*. The little guy was blown away by watching a movie outdoors in a recliner while wrapped in a warm blanket and looking up at the stars.

So again, think outside the box when it comes to getting out while you're "faking it" during the tough times of your divorce. If you pick the right activities with your kids and friends, you'll be able to zone out as necessary.

I can't tell you how many times my son and I would be on a bike ride along the beach boardwalk. He'd be laughing and peddling his ass off while I just cruised in a fog of reality. It got me out while taking care of my son. (two birds with one stone)

However, I strongly caution you to not become one of these dads who think they can simply buy their kids. Kids are so smart nowadays, and most see right through that shit. Here's an example.

My sister is divorced and she has two boys. When one of the boys was about five years old, he went on a typical weekend away at his dad's. As usual, my nephew came home with several new toys—clearly his dad's attempt to compensate for only seeing his son every other weekend. My sister was talking to my nephew about the weekend at his dad's when he suddenly blurted out, *"I like going to daddy's because he buys me stuff, but then I like it better when I get to come home."*

Kids need love, attention, and the commitment of your personal time. Fortunately for those of us in the divorce poor house, all of these things don't cost a dime. And even if you do have money, take your kids to the beach, the lake, a river, the park, on a hike, to an aquarium, etc. Those of you parents should know exactly what I'm saying.

If you've been trying to buy your kids, I can almost guarantee they're on to you. Of course this doesn't mean you should never get your kids a gift. Just take a good look at the balance between material possessions and true commitment and parental caring.

Writing this book was also a big help because it allowed me to gauge my progress. When I decided early in my separation to write much of this book as I actually lived my divorce, compiling accurate daily records of my emotions, thoughts, and experiences became essential.

But there were plenty of days I just couldn't write because I was so out of it. When that happened, I'd simply play catch-up a few days later when I felt better mentally. I can't stress enough that your journey through divorce is not some regimented military campaign. Have goals and make lists, but take each day as it comes and roll with the punches.

I specifically recall that my notes for this book, along with my aforementioned lists, really came to my rescue on about four different nights during the toughest part of separation. These were times when I was literally having a physical panic attack and feeling like my life was out of control.

Each time, I was able to review my ever increasing pages of notes and lists and see my progress. Although these were still the epitome of shitty nights, my notes always helped as a major source of comfort.

And this doesn't need to be some elaborate diary like a chick would keep. You don't need to spend a whole day hunting through every bookstore in town to find just the right Hello Kitty Diary with the pretty pink embossed gold line pages. It can be as easy as writing notes on your favorite Snap-on shop calendar hanging in the garage. (You know, with pictures of the hot girls you'll never get to date. Sorry, I couldn't resist, again…) Remember, this is your journey, and I can't encourage you enough to truly customize it as much as possible.

Divorce is in no way a fast process, especially if you're going to do it right. I know I keep repeating myself, but this is truly the central concept around existing through the dark days of divorce. I can't stress enough how divorce is a long compilation of small milestones that are so minuscule they're often overlooked. (especially in your deteriorated mental, physical and emotional state) By maintaining notes, it can really help when you're wondering, "Am I getting any better?" You must develop some kind of personalized system that works for you.

I even knew a guy who cleaned his car religiously almost every day during his divorce. As weird as it sounds, he said cleaning his car relaxed him. It's certainly not the norm, but it worked for him. So please think outside the box. Maybe you have a strange ritual that will help you through. If you do, go for it.

In the end, I found faking it really came down to one simple concept—fighting the routine of negativity. It's perfectly fine if you need to sleep more than normal or you need to take some sick days and simply pass out alone. God knows I burned a few sick days lying around as a blob of useless shit glued to the couch watching the same movie over and over.

Don't laugh, but on my worst divorce days I would start a DVD that I'd seen a hundred times and then plop back down on the couch or in bed. The next thing I knew, I'd be awakened by the credits, realizing I'd literally dozed throughout the entire two hours. Then I'd simply restart the movie and do it all over again. I guess I found the background noise of a familiar movie very comforting. Hey, whatever it takes, right?

I still can't believe how tired I was throughout the entire process. If I could have slept 15 hours a day, it still wouldn't have been enough. There were even times I thought I was sleeping too much, so I tried cutting back to six or seven hours, but it just didn't matter. I felt like a brick shit-house every minute of every day until about the four month mark.

I also know one of the reasons I was so tired all the time was because of my crazy imagination. Throughout the emotional ups and downs of divorce, my out of control imagination caused me more trouble and pain than anything else. I was the master at telling myself stories about so many different aspects of my life.

As I interviewed more men about their divorce experiences, I began to see how a "runaway imagination" can be such a problem for so many men. It seems a lot guys tell themselves stories. We then let those stories (mostly negative ones) begin to destroy us from the inside out. But fortunately, controlling one's imagination is something each guy can do to quickly bring relief and begin heading toward emotional recovery.

If you're a dumpee, you're probably being bombarded with constant images of your ex living the good life while you're stuck in emotional hell. Or, maybe you're a dumper and she's not doing so well, so you're haunted by feelings and images of guilt. Maybe you were finally able to break free from a bad marriage and you're now trapped by your imagination telling you bad things about your ex's situation and her misery. Or, maybe you could care less about your ex but your imagination is running wild with thoughts of your own financial ruin, etc. Hell, I'm exhausted after just writing this paragraph!

For me, my imagination was "The Godfather" of my emotions during the four months immediately following my separation. Imagine Marlon Brando as the Godfather saying in his slow and raspy voice, *"Joey, ya ex is havin da best time in da woild. She's got it made and ya might as well trow in da towel—ya nevva gonna be back in da saddle again."* It sounds a bit stupid, but I'm sure you get my drift.

These crappy imaginative thoughts and self-destructive talk left me increasingly vulnerable to ongoing emotional pain. For several months I actually believed I was getting emotionally worse rather than better. This obviously delayed the healing process which, in the end, only resulted in hurting me—and me alone.

Okay, I'm going to get a bit weird and "out there" for a minute. Have you ever read any self-help books? Maybe you've even seen or heard of The Secret? I told you self-help books have their place in the divorce process, and this is exactly where I feel they fit in. The Secret is a wonderful book that explains the quantum physics behind positive thinking and the law of attraction. The author, Rhonda Byrne, stresses how good thoughts attract good outcomes and how negative thoughts attract negative outcomes.

If you've ever had any type of sales job, it's almost certain you've been to trainings that deal with the power of mental imaging and positive thinking. Well guess what? The crap really works! (It's not really crap. I just said it for the "man effect!")

I'll try to make this the only time I get far out into the touchy-feely realm of the cosmos. I know most guys don't like this kind of stuff. However, when discussing the concept of positive vs. negative imagination, we must get a bit philosophical.

I'm a firm believer that as humans we want to create this false sense of control to comfort ourselves. By this I'm referring to the need for security. Watch a child (or think back to your own childhood) and see how they're always looking for reassurance and comfort. A child needs to feel everything is okay before they can generally relax and have fun.

Well, you guessed it, we men are nothing but little boys at heart. (just accept it, it's true) Therefore, if we as men still think like little boys, then we can learn a lot from looking at how a boy's mind works, especially a boy's imagination.

I recently received an email story that epitomizes this discussion:

> One evening, an old Cherokee told his grandson about a battle that goes on inside people. He said, "My son, the battle is between 'two wolves' inside us all. One wolf is evil. It is anger, envy, jealousy, sorrow, regret, greed, arrogance, self pity, guilt, resentment, inferiority, lies, false pride, superiority, and ego. The other is good. It is joy, peace, love, hope, serenity, humility, kindness, benevolence, empathy, generosity, truth, compassion, and faith." The grandson thought about it for a minute, and then asked his grandfather, "Which wolf wins?" The old Cherokee simply replied, "The one you feed."

So feed the positive and try your best to manage the negative. Notice I said, "manage the negative." Don't even try to make it go away. For most of us that's just not possible. I'm not suggesting you fight reality; you should simply work toward keeping things in perspective.

Your life may suck now, yes. You may be in the poor house, yes. You're ex may be a real bitch, yes. You may feel like a real pussy, yes. But you do have a future, and you must develop your own personal system that helps you make it through each day while slowly moving toward emotional progress.

This is also a great time to talk about another question that so often plagues both men and women during the break up process: "To snoop or not to snoop?" Many of you already know exactly what I'm talking about. This is more of an issue faced by dumpees.

I remember a specific conversation I had with a divorced man named Keith who told me the following:

> *"I'll admit it, I was a snooper. When my ex said she wanted a divorce, I became James Bond 007! It was my mission in life to find 'The Evidence.' I was sure she left me for another guy and I was gonna find the proof. The problem was that I found evidence way before I was ready to. It wasn't anything bad or juicy [sorry fells], it was simply a picture of my ex standing with a guy at a party—they had their arms around each other. It was just something that I didn't need to see at that point in my divorce."*

Although you may not believe me in your current mental state, someday you'll be ready to see pictures of your ex with another guy. I actually hope you get to the point where you see your ex in a healthy relationship as a good thing. However, if you're still hurting and upset, you don't need to see that shit right now!

Keith then added:

> *"But later on, when I was about 10 months into my separation, this kind of stuff no longer bothered me. I was at my ex's house the other day and saw a picture of her and the new man hanging on a bulletin board. Now that I'm healed and in a good place in my life, seeing her with someone else is cool. After all, when she's with someone else she's less likely to hassle me for money and kid issues. It's also good for my kids' stability for her to be in a healthy relationship. But it was just the opposite when I found the pictures of her and the new guy while snooping around shortly after we separated—it made me sick to my stomach!"*

So when one asks me the question of whether snooping for evidence about a new man (or men) is a good idea, I tell them it's something each guy must decide for himself.

You must seriously ask yourself, "What do I truly stand to gain from finding the evidence?" If you're already getting divorced and she's open about the fact she's dating, you already know what you need to know—yes, she's dating. Is it worth torturing yourself even more? And by snooping around are you being able to stick with your goal of trying to "Fake it 'Til You Make it?"

I've seen this very issue become such an unhealthy obsession for too many men. Another divorcing man named Mel once said:

> *"I had such an issue with this; I would snoop around and then do things like pick fights with my ex about us getting divorced. It's like I needed my ex to remind me every few weeks that we were really getting divorced. But each and every time after I picked this same old fight, I felt ashamed and insisted to myself that I would never do it again. But low-and-behold, just like clockwork, I'd pick another fight a week or so later."*

My therapist once used the following analogy to describe the ending of a relationship:

> *"A relationship ending is very similar to the cutting of a rope. Ropes are not made from one solid strand; they're created from many smaller strands woven together into a single rope. As a rope begins to fray, these little strands break a few at a time. Each broken strand weakens the rope until it finally breaks completely. A relationship is the same way. Many people [especially dumpees] can't just sever the relationship with one cut. Instead, they cut the fibers of the relationship a few at a time."*

Arguing is a very common way of cutting the relationship fibers. Another common way is by having "ex sex." Many couples continue to have decreasing numbers of sexual encounters as they cut the fibers of their relationship.

Just knowing that this could happen (or maybe something similar is already happening to you) can help you find a way to limit this process of prolonged emotional suffering. Once again, there's no way to properly get divorced without living through some amount of hurt. You just don't need to torture yourself excessively.

Here's another analogy I thought of one summer day as my son and I were at the beach. You may have experienced what I'm about to share. Even if you don't live near the ocean, I'm sure you've swam in a lake or a pool.

My son and I arrived at the beach, set down our things, and headed into the water. It was pretty cold and I was inching slowly into the surf. It felt torturous as each wave splashed me more and more with cold water. I eventually got all the way into the water and began to warm up after a few minutes.

I began thinking to myself that getting into the water slowly is just like cutting the rope fibers of a relationship. We all know the pain of getting into cold water can be sped up by simply jumping in rather than inching our way in slowly. Yet, so many of us avoid the initial shock and pain of just jumping into our divorce. Instead, we inch our way through the process and delay getting the warmth offered by emotional growth.

Think about which will be better for you; do you cut the emotional rope more quickly, or do you weaken it slowly over time until it finally breaks? Are you going to jump right into the cold water of divorce (hopefully getting it over with more quickly), or are you going to inch-in slowly and prolong the discomfort? These are questions only you can answer.

Maybe you're just not capable of severing the emotional ties with your ex so quickly. Maybe your specific personality traits determine how you're going to handle things. I'm simply hopeful this chapter gives you something to think about and opens your eyes to some of the many options.

Faking it 'til you can make it is one of the most difficult aspects of any divorce. In retrospect, I guess I did okay. After all, I did keep my job, protect my son, and pay my bills. I know I was a bit of an emotional sap and sometimes looked like a real pussy in front of my ex and my close friends. Maybe that just shows I'm only human and not an insensitive bastard. I can't really say for sure. But what I do know is that, had I been armed with a little better information about the process of divorce, I might have limited my emotional suffering.

I hope this chapter has opened your eyes to a few ways of making it through the tough times, especially during the days and nights when the tears won't stop flowing and your wild imagination may be out of control.

Let me close with this final analogy. Faking it 'til you make it is just like staying dry in a rainstorm. It's not always easy to do, but it must be done if you want to keep from getting sick. However, if there were never any rainstorms, the world would be an awfully dead place. Life after divorce is the springtime following a rainy winter. The tough thing is staying dry through the miserably cold and wet winter of divorce…

CHAPTER 4

YOUR EX IS DATIN' SOMEONE ELSE... (OR SHE EVENTUALLY WILL BE)

The idea that your ex may be dating a new guy is a strange topic. That's because it seems to either be a gut-wrenching issue or you couldn't care less about what she's doing. But for so many men this is one of their biggest problems. I remember discussing this issue with one particular friend who'd actually been divorced three times. (shit, maybe he should be the one writing this book) I asked him, *"How does a guy deal with the mental image of their ex dating some other guy?"*

He looked at me as if I were an idiot for even asking such a stupid question as he replied, *"Dude, who cares? The new guy's gotta deal with all her shit!"*

What my friend said made a lot of sense. But for men affected by this issue, such simple words bring little relief to their emotional turmoil. If this concept bothers you, there's no other way around it—it just sucks. (at least in the beginning)

Even if you know in your heart that your marriage was not healthy for either of you, this in no way, shape, or form helps with the pain of your ex possibly doing "the horizontal mambo" with someone else in the beginning stages of your divorce.

Think about it. One of the first questions divorcing men and women ask mutual friends/family about their ex is, "Do you think my ex is seeing someone new?" Almost every divorcing person wants to know what the other one is doing when it comes to dating.

Even if you're the one who initiated the divorce (the dumper), you almost always want to know about your ex's dating life. Come on, be honest, you know it's true. And if you really don't give a shit who you're ex is doing, I believe you to be in the extreme minority.

I spoke about this very issue with a divorced man named Jay who said:

> *"I had to deal with this issue very soon after my separation. Shortly following our break up, it became very clear my ex was seriously dating someone else. In retrospect, she really wasn't doing anything wrong. We'd separated with the clear intentions of getting divorced, and she was legally and morally free to date whomever she pleased. But God, it still fuckin' sucked! I also cannot tell you how many times I wondered if I was the only guy who ever actually visualized their ex doing 'the dirty deed' with someone new."*

As I did more research and talked with endless guys, it seemed like a vast majority of men are troubled (to one degree or another) by this issue. I guess it only makes sense; men are visual creatures. We often watch porn (don't deny it, pig!), we like to have sex with the lights on (unless it's with some chick we picked up during last call!), and we spend a lot of time looking at women and imagining "stuff!" So it's only logical we as men develop the mental images of our ex dating and possibly having sex with other guys.

The first bit of advice I have is to just accept these feelings. Yup, I said it—you need to accept it. The bottom line is that these images will leave your head when they're good and ready, or when you can learn to make them unimportant. Although there're some things that can help minimize the mental images of your ex prancing around with some new guy in a sexy cocktail dress and lingerie, your upset feelings won't simply go away overnight.

Let's really think about why this bothers so many men to such an extreme. After all of my soul searching and extensive research, I believe it comes down to one word. Are you ready for this? It's an "ego" thing. Yup, it's your ego that's causing you so many problems.

I think this ego thing is also a result of the ongoing "cat-and-mouse" game we play with each other as men and women. You know the game:

> Person #1 has a crush on person #2, but person #2 wants no part of person #1. So, person #1 eventually moves on and no longer wants person #2. But then, person #2 suddenly realizes they now want person #1.

I know it's confusing and sounds stupid, but this game plays out constantly. We often want what we can't have, and vice versa. Maybe this is not the direction you'd expect me to go with this topic, but I'm pretty confident I'm right based on a hell of a lot of research and discussion.

We've already discussed the need to openly admit you weren't happy in the marriage. Even if you're a dumpee, you know you weren't happy. And if you're still caught up in telling yourself you were happily married and your divorce came as an utter shock, you're lying to yourself. If this is the case, do you take yourself for stupid? I guess maybe so.

In all my years of speaking with divorced people, I've only known one man whose divorce truly came as a total and utter surprise. This fella was a lieutenant on my police department (a mid-management position) and someone who I believed was a relatively intelligent person. Yet it was so obvious he truly never saw it coming when his wife divorced him. But other than this one single dumbass, everyone else I've ever met (both dumpee and dumper) has admitted they were not happy during the time leading up to their divorce.

Once again, we always seem to want what we don't (or can't) have. So when you think of your ex possibly having sex with another guy, what is it that really bugs you? Is it that she will enjoy sex a lot more with someone else? If that's the case, then it's an obvious blow to your ego.

I take you to back to Chapter 1, "Face it, You're Gonna be a Bastard." Remember, she's supposed to find someone she likes (and likes having sex with) better than you, just as you're supposed to do the same.

I was discussing this issue with a friend of mine, Jeremy, when he said, *"As I look back, having sex with my ex when we were married was not the greatest. I mean, it wasn't bad sex. But it's very far from the fun, crazy, and very intimate sex I've had since my divorce. And now that I'm free, I can honestly say I hope she's having much better sex, too."*

I commend Jeremy's elevated grasp of reality; however, it can be a tough concept for many men to swallow. But think about it. I just shared how Jeremy was having far better sex since his separation, so logically why should he have cared that his ex may, or may not, have been doing the same thing?

Every guy has seen *Star Trek* and knows Mr. Spock—imagine his take on this topic:

> *"You are no longer together and now happier and having much better interminglings with human females. The fact that you are troubled by your former mate doing the same with someone else is irrelevant to your feelings. It is not logical."*

So, you get my drift there, Scotty? The sooner you can deal with these feelings and realize they're a non-issue, the better off you'll be.

A fella named Juan gave the best comments ever about this topic. Juan basically said:

> *"I'm so happy my ex met a good guy. I've been separated from my ex for about 15 months, and our divorce has been final for about seven months. My kids are doing great and my life has really turned around. My ex is living with her new boyfriend whom she's been dating for over a year. He seems like a nice guy and does very well financially. In fact, he does so well that my ex can work part time, which allows her to drop off and pick up my kids everyday from school. But what if my ex broke-up with her boyfriend? She'd have to go back to work fulltime. My kids would have to be dropped off early at school and stay in one of those after-hours programs. She may even come after me for more money. My life, and the life of my kids, would be greatly impacted in a very negative way. It's to my benefit that my ex is seriously dating someone else. In fact, each*

time I see her I look to see if she's got a nice new rock on her finger. I want them to get married to bring one more level of stability into her life—subsequently doing the same for me and my kids. So, I hope she's swinging from the chandeliers and doing every wild and crazy thing with her new guy that I was never able to bring out in her. But when I was newly separated and my ego was bruised, I wanted my ex to crash and burn."

Later in the conversation (and after a few more beers) Juan was honest enough to admit:

"I was also a bit of a hypocrite during my divorce. I was emotionally upset about my ex dating, yet I was having more sex than ever. It [sex] was just all around me."

We'll cover how easy it is to get laid nowadays in a later chapter. As for now, just take Juan's word for it. But again, I point to the cat-and-mouse game, and Juan is the perfect example. He was having better sex following his separation, yet he was devastated over his ex also beginning to date.

I know this sounds crazy, but if you're not affected by this issue you simply cannot understand the near inanity of the worries. It's like that scene in Austin Powers when he confused himself about time travel. He suddenly looked at the camera and said, *"Oh no, I've gone cross eyed!"* That's what this entire topic is, one big, crazy, "cross eyed" waste of time.

I remember one specific friend-of-a-friend, Mark, who went through a very painful separation this past year. It was so bad we even had to take Mark's guns away from him; that's how bad this dude became.

Mark's is your typical married story that so many of us have lived. (or might still be living) Mark and his wife had been married for about 13 years with a few kids in elementary school. Mark had put on a little weight; however, his ex had ballooned up like the mean aunt in *Harry Potter*. For those of you who don't have kids, *Harry Potter* put a spell on his mean aunt and made her grow like a balloon until she floated away. That was Mark's wife—she was huge.

The situation began when Mark got word that his wife was cheating. He was devastated. Mark and his wife subsequently separated and he moved out. Shortly thereafter, Mark began dating a very attractive lady. I'm serious; this new girl was a real looker and a wild one in bed.

And it wasn't like Mark was bragging about how great the new girl was in bed. We had to pull, and pull, and pull, (and get him drunk) for him to spill his guts about his new chick being a sexual freak. (which is always a good sign it's true when a guy is not eagerly bragging) The new girl also fell hard for Mark and wanted him to be her steady boyfriend. Yet, even with all this, he was still an emotional wreck about his ex "doing it" with some other guy.

Again, please don't misunderstand me. I'm not suddenly advocating you becoming some macho guy who deals with your divorce woes by screwing everything in site. As you're probably tired of hearing, "healthy grieving" is the name of the game. But being upset over your divorce is far different than obsessing about your ex dating someone else.

Here's another situation that's much deserving of mention. I've known numerous guys who constantly cheated on their wives while they were married. However, when the couple splits (often initiated by the woman), these guys frequently go "nuts-o" as she begins dating. What's that? Talk about being an egotistical control freak!

I once had a guy named Vernon tell me the following after being separated from his wife for nearly a year: *"Every time I see her I'm reminded of what I had, and what I fucked up."*

Vernon was one of those guys who repeatedly cheated on his wife while they were married. But when she filed for divorce, Vernon suddenly couldn't get over her beginning to date. I'm confident Vernon also fits into the category of "Big Bumbling Idiot."

Vernon openly admitted that he had been a complete asshole to his ex about her beginning to date someone new. Although it's great Vernon finally realized he did some things wrong in his marriage, he shouldn't be dwelling on the situation a year later.

I wish I had more to offer you about the topic of your ex dating some new guy, but it's really not that complicated of an issue. As I've mentioned, the divorce process can be quite lengthy and tasks the very fibers of your emotional sanity. But worrying about your ex "bumping nasties" with someone new is really wasted energy.

Back to our friend Juan. He also said, *"I personally wish I could have gotten over this issue sooner. After all, this situation that I previously viewed as detrimental has since turned out to be a blessing of peace and stability for me, my two kids, and my ex."*

If this is still eating at you, I recommend referring to the lists you hopefully made following my recommendations in "Fake it 'Til You Make it." As you worry about your ex dating, refer to the reasons you're getting divorced. Remind yourself of the reality of the situation and that your marriage wasn't what you wanted it to be.

As I stressed earlier, lying to yourself is the worst thing you can do. Don't look at things through the "rose colored glasses" of the cat-and-mouse game. If she's dating and no longer wants you, that's a good thing. She's not supposed to want you, dummy! You're getting divorced.

Remember how our logical friend Mr. Spock would see this: *"Wanting your former partner to desire you after the legal dissolution of relations is not good. It is not logical..."*

Chapter 5

Going Into Battle: "The Ex Wars!"

I'd like to begin this chapter by reminding you of something I wrote in the Introduction of this book:

> *"I was looking for a Cliff Notes version of the things a man will face throughout the journey of divorce. I wanted a book I could keep with me that contained quick reference chapters to almost everything I would have to confront. I hope this book will be that guide for you. Something you can refer to when you need a pep-talk, a reminder that things will get better and you're truly not alone. I'd be quite happy if, at the end of your journey through divorce, you were forced to throw this book away because you'd referred to it so many times it simply fell apart. I hope you'll keep this book in your glove box, your lunch pail, or your brief case, so you can turn to it when you need words of encouragement."*

I remind you of this quote because the topic of dealing with a difficult ex-wife is something that can take a very long time to master. And I'm not speaking about mastering your ex; rather, I'm referring to mastering your own attitude toward the entire situation and how you let your ex-wife affect your life.

A good friend of mine, Aaron, has a really difficult ex-wife. Aaron would call me every few weeks with some type of new drama caused by his ex. To try and help, I actually gave him a printed copy of this chapter well before the book was published. Aaron later told me that he re-read this chapter about once a week (and sometimes more) for months. Each time Aaron read the chapter he got a little better at not allowing his ex to negatively affect him so much.

As a friend, and now as an author, hearing these words from Aaron is the true reward for my efforts. (okay, so the extra money is cool, too.) This is exactly what I hope to do for thousands of men. If you've got a difficult ex-wife, I hope you do exactly what Aaron did—re-read this chapter over and over when times are tough.

With that being said, I hope you recognize that so far I've done my best to paint a good picture of "the ex." It really does us no good when we verbally bash one another and hold onto hatred. Again, that's not some book-writing, touchy-feely crap—it's really true. Remember, hate only hurts the hater!

But what if your ex is the hater? What if she takes out her anger and rage on you? How does a man deal with a crazy ex-wife who won't work together civilly toward the best interests of everyone, especially when there're children involved? This type of behavior is truly the ugliest face of divorce.

I must also warn you that men can just as easily be the ones who cause the ex wars! Oh yes. You could be the drama person in the divorce and continue with the hateful behavior. I've met many guys who've been the source of difficult ex-spouse relationships.

Remember Erica's story from Chapter 1? She was the lady with the ex who forced her to struggle through the divorce "by default." What a jerk! If this at all describes you, it's time for some serious personal reflection.

Furthermore, this chapter is not just for those of you with an "evil" ex-wife. This information pertains to just about every guy at some point in their post-divorce life. You may get along well with your ex for now, but disagreements and problems will surely surface at some point in the future.

In Chapter 9, "Divorce, the Law, and the Money," I share a story of a man and woman who were divorcing amicably until a very small disagreement sent them spiraling into an all out legal war in the courts.

If things have gone well for you so far, consider yourself lucky. Just be prepared. Even if your ex is a nice person, there may come a time when you two have very hostile feelings over any variety of unforeseen circumstances.

Maybe it will get ugly when your ex goes through menopause. (ohhhh shit) Maybe you and your ex will seriously disagree over the school placement of the kids. Maybe you and your ex will fight over the right time for your teenage daughter to begin dating. (I'm so glad I only have a boy!) I cannot stress enough the importance of mentally preparing for confrontations with your ex.

But as with most aspects of divorce, there's not some all-knowing "Divorce Bible" that reads:

When the ex is PMSing and wants to kill you:
Page 120
Your ex's new boyfriend dumps her and she's being a bitch:
Page 323
The ex is brainwashing the kids against you:
Page 460

Divorce is confusing enough without adding into account that most of us still have to deal with our ex-wives on a daily basis. Yet so many men can't even have a civil conversation with their ex. Of all the aspects of divorce, dealing with the ex-wife can be enough to drive you mad!

We as men must learn new techniques to interact within the parameters of the challenging and unique relationship called divorce. History shows us that, for many men, dealing with an ex-wife can be pure hell. Years following divorce, your ex-wife may cause unbelievable problems that can easily ruin an entire day or a very special event.

Here's an example of just such an incident. This story really sucks:

> I remember one day when I was working uniform patrol and was dispatched to investigate a report of a "child abduction." I arrived and met with the reporting party who happened to be a man. He seemed like a

> nice, regular guy. The man explained that he had been divorced for several years from his first wife. Together, they had a four-year-old son. Two days prior, the man had gotten re-married to a new woman, and his son was supposed to be the ring boy in a very big ceremony. The morning of the wedding, the man drove to his ex's house to pick up his son, but no one was home. The man frantically called his ex on her cell phone. When she didn't answer, he began calling his ex's mother and several of her closest friends, but no one knew where she was with his son. The man had no choice but to head to his wedding without his boy. The ex-wife called the guy just as the wedding was about to begin. She said there was an emergency with her air conditioner (what the hell?), and that's why she couldn't exchange their son. (I know, bitch!) So, the man was forced to get married without his son there—how shitty. He remembered looking over at his son's little tux hanging up and wanted to cry…

Tragically, as I researched information for this book, I found stories like this are far too common. It's just amazing how some parents use their kids as pawns in the childish attempts at some kind of revenge plot toward their ex. I wish things were different. I wish parents put their kids first and could let go of the hatred toward each other, but that's not reality for so many of us.

I once interviewed a guy named Matthew. Dealing with his ex was so hostile and stressful that Matthew was hospitalized for an irregular heart beat. At one point, the doctors had to stop his heart and then restart it because they'd exhausted all other options to get it beating in a normal rhythm.

Okay, so you get my point? Although I could write volumes of books with thousands of examples just like these (and much worse), it's time we talk about how to handle the difficult ex. And I hate to say it, but calling your ex every bad name in the book will not help. Let's do this; read the following quote out loud. If you like, scream it at the top of your lungs.

> *"My ex-wife is a no-good, slutty bitch who is the biggest 'C-word' ever to walk the face of the earth! She's a selfish tramp who never thinks of anyone but herself!" (And please feel free to add whatever expletives you'd like.)*

So there, do you feel better? Probably not. (Okay, well maybe just a little? Ha!) I know these are some extreme words, but I only use this example because I've found that many men harbor exactly this degree of hostile feelings. But name-calling and ex-bashing is just not the answer. At some point we must all let go, even if the other person won't.

There're even people who've been divorced for over 20 years and their ex still treats them like crap. Wow, talk about unproductive! Things are so bad between some divorced couples that they must exchange their children at a police station to ensure everyone behaves.

When researching "divorce hostilities," I actually found so much information (and ex-wife horror stories available) I initially thought it would be easy to write this chapter. I actually got excited. I thought to myself, this will be the juicy chapter! There's so much stuff out there about bitchy ex-wives that this should be super easy to write.

But I quickly discovered just the opposite. That's because, other than simply telling you a bunch of ex-wife horror stories, I soon realized I didn't have the answers.

I remember thinking, *"So, what do I actually tell my readers about fighting the wars and battles with their crazy ex-wives? What are the answers that will help every man free himself from the emotional burden of the angry and hostile ex-wife?"*

As I reviewed my pages of notes, I realized most of my conversations with men about their bitchy ex-wives went something like this. See if this sounds familiar:

Me: *"Dude, what's wrong?"*
Divorcee: *"It's that bitch! I'm so sick of her ass! I fuckin' hate her!"*
Me: *"Wow. She sounds like a real piece of work."*
Divorcee: *"I must have been crazy to marry her. And now she's telling my kids shit about me."*

Me: *"So what are you gonna do?"*
Divorcee: *"I don't know. Shit!"*

Conversations like this happen each and every day between men who are at their wits end with their ex-wife. Furthermore, our inability to help the situation often makes it worst. Neither the man nor the woman is under any obligation to listen to other.

Think about it; it's often tough enough trying to work with someone who respects you and your opinion, but then consider the fact that both communicating parties may truly hate each other. Makes you wonder how the hell one accomplishes anything.

It wasn't until I finally went to therapy about this issue that I received some good advice. The conversation went something like this:

Me: *"So I'm unsure about how ex-spouses should communicate. I'm also trying to write this chapter about battling with difficult ex-wives; however, I just don't have the answers. What is a guy supposed to do? How does a guy win the war with his ex?"*
Therapist: *"It's really simple, you don't."*
Me: *"What the hell? I don't win the war?"*
Therapist: *"No, you don't fight the war. You don't go to war with your ex."*

Wow! Now that's some really deep shit. My therapist's response completely threw me for a loop. I tried to explain to her how so many guys don't want to deal with a hostile ex, yet they have no choice.

My therapist stressed to me just the opposite when she said:

> *"Tell every man you know that their ex is gonna do whatever it is that she's gonna do. You have absolutely no control over her. What you do have control over is how you emotionally react to her and how much you let her get to you."*

As you can imagine, I pondered this issue for several days. I was still in "fight mode." I was living under the illusion that I was somehow going to find just the right words to tell my readers how to win the battles with their exes.

I racked my brain until it finally made sense. I guess you could say the light finally came on in my little brain. I thought back to my comments in the beginning of this book about divorce being "the ultimate argument" because there can be no real winner. Neither party is under any obligation to respect the other or treat them with any sort of dignity.

Although we hope and pray for civil (even friendly) retaliations between ex spouses, there're no laws or regulations that can mandate mature behavior. No judge can order both parties to like or even respect the other. You can't call the cops and tell them, *"Officer, my wife is being a raving bitch!"* Sorry, but there's just no law against that kind of behavior.

I finally began to see how my therapist was completely right. It's a man's mindset toward his ex that he must seek to master. If you're looking to win in this situation, your mindset will be the driving force that frees you from this burden.

Again, I'm only talking about winning in this situation for you and you're kids. Forget your ex-wife. I don't mean that in a derogatory sense, but rather as a statement of assertion. Your ex is now a non-entity. You no longer care for your ex-wife as an intimate companion. You likely only care for her as the mother of your children. Of course there're some exceptions, and many of men actually do care for their ex as a person.

A man named Tony once told me:

> *"For me, my ex is neither friend nor foe. We generally get along well, but our contact is limited to our children. And I think my situation is the most common among divorced couples. I'd estimate that, for nine out of ten people, an ex-spouse is neither loved nor hated."*

In fact, let's actually take a moment to examine the phrase, "we're friends." First off, I believe you're in the minority if you actually consider yourself to be true friends with your ex. In fact, you two are probably not friends at all. Think about it. A friend is someone you do things with, chat with on the phone about things in your life, lean on for support, etc.

Ask yourself this question: "Would I hang out with my ex or even talk to her if it weren't for the kids?" I'm betting over 95% of men and women would answer, "No."

In reality, although you might be "friendly" with your ex, most of men are certainly not real "friends" with their ex. Tony added:

> *"If not for my three kids, I probably wouldn't even talk with my ex. We might chat for a few minutes a couple of times a year over a piece of mail or something trivial, but that would be it. Again, it's not that I dislike my ex. I'm just not friends with her. We simply interact on a friendly and professional level—almost like business associates."*

Based on hundred of interviews with divorced men and women, I'm certain the majority feel almost nothing for their ex. We generally reach a stage of true detachment. As time progresses and we gain the powerful emotional distance from our ex, nostalgia over the past, intimate emotions, sensitive feelings, etc., all seem to fade into the oblivion of time and divorce.

For most men, the ex just becomes one more thing in life they must simply deal with. She's another credit card bill in the mail, another irritating co-worker who sits in the cubicle next door, or another nosy neighbor you try to avoid by quickly pulling into the garage before being seen.

It took me almost two years to master this concept. That's because it wasn't until I realized the abnormality of the "ex-spouse relationship" that I truly understood the unique dynamics. We must learn to take a very indifferent approach when it comes to our exes.

She cannot upset you if you don't let her; she does not have a say in your life if you don't give her the power. I know this is far easier said than done, but it's possible with practice and the right outlook.

Allow me to elaborate by exploring a very common situation faced by probably 99% of divorced men—the "bitch session." I've watched dozens of my buddies deal with this, and it usually happens when they least expect it. Something just seems to set off the ex and she goes on the war path. See if this sounds familiar.

> You'll be going about your day when the phone rings—it's your ex. You answer in your typically pleasant but nonchalant tone. You don't even finish with your "hello" when she launches into the tirade of pissed off rants about something you failed to do or something you did wrong, or just the fact that she hates your living guts. Quite often, she's pissed about something rather simple, but her bad mood has made the situation much worse.

Most of the men I've interviewed (and watched/listened to as I've sat nearby when they received the "bitch session" phone calls) adamantly try to defend themselves. The call quickly turns into an argument with insults flowing back and forth like spitballs. Although there may be valid issues that require some discussion by both parents, they're certainly not going to get anywhere during that kind of confrontational interaction.

My friend Tony further said:

> *"In the beginning, I would personally feed into these conversations—as do many other men. I'd try to defend myself only to be verbally beat down by my ex. I now realize I fought back so hard because I wanted to be right! I wanted to win! I wanted to go into battle and was speaking from the perspective of anger. But in the end, I only caused myself unnecessary worry that often ruined the remainder of the day."*

Tony also offered this great story to really illustrate his point:

> *"I remember one day my new wife and I were taking our kids to the snow. It was about a 45 minute drive from our house. The kids were having a great time sitting in the back playing video games and watching movies. It*

> *was a sunny day with lots of snow on the ground—the mountains were beautiful. It was also my new stepson's first trip to the snow. He was three years old and beaming with excitement. He couldn't wait to touch the snow for the first time. My older kids (a boy and a girl) had taken many prior trips to the snow and were excited to show him everything. The stage was set for a great family day. But my ex and I had been fighting about some trivial issues, and it was really eating me. My new wife could tell something was wrong and quickly figured out it was my ex that was bugging me. Although I did my best to hide things from the kids, I was disappointed that I let the issue tug at me all day. It was just like a thorn in my side. So there I was, a day off from work with my beautiful new wife and our three great kids playing. Everyone was having the best time, yet I was troubled by an issue stemming from my ex—it should have never affected me so much. My new wife and I were later talking about the day when she said, 'It really bothered me that she [Tony's ex] was able to affect our family day.' And my new wife was right. I should have been able to brush off my ex, but yet I wasn't."*

Tony stressed how he felt a bit ashamed that he let the situation affect him so much. But like I already mentioned, Tony didn't have a divorce manual to help guide him through. Dealing with an ex-wife is truly one of the most unique relationships a person can face, and I have yet to find the detailed instructions.

I firmly believe a man won't be able to put and end to these types of confrontations until he takes an entirely different approach when dealing with a difficult ex. I was discussing this issue with a man named Curtis. His story is a great example of how to win over "the bitch sessions." Curtis basically said:

> *"It took a while, but I was finally able to put a stop to these confrontations. My new technique was actually to end the phone call and not to deal with it. I'm not a fan of being rude and hanging up on someone. That bullshit hang up game is*

stupid and only adds gasoline to the raging bonfire. I know couples that have been divorced for many years that still hang up on each other, even though it gets them nowhere. It was actually my therapist that really helped me with this. [See, aren't I always praising therapy?] He prompted me to create a pre-scripted response to my ex." [I know, another thing to write down. Just shut up, Curtis is on to something!]

Curtis said his script to his ex read:

> *"I know this is an important issue for you and I value your opinion. However, we're not going to accomplish anything with you yelling at me. I know you don't think you're yelling, but your tone is bad. So I'm gonna hang up now if you can't calm down. We can talk about this later."*

Curtis added, *"If my ex kept yelling, I'd simply hang up. However, it wasn't the typical hanging up; she was given fair warning before the call ended."*

Curtis' story is the perfect example of why it's so important for men to begin to share our divorce experiences. Again, not the typical "sit around and trash our ex" talks. Rather, we need to open up about what has really worked to productively move through divorce and build the better life we should be striving toward.

But back to the topic of "the bitch session." I was actually discussing Curtis' technique with a female friend, Mindy, and she said it worked on her. Mindy's face got a bit red as she smiled with slight embarrassment while saying:

> *"I used to yell at my ex over the phone for any little thing. I was a real bitch. But he quickly put a stop to it by putting me in my place. I finally learned he was not going to stay on the phone with me if I yelled at him. He'd insist that I stop yelling at him or he'd hang up. When I didn't stop shouting, he'd simply hang up. After this happened two or three times, I figured out that I'd better be calm if I wanted to talk with him or my kids when they were together."*

Again, you don't have to be rude. You only need to be stern enough to set the tone. No one has the right to yell at you—especially not your ex. The worst-case scenario is your ex may just never learn. If that's the case, you're going to need to work with your attorney.

I've known several couples that had to communicate directly through their attorneys for everything, especially in the beginning. This is the epitome of a parent (or parents) being childish and holding onto their hate, but it's just the reality for many divorced couples.

Another thing that works is to make yourself appear too busy to talk with your ex. For example, let's say your ex calls you pissed off because you let your kids watch a movie that she doesn't approve of. You answer the phone and she launches into a tirade of demands and insults.

You could reply, *"You know, I'm just really busy right now. I need to call you back later."* Chances are she'll ignore you and continue with her rant. Just repeat, *"I'd love to talk about this, but I can't right now,"* and then hang up.

I've got a really good friend, Eddie, who made this response his mantra every time his ex got angry with him. It didn't take long for Eddie's ex to realize he just wasn't going to tolerate her hostile behavior. Eddie's ex is no dummy, and I'm sure she realized he is not always that busy and he was really just blowing her off. But Eddie's stance was simple—he was not going to entertain his crazy ex.

Eddie once told me:

> *"What's she [Eddie's ex] gonna do to me? She can't take my kids away from me. My kids know she's crazy. They love being with me. I put up with her crap for years. I got divorced so I wouldn't have to listen to her yell at me anymore, so why would I allow her to continue?"*

I've watched Eddie in action. It's truly amazing to see him interact on the phone with his ex. Not only does he appear calm when he speaks to her, but he also truly feels calm. His words and soothing tone are not an act. Eddie has arrived at a place where his ex has absolutely no emotional effect on him.

I also recall a very similar outlook from another man I once interviewed. Phil had to deal with an extremely difficult ex-wife. Phil's story stands out in my mind because of his calm nature—very similar to Eddie. As Phil spoke, I noticed how he seemed to be at real peace with the troubles caused by his ex.

However, during the first five or six years following Phil's divorce, his ex put him through a literal hell as he tried to remain an active part of his kids' lives. Phil religiously paid his child support and was always early when picking up his children. But it was clear Phil's ex just hated him and everything about him. Think of all the horror stories about ex-wives that you've ever heard or experienced, and Phil had lived them.

As we dove deeper into conversation, I truly began to admire Phil's attitude toward his ex. Phil explained:

> *"For years I lived on pins and needles. Every time the phone rang my stomach would drop as I looked to see if it was my ex. She did everything she could to try and keep me away from my kids. I would constantly worry about worst-case scenarios where a judge may side with her and take my kids away from me. Even though I knew I was a great dad, I couldn't stop the worry, the stomachaches, the headaches, and the lack of sleep. But then one day, I just accepted that this is what I have to deal with and she can't keep my kids from me. I wish I could tell you why the change, but it was just something that happened. A true revelation."*

Phil also shared a very memorable conversation he had with his ex about their kids:

Phil: *"What is it with you? I've tried everything and I just don't know what you want from me."*

Ex: *"I just want you to go away! I want you to leave me and the kids alone!"*

Phil: *"That's just not gonna happen. I'm their dad and these are my kids, and I'm here to stay. You're just gonna have to accept it…"*

After that conversation, Phil said his ex began slowly backing off. She was still a bitch, but she didn't fight with him every single time they talked on the phone about even the most trivial of issues.

Although it took years, and an unbelievable amount of mental and physical stress, I got a real sense that Phil had won his war because he finally stopped trying to fight it. Phil's kids are now grown and much closer to him than their mother. Although his ex continues to live a very angry and miserable existence, she leaves Phil alone.

Phil is actually at such an elevated place that he even told me:

> *"I truly feel sorry for my ex—she's a miserable person and it shows. You may think I'd be happy that my kids like me much more than her. I guess you could say that, after years of fighting, I won because my kids spend all their time with me and very little with their mother. But I don't feel good about that. I wish my kids had a better mother. I wish things could have been different and my daughter could have had that special mother-daughter relationship all girls should enjoy with their mom."*

What amazing words from Phil. He really wanted what's best for his kids, not what gives him some superficial sense of victory over his ex. As I've said, Phil's level of acceptance and peace has taken years to achieve, but maybe you could get there sooner with the right attitude and perspective. And I remind you, Phil had a horrible ex. So, if he can get there, why not every man?

Tony, Phil, Eddie, and Curtis all represent a growing trend I found among men who were very willing to talk about their own personal ex wars. Although most men are generally leery of speaking about the emotional aspects of divorce, I've found it's just the opposite when asking men to share their ex horror stories. Just try it sometime. If you're chatting with a guy and the topic of divorce comes up, try sharing one of your own crappy ex-wife stories. Most of the time you'll find the other fella will jump right in and begin sharing one (or more) of his.

Although I once again caution you about simply engaging in the typical ex-bashing session with other divorced men, participating in productive discussions is a great way to learn from another guy's experiences. As I've said, I got a lot from Phil's conversations that he shared about his ex-wife.

I know many of you may be shaking your heads right now. I acknowledge this is a very different approach than many of us have taken, especially in the beginning. You may still be harboring angry feelings toward your ex and want to tell her to "F-off." But the more you honestly examine the negative results of this kind of behavior, the more you'll come to accept that going to war is not the answer.

Do you actually think your ex will eventually submit to you and say, *"You're right; I'm a bitch and a crappy mother. I wish I'd have seen this sooner. I'll never talk mean to you again. Let's be friends."*

I'm laughing as I write this. Just face it; if you're ex is a bitch and yells at you, yelling back will simply not work.

It's also time you take an honest assessment of your ex. Think about how she is now as opposed to how she was when you got married. I once spoke with a guy named Manny whose ex-wife was literally diagnosed with Bipolar Disorder. (a chemical imbalance causing crazy mood swings for no reason at all) Manny rambled on about his ex's crazy mood swings and her evil ways. Manny was desperately looking for some answers about how he could get his wife to stop acting Bipolar when he dealt with her.

I replied, *"Dude, was she Bipolar when you married her?"*

Manny thought about it for a good 30 seconds when he answered, *"Yeah, I guess so. But it was never this bad."*

I then said, *"Of course she was just as bad back then, you were just in love at the time and you guys actually liked each other. Now that you're divorced and she hates your guts, it just seems a lot worse."*

In short, the things we often overlook for new love (and lust) now seem a lot worse because we've taken off those good old "rose colored glasses."

So take stock in the reality of what you're dealing with. If one of the reasons you got divorced is because your ex is a super control freak, she's probably not going to stop trying to control you and the kids just because you're now divorced. In most cases, you couldn't communicate with this woman when you were married, so what on God's green earth makes you think you'll be able to talk with her now.

This is not some defeatist attitude. I'm in no way insinuating you lie down and take shit from this woman. I'm actually stressing just the opposite; you definitely don't have to take her shit.

But the road to freedom from a bitchy ex can't be found in going to war with her. Your peace lies in freeing yourself from the burden of dealing with her negative, controlling, and often demeaning comments.

This may be getting a little weird for some of you. I don't mean to sound like some metaphysical self-help guru saying, *"Just accept reality and flow with the heavens..."* I'm simply stressing that you accept the reality of what you have to work with.

This is another place where a lot of self-help information can come into play. As I've said, men are much more emotional and spiritual than we're given credit for. For example, take a look at the almost overnight explosion of Mixed Martial Arts and Ultimate Fighting. I know most of us watch it because it's truly amazing the way those guys beat the living shit out of each other and don't die. But there is also a very spiritual side to these arts, and most champions explore the metaphysical side of life as a regular part of their training.

One of the best self-help books I've ever read is Loving What Is by Byron Katie. This is a great book for accepting reality. Katie has developed a process she calls "The Work," and it's as simple as it is complex. I say complex because I found my mind pushing back toward the complicated rather than accepting my relatively simple reality as explained by Katie.

But once I practiced "The Work" repeatedly, I noticed myself wondering why I made such a big deal out of so many things that were outside my realm of control. My favorite quote from Katie's entire book is, *"Reality is always kinder than the stories we tell about it."* Another great quote from Katie is, *"When I fight reality I lose, but only 100% of the time."*

I hope I'm not scaring you and turning you off to my advice by delving into the self-help arena. I'm only sharing what has worked for so many men. I fought reality for years, especially following my divorce. I kept fighting for control of things that were outside my scope. It wasn't until I recognized my true reality that I gained a clear understanding of what is mine to master, and what I could never possibly begin to control.

Katie also writes:

> *"The Work [Katie's system] always brings us back to who we really are. Each belief investigated to the point of understanding allows the next belief to surface. You undo that one. Then you undo the next, and the next. And then you find that you are actually looking forward to the next belief. At some point, you may notice that you're meeting every thought, feeling, person, and situation as a friend. Until eventually you are looking for a problem. Until, finally, you notice that you haven't had one in year."*

I'm nowhere near Katie's elevated acceptance of reality. I'm still a pretty average guy who gets pissed over everyday shit (work, house repairs, car problems, money issues, etc). I seek to control that which will never fall under my command. But I do credit Katie (and much of the other self-help professionals) for bringing me to a place that forever encourages me to understand and deeply accept the truth about my reality.

I don't get nearly as upset as I used to about most things. Each time I now deal with hostility from any source, I get better at deflecting negativity. But this entire concept is something we must practice forever to ensure continued perfection.

None of these personal changes within you (within your thought process) will take place overnight. Take me for example. The majority of my life I was very much a "the glass is half-empty" kind of person. From my early childhood, I frequently dwelled on the negative. I've always focused on the fear in life, the challenges, and the struggle.

But as I began to grow during my divorce, I also began to improve in many other aspects of my life. Maybe I just figured, "What the hell? My entire life is in a state of disarray, so why not try to improve everything, not just my attitude toward divorce and my future relationships with women?"

In the beginning, this new "the glass is half-full" attitude took some getting used to—it actually took a lot of work. When negative thoughts about anything (not just my divorce) entered my head, it took a *conscious effort* to push them from my mind and replace them with positive ones.

I know I'm going off on a tangent, so maybe it would help if I gave you an example. Take my finances. As with most other men, money was a real issue during and after my divorce. Although I had developed a sound financial plan, it was going to take me at least a year to pay off my divorce bills and then be able to start building a savings.

I was essentially living paycheck-to-paycheck. It was stressful to say the least. But when a scary or depressive thought entered my head about my finances, it took an *active effort* to transition (shift) to feeling good about my financial plan.

After about six weeks, I noticed it becoming a lot easier to make the transition from negative and fearful thoughts to positive ones. I'm not saying I didn't still get scared or nervous about a lot of different aspects in life, but it really did get easier to think more positively—it wasn't the same fight within myself to see the forest for the trees.

Just go to the bookstore or library and look up literature on "positive thinking." There's hundreds (if not thousands) of books available. As I paroozed a few dozen of these books over an 18-month period, I discovered one very common (yet simple) theme: countless people have changed their thought processes and personal perspectives through an *active effort*—pushing themselves to literally switch the way thoughts run through their minds.

"Nothing from nothing leaves nothing." What a true statement. If you've got a negative attitude toward your ex—or anything else in your life—it will take an *active effort* (I know I keep repeating that phrase) on your part to change it. Sorry, but I've never found any magic words that instantly changed my perspective about anything, especially regarding my divorce.

Choosing not to go to war with your ex has everything to do with how you look at things—the perspective you take toward the trying circumstances of divorce. In her book, Divorce and New Beginnings, Genevieve Clapp writes:

> *"As you come to accept that your marriage is truly over, a dam may seem to break inside of you, spilling out a*

> *torrent of anger—or perhaps even rage, more intense than you had ever thought yourself capable. Unfamiliar feelings of bitterness and vindictiveness may become your new companions, consuming a good share of your thoughts and energy each day. You may become obsessed with old hurts you had almost forgotten [and women don't forget shit!], reliving each as vividly as if it had occurred yesterday, each memory pouring fuel on your seething anger. Your friends may even notice that you are unable to have a conversation with your former spouse without the anger erupting into a full blown battle."*

Clapp further writes:

> *"Researchers Judith Wallerstein and Joan Kelly found that 80 percent of men and a somewhat higher percentage of women they studied experienced such anger and bitterness after separation. Both leavers and those left become victims of their own rage. Frightened children heard their dads called disgusting, crazy, liars, and bastards, while they heard their moms called whores, drunken bitches, greedy, and grasping."*

These quotes epitomize the deep hatred and disgust many ex couples have for each other. You may share equally bad feelings toward your ex; you may be just as big of a hater. If that's you, I must repeat that a certain amount of anger is completely normal, acceptable, and even healthy.

In *Terminator 3*, Arnold Schwarzenegger says, *"Anger is a more useful emotion than despair."* So if it's between being angry and being depressed, I'd recommend being angry.

However, anger in a completely unchecked state can lead to near insanity. The following is one crazy story that exemplifies "The Ex Wars" being caused by both the husband and the wife—basically a couple that is openly warring with each other.

I had known this couple (lets call them Marco and Sylvia) for over 15 years. I worked with Marco for years and met Sylvia when they began dating. Marco is your typical womanizing macho guy, and he's always been that way. I've watched Marco in action, and he always has a smooth line at the perfect time to get any girl.

Marco and Sylvia got married and had two kids over the course of about ten years. Marco also had a teenage son from a previous relationship. According to Sylvia, there have always been other women.

Marco has also had several instances where other women have made allegations against him. Marco was even transferred from a very prestigious assignment at work because of allegations that he was involved with a co-worker's wife. I cannot say for sure if there's any truth behind these allegations, but from knowing Marco for nearly 20 years, I can only imagine.

One morning, I was at a Starbucks having coffee with my girlfriend when I saw Sylvia walking in. I actually hadn't seen Sylvia for many years, but she immediately recognized me.

Once inside, Sylvia walked up, gave me a hug, and immediately started crying. She spilled her guts about her and Marco's separation. Sylvia was so distraught I felt she was about to throw her arms around my neck and collapse in pure grief.

Sylvia explained that she and Marco had separated about nine months prior. According to Sylvia, Marco just stopped coming home because he was *"staying with one of his many girlfriends."*

On that morning, Sylvia was scheduled to meet Marco at the Starbucks to exchange their kids, and Marco arrived about five-minutes later. Marco stopped in the parking lot and remained seated in his truck—I walked out to greet him. Marco and I no longer worked together, so I actually hadn't seen him in a few years.

Marco saw that I had been talking to Sylvia and he immediately greeted me by saying, *"I'm not dealing with her shit!"*

Now, keep in mind I had not talked to Marco for several years, and those were the first words out of his mouth. Talk about living a stress-filled-life.

Marco then launched into a tirade about how Sylvia had kicked him out and he was forced to leave with just the shirt on his back. Marco said he had no choice but to park his motor home at a campground and live there for over a month until he found a place.

My girlfriend, who also knew Marco and Sylvia, remained at one end of the parking lot with Sylvia while I stood at the other end with Marco. Sylvia sobbed to my girlfriend about how Marco only sees the kids about one or two days every few weeks. According to Sylvia, Marco never makes an effort to see the kids. But, according to what Marco told me, Sylvia keeps the kids from him.

Yeah, I know, you're tired and confused with this story. My girlfriend and I felt exactly the same way for the 45 minutes we were trapped in the middle of the two.

But the strangest thing about this situation is that Marco chose to only take the two older kids with him and he left the youngest (his four-year-old girl) with Sylvia. My girlfriend actually walked over and asked Marco, *"You want the baby, too—right?"*

Marco was very short with my girlfriend as he replied, *"No! She* [Sylvia] *can keep her!"*

I didn't even ask Marco why in the world he didn't want to take all three of his kids. Being that my son is the most important person in my life, and I'd kill to spend every moment with him, I can't understand why Marco would only take two of his kids and leave the third, especially since he openly complained to me about Sylvia limiting his visits with the children. This was a perfect opportunity to see all of his kids.

After about ten more minutes of listening to Marco rant and rave about Sylvia, I was finally able to leave.

There's so much that can be learned from this situation. First, the vast difference between Marco's and Sylvia's stories clearly indicates someone is lying and being overly dramatic, and that the truth probably lies somewhere in between.

And regardless of whether Sylvia was keeping the kids from Marco, or if he was just not trying that hard to see them, it was not a healthy situation for the children. Kids need both of their parents actively involved in their daily lives.

Furthermore, the fact that this level of fighting and mutual hatred still exists after nine months of being separated is a clear indication of how both people are not moving forward. Actually, it's obvious that Marco hates Sylvia, but Sylvia actually said, *"I haven't filed any paperwork yet because I still hope we can reconcile."*

What a crazy statement—literally! Sylvia couldn't stop talking about all the grief and emotional trauma Marco had put her through, yet she still wanted a chance to work things out. I don't get it.

I can't think of a better example of a couple that is actively engaged in a war of words, hurt, and negative emotions. And worst of all, I could see the fear and pain pleading from the eyes of their children. It was so sad.

Most of you are reading this thinking that Marco and Sylvia both need to just move on and do what's best for their children. However, it's very different when you're the one living through the situation. When it's your life, it's almost never that easy.

This is why in the Introduction I use the analogy of the battered women who remain with their abusive husbands. Everyone who isn't involved in these types of situations can ever-so-clearly scream at the woman to leave. But when you're the one living through the events, the emotions cloud everything.

It's essential that you continuously strive toward the goal of eventually moving beyond anger, hate, and depression. I'm not trying to demean you by repeating myself. I'm only reminding you of an important fact—many men are the ones who cause the ex wars because they never move forward.

I'll detail the concept of moving forward much more in Chapter 10: "Emotionally Getting Over This." For now, I'm just planting the seed for further thought—free your thoughts and you'll no longer be trapped by your hate.

It's also a lot easier to do damage control for your kids if you're not possessed with hateful and vindictive feelings toward your ex. A great book for helping to deal with a negative ex who is insulting, abusive, and even hostile is called Divorce Poison, Protecting the Parent-Child Bond from a Vindictive Ex, written by Dr. Richard A. Warshak.

The book was a bit long and sometimes dry, but I highly recommend it for any person dealing with a difficult ex. The most important thing I got from this book was how to counter negative comments an ex makes to your children about you. I have met so many men who have been literally tortured by an ex-wife who is on the warpath to turn the kids against him.

My experience shows me that most men still subscribe to the concept that "silence is golden" when dealing with an ex who trashes them to their kids. It was not until I truly educated myself that I realized this may not always be best. There is a time and place for a parent to counter certain negative comments an ex makes to the children.

I really enjoyed Warshak's different and unique approach. He says, *"Children deserve an explanation equal to their age and maturity."*

Although in Chapter 1, "Face it, You're Gonna be a Bastard," I give several successful examples of men who chose to ignore their ex's derogatory comments, I now see how this can be very risky. Warshak shares some terrifying stories of men who emotionally lost their children as a result of an ex-wife turning them against their dad. If your kids frequently come to you asking for explanations about horrible things their mother said about you, you'll definitely want to read Warshak's book.

Warshak helps you navigate the difference between "badmouthing" and "brainwashing." So many men deal with an ex-wife who verbally trashes them in front of their kids. I think this is pretty easy to counter by your words and your actions.

If your ex is constantly telling the kids you are a "no good, deadbeat dad," yet you constantly spend time with your kids, work hard to provide for them, ensure a loving and nurturing environment for your children, and do not force them to choose between you and their mother, most kids will generally figure out your ex is a nutcase by observing the good behaviors you consistently model.

The really scary thing is dealing with an ex who is strategically working to brainwash your kids against you. I couldn't even begin to try and rewrite Warshak's book. He does such a great job of differentiating between badmouthing and brainwashing that you really must read his book if you think either of these two situations affect you.

Brainwashing has become such a well-known problem that it has been given its own official title, "Parental Alienation." According to the Canadian Children's Rights Council:

> *"The parental alienation is a disorder that arises primarily in the context of child custody disputes. Its primary manifestation is the child's campaign of denigration against*

> *a parent, a campaign that has no justification. It results from the combination of programming [brainwashing] parental indoctrinations and the child's own contributions to the vilification of the target parent. The alienation usually extends to the non-custodial parent's family and friends as well. Many children involved in divorce and custody litigation undergo thought reform or mild brainwashing by their parents. This disturbing fact is a product of the nature of divorce and the disintegration of the spousal relationship in our culture. Inevitably, children receive subtly transmitted messages that both parents have serious criticisms of each other. Parental Alienation, however, is much more serious. It involves the systematic vilification by one parent of the other parent and brainwashing of the child, with the intent of alienating the child from the other parent."*

Simply Google "Parental Alienation" and you'll find pages and pages of information. As with all aspects of your divorce, I strongly encourage you to research this important aspect of the journey. The information is out there if you are willing to put forth a very minimal amount of time and effort.

Warshak touches on so many tragic issues, such as:

- Parental Abduction (Wow)
- Your ex wanting to move away with your children
- Bridging the gaps with alienated kids
- Dealing with childhood depression
- Lies and the corruption of reality
- An ex who wants you to disappear
- How to deal with a new stepparent trying to replace you
- Using mediation to resolve custody disputes

Many men and women make it a point to carry over the ill feelings of the past into their new relationship as divorced parents. The fact that you have children means you must maintain some type of relationship with her for the rest of your life. I know this is all very obvious. I'm simply trying to push you toward a real and proper understanding of the dynamics involved. We already know your ex might be a bitch. Now what can you do about it?

This is why it's time to begin transforming those feelings toward your ex. If you are reading this book early in your separation, this may be a real issue for you. The memories for both you and your ex may be very raw, and it will probably take more time to let go of the old and form into the new. If you have already been separated/divorced for some time, you may have made this transition long ago.

The right attitude toward your ex will also help with another important concept you may have already experienced (and I've been stressing), *When she's happy, you're happy. When she's miserable, she often does all she can to make your life miserable.*

This is one of the few things that truly drives me nuts about women. In comparison, I've found men to be generally even keel. I mean, if a guy is a jerk, he is generally a jerk most of the time; if he is mostly calm and mellow-natured, it usually takes a lot to get him pissed. But women often have more emotional ups-and-downs than the Space Shuttle!

A friend of mine named Bob stands out in my mind regarding this subject. Bob was married for several years with two small children when his wife initiated a divorce. It has now been about 10 years, and Bob's ex-wife has been through several long-term boyfriends. When Bob's ex is in a relationship, she is always nice and sweet to Bob.

But when she is single and between boyfriends, she is an absolute bitch. Bob can't do anything right; he is a horrible father and she always wants more money. This was especially bad when Bob got remarried about seven years after the divorce. His ex-wife bordered on psychotic.

Another friend, Mike, called me one day almost in tears about his ex. It was two days after Valentine's Day when, out of left field, Mike's ex called him and began yelling about movies the kids watched at his house, what they ate, and how sometimes both kids slept in his bed, etc. She was going off about everything.

I found this really odd because I know Mike's ex-wife and she is generally pretty mellow. But for approximately the following three week period, Mike's ex was brutally mean and rude about everything.

Eventually things calmed and Mike's ex went back to being nice to him.

Mike then called me several months later because he had discovered why his ex had been so mean around Valentines Day. A reliable friend-of-a-friend had told Mike that his ex was bragging around New Year's Day that she would be getting engaged by Valentines Day.

But I guess her new boyfriend was not quite as ready to tie the knot as her, so there was no ring attached to Cupid's arrow. In the end, it became very apparent Mike's ex had given him the brunt of her anger about not receiving her expected engagement ring.

So be prepared. More often than not, an ex may frequently be a problem over things in their life that are completely unrelated to you; you just may bare the brunt of her anger.

And next to your own personal attitude, a solid court order will be your most important ally. In the beginning stages of your divorce (often before a real court order exists), things may be somewhat difficult, even downright horrible. You won't have the support of a legal order signed by a judge defining when and where your children are to be exchanged.

You may have to fly by the seat of your pants. In some states, divorcing couples can be granted a temporary custody order pending the permanent divorce proceedings, but that is very inconsistent and you should do your own research.

In Chapter 9: "Divorce, the Law, and the Money," I provide information about selecting an attorney and using the courts to your benefit. That chapter also contains information and Internet links to divorce resources and legal references for individual states. If you have a difficult ex, I strongly recommend you invest in a good attorney who will ensure a court order is created to protect you and your relationship with your children.

You must also make sure you do not give your ex one iota of ammunition to use against you. From the moment of separation, ensure that you regularly pick up your children as much as possible, provide appropriate financial support, and maintain accurate records. I'm not trying to belittle you, I've just interviewed far too many men who half-assed things and it came back to bite them.

For example, I interviewed a guy name Ben who actually saved himself in court with the accurate records he kept during his separation and divorce process. Ben's ex was extremely difficult. Ben could have given her 100% custody of their four kids and his entire paycheck, and she still would have hated him.

When Ben and his ex finally got into court, she made false allegations that he rarely saw the children and had not given her a dime since their separation. But Ben was smart; he maintained detailed records of all the time he had spent with each of his kids. He also produced certified bank records and copies of cashed checks that clearly detailed all the money he had given his ex since their breakup.

Oh, winning for you and your kids is ever-so-sweet. I laughed as Ben explained the look on the judge's face when he reviewed this evidence that directly contradicted his ex's lies. The judge ruled in Ben's favor and things went very well. Although this didn't keep Ben from having shared custody and paying some child support, it could have been much worse.

And regarding court preparations and appearances, Warshak also comments:

> *"To show that you have previously enjoyed a good relationship with your children, provide the court appointed evaluator with objective evidence. Bring in videotapes, photographs, gifts, and greeting cards that demonstrate your children's affection towards you. Give the evaluator a list of names and phone numbers of adults who have observed you and your children together. Make sure the list includes people who would not be expected to be biased in your favor. Your mother may give you a glowing endorsement as a parent, but the court is not likely to view her as an impartial reporter. The list should include teachers, coaches, and parents who have seen you at extracurricular activities. Ask the evaluator to contact these people. Why? The evaluator will hear vastly conflicting accounts of reality. If your children are alienated, their fears and complaints may appear very convincing. You will have a better chance of proving that their negative attitudes are a response to*

> *the divorce poison if you can provide the evaluator and the court with evidence that your past involvement with the children was generally positive."*

Warshak also cites the following example:

> *"One father had his former mother-in-law describe the close relationship that used to exist between him and his son. This was the most convincing because, if anything, the court would have expected her to be biased in favor of her own daughter. One mother, whose children claimed that she was never fun to be with, brought in videotapes of her and the children playing happily together throughout their early years. This showed the court appointed evaluator that her children's complaints were the product of recent attitude changes and were not characteristic of their relationship."*

Warshak's book is filled with many examples of ways to address the worst situations. Again, I highly recommend it.

So it's now time to ask yourself, "Am I doing everything right?" Are you paying your child support, adhering to the court ordered custody decree, being a truly active part of your children's lives, etc.? If the answer to any of these is "no," then you have no room to complain about a bitchy ex! I mention this because maybe you're giving your ex reasons to be a bitch—to go to war with you.

And I'm not talking about whether or not your ex would speak highly of you when answering these questions. It's probably a given that many of you could be the perfect dads ever, yet your ex would still paint you as "The Antichrist."

I'm challenging you to do an honest assessment of your parenting. If there're things you need to improve, then start today. Remember, it doesn't take a lot of money to be a great dad or to fulfill your responsibilities.

You will hear me repeatedly stress that money is nice, but it's not the end-all. I have met many poor families that were beaming with pride and love for their children. A great movie for this is *The Pursuit of Happyness* with Will Smith. And yes, I know I spelled happiness wrong.

For those who have not seen it, they spell it that way in the movie for a reason.

The story is about a man (played by Will Smith) who loses everything financially while his wife runs-off and leaves him and their son to fend for themselves. At one point, the man and his son become homeless and are forced to sleep in a subway. It's a heart wrenching movie (a real tear jerker, too), but it speaks strongly about the idea that being a good person and a good parent does not mean you must have money oozing from your pockets.

For example, when my son was about to turn three, I bought him a little 50cc dirt bike. (What, so I was an overzealous dad!) I attached these super heavy duty training wheels so he could go anywhere in the dirt. This thing was really tricked-out.

For several years we frequently went camping and I would practically beg for him to ride along side of me. But he never really took to riding. Oh no! My boy was more interested in playing all weekend in the dirt with a ten dollar toy I bought him at a gas station. The bike eventually got sold and he never missed it one bit.

So whatever the excuse (money, your work hours, a long drive, etc.), you must do what needs to be done as a father. Only then can you begin to stand with pride when facing a difficult ex. This may sound elementary and repetitive to a lot of you, but there're far too many men that need this reminder.

Remember, someone has to steer the ship. The difference here is that your ex is now on a completely different ship than you. But look at it this way; when she has to deal with you, make sure she has to step onto your ship, where you're the captain. If she will not be respectful (or at least professional), then she only gets to pull up alongside your ship and have very minimal contact. You set the tone of the meetings.

The only catch will be if she has a vindictive nature and uses underhanded tricks to affect your children. If that's the case, you must fight the good fight for the sake of your children, your relationship with them, and your own sanity.

And no matter what, always remember that there's some other guy who has it worst than you. The following story has stuck out in my mind since the day I heard it. It's about a fella named Jerry.

When Jerry was younger he was always the guy that was adamant he was never getting married. Jerry got into a good career a few years after high school and began saving a lot of money. At about 25, Jerry had saved enough money to put almost half down on a new house.

A short time later, Jerry allowed his girlfriend to move-in; however, Jerry had no intentions of ever getting married or having children. But, Jerry's girlfriend had other plans.

She "accidentally" got pregnant about six months later. Jerry then felt obligated to marry her before the baby was born. Some of you're shaking your heads right now, but the story is far from over.

When the baby was about a year and half old, Jerry began developing suspicions his wife was cheating. Jerry and his wife actually worked for the same company but in different divisions. This made it easy for him to access her desk at work.

One afternoon, Jerry went to his wife's workstation and began snooping around. (he actually broke the lock on her desk) There he found the hard truth—numerous love notes between his wife and another guy that also worked for the company. In fact, Jerry knew this other guy quite well and the two had shared several work assignments. But wait, there's more!

So Jerry confronts his wife and, after about six months of couples counseling, his wife chooses the other guy over Jerry. Upon separating, Jerry's wife actually moves in with the guy she had been having an affair with. So, not only did Jerry have to deal with the break up of his family, but he also had to regularly drop off his baby at his ex-wife's house where she was living with the guy she cheated on him with.

Wow, I'm tired after writing that story! It has now been over 15 years and Jerry has happily remarried. Surprisingly, Jerry's ex and the guy she had the affair with got married and are still together. What an unbelievable test of emotional fortitude for Jerry. I could not imagine going through all that and then having to leave my infant with the very guy who I considered a friend but was having an affair with my wife.

So whatever your individual story, remember there're millions of us guys who have walked, who are still walking, and will walk, in your shoes. You're truly not alone and things will get better as your develop a plan to specifically deal with your ex and the severity of your individual situation.

Finally, please don't be too tough on yourself if it takes time for you to reach a point where you truly feel comfortable with ex-wife confrontations. As I said in the beginning of this chapter, the dynamics of an ex-spouse relationship can take years to master.

And again, I'm not speaking of mastering your ex. I'm referring to mastering the way you interact with her and allow her to affect your emotions and happiness. Just draw on the experiences of those who've gone before you, and work to develop a mental perspective that is best-suited for your situation.

CHAPTER 6

OUR FATHERS FAILED US

First off, I must clarify the title of this chapter. It doesn't mean I had a shitty dad. He was actually a great dad, and we're very close to this day. (Hear that, Pop? Don't cut me out of the Will!)

The term "Our Fathers Failed Us" is a bigger commentary about society and how we don't train our young men about relationships. In comparison, most states require at least a semester-long class just for teenagers to get a driver's license. And what about the hundreds (even thousands) of hours our fathers/mentors spend coaching our sports teams and throwing the ball around with us in the backyard?

Yet the majority of our fathers spent little time even scratching the surface of relationship coaching. Maybe it's because relationships are just so complex that most adults never even truly understand them. We already know 50% of first marriages, and 75% of second ones, end in divorce.

With those kind of odds, it's no wonder we've been failing our young people for decades. When it comes to our children and relationships, it's as if adults have simply thrown up their hands and reverted back to the argument, "Everyone needs to make their own mistakes, and we can't do it for them."

So what is my real goal in this chapter? It's to give you examples that spark your understanding of society and how we've been trained (or not trained) to view relationships. I'm certainly not trying to take the responsibility away from you and your ex for the end of your marriage. But this chapter should be a moment to take a break from beating yourself up. I'd like you to seriously consider the way you were raised and how it instilled within you a certain perspective and approach to relationships.

The totality of our childhood experiences have subconsciously created how we choose a female partner—along with the reasons we behave certain ways once we're in a relationship. I hope you can attain a new perspective that further helps you understand deeper reasons you both did what you did during your marriage.

Take me for example. I personally grew up in the 70s and 80s, a time I think truly saw the end of the "Tough Guy Generations." Whether your parents remained married, or whether they divorced, men of the pre-1990s generally got up early, went to work, came home, plopped down in front of the TV, and didn't say shit. Of course there were limited talks about sports and stuff like that, but not much else.

The 60s and 70s also saw the ballooning phenomena of broken homes. This obviously led to more and more kids being raised without dads in the home. The emergence of the "every other weekend dad" really became an accepted norm. Tragically, this meant many dads were even more emotionally unavailable than ever before.

A very applicable story from the movie *City Slickers* helps illustrate my point. Mitch (Billy Crystal), Phil, and Glen were all sitting around in the middle of the country having lunch with the rest of the vacationing city folk. The three guys are rambling about baseball when the only woman on the cattle drive chimes into the discussion. She makes a big deal about how men always talk so much about sports.

Glen snaps back at her, *"Okay sweetheart, so what do you and your friends talk about?"*

The lady replies, "*Well, we talk about life; real life; relationships; are they working; are they not?*"

I love Glen's witty comeback in his sarcastic New York accent. He said, *"Lady, if dat were as interestin' as baseball, they'd put it on cards and sell it wit gum!"*

Phil then adds to the conversation by saying, *"I guess it is kind of silly. But when I was a kid and my dad and I had nothing to talk about, we could always talk about baseball."*

I'm sure you follow me. It was just not the norm for men to talk about relationships. Of course there's an exception to every rule, but it was definitely not common.

I was once discussing this very topic with my childhood friend, Don. He had a grandfather who actually spent three years as a frontline soldier in WWII. Don's grandfather served in the Pacific and fought in places like Guadalcanal, Iwo Jima, and Okinawa. He actually won the Silver Star for bravery. (a really big deal!)

In fact, the WWII generation was so tough that Don's grandfather didn't even know he had Post Traumatic Stress Disorder (PTSD) until he was in his 70s and had to seek services from VA. Not to mention, Don's grandfather (along with all of my own grandparents) were raised right in the middle of the Great Depression. I've heard their stories about how they lived—people at that time were just dead poor! When I hear their stories, I feel like a real wimp in comparison.

But unfortunately, a big part of these men being "tough guys" meant that our dads and grandfathers never really talked to us about women and relationships. The only advice Don or I ever got about women and dating was something to the effect of, "*Kid, you betta nevva knock-up a girl and I betta nevva catch ya doin drugs, cause I'll kill ya!"* And believe me, both Don and I absolutely thought our dads and grandfathers would kill us—no kidding!

There was also something very strange and confusing about these tough guys of years past. Most of them were "manly-men" outside of the house, but were then real "lap dogs" once they got home. It was ever-so-clear the women were the bosses once inside of the home.

Think about how many times you've heard an older guy say, "Well, let me ask the boss," referring to his wife as the person in charge. In past years, we also heard many-a-man say things like, "I don't deserve her." (referring to his wife or girlfriend) Another good one was, "I can't go. She won't let me." God that one bugs the hell out of me!

Don's grandfather (the aforementioned Silver Star winner in WWII) is the most classic example of this. As I told you, he fought on the front lines for three years only to come home, get married, have four kids, and work fulltime while going to night school for a Master's degree in something related to construction. He even rose to the executive level of administering a welding shop for a very large New York construction company—they built skyscrapers. Toward the end of his career, Don's grandfather supervised over 500 workers. Those of you in construction know what a gold hard hat means—yup, he was "The Man" at work.

But then, oddly enough, when Don's grandpa got home he definitely checked his balls at the door. Don's grandmother was a tough old Scottish lady who ran the show inside the house. These vastly different roles most men played between work and home is almost mind boggling.

I know this can be a bit confusing, but I hope you're following me. So many of us were being raised by these tough guys, yet we watched their women run the show at home.

This dichotomy translated to the men being generally quiet in their personal life while the women did all the talking. As a result, so many of our male role models did the absolute minimum when it came to mentoring us about relationships. Again, this is not because they didn't care. My entire life I could call on my dad whenever I was in trouble or needed anything, but it was the relationship advice that was simply not the generational norm.

I remember one particular day when I was especially down about my divorce. I was talking to my mom when she told me to call a long-time family friend, Chris. He had divorced about 20 years prior under very similar circumstances to mine. I was 14 at the time and I actually remember Chris' divorce quite well.

Back then, I overheard my mom talk to Chris for hours on the telephone about his divorce. He was in really bad shape emotionally for almost an entire year—not in danger of loosing his job or anything like that, just really depressed.

So, I actually got excited. I remember thinking, *"Chris is a good dude. He went through this hell with his divorce and he'll be able to tell me exactly how to make it through mine!"*

I eagerly called Chris, left a message, and waited for his response. However, I was completely disappointed a few days later when Chris returned my call. Chris spoke as if his divorce had been no big deal. In a nutshell, he gave me the typical response—just grin and bear it and things will eventually get better!

Although Chris was really nice and compassionate with his words and demeanor, I could tell he was just not motivated to give me a lot of advice. Maybe it was too difficult for Chris to go back and relive his divorce experiences? Maybe it had been so long he actually didn't remember? But no matter what the reasons, Chris wasn't full of the answers I was starving for.

I also remember another time when a friend of mine, Ted, was dating a girl who was kind of "drama." Ted and I were at a baseball game with Ted's father when this girl and her drama became the topic of conversation. Ted's dad joined the conversation by telling Ted, "*I had heard that she was kind of a drama queen from some other guys that know her, but I didn't want to say anything.*"

Ted got pissed at his dad and snapped at him. Ted insisted that his father was obligated to share information like that about any woman he is dating. Ted's dad seemed very uncomfortable as he fumbled for the words to convince Ted that he didn't want to upset him. Ted insisted that he felt it was a father's duty to tell his son things like that. Ted's dad reluctantly agreed and said he'd do so in the future. We then went back to enjoying the ball game.

I was then discussing this incident with my mom about a week later. It was a positive discussion; however, my mom knows Ted's dad and she basically supported his position. Mom said it's a big risk for parents to give their opinions about how they feel toward a girl their son is dating.

Although I understood Mom's position, I adamantly argued that it's a parent's duty to impart their observations and wisdom onto their children. In the end, Mom understood my position, but we agreed to disagree.

I respect most parents for giving us the courtesy and confidence to let us live our own life, but I'd still like to see a bit more relationship guidance. I then shared the following story with my mom to help illustrate my point:

> My therapist once met with a 45-year-old female patient who had a 19-year-old daughter; the daughter had been dating the same serious boyfriend all through high school. The boy and girl were deeply in love (ah, aren't we all at 19!) and planning to get married. As one can imagine, the mother was extremely concerned about her daughter being such a young bride. Although

> mom really liked the boy, she knew her daughter was far too young to wed.
>
> So, the mother and father developed a very interesting solution. They took a second mortgage on their home. (they were not wealthy, but regular middle class) They told their daughter they would completely pay for her to live abroad anywhere she wanted for one year. They never attacked the boyfriend. They simply insisted they wanted their daughter to see some of the world before she got married. The parents even offered to pay for the boyfriend to visit their daughter several times during the year she was away.
>
> The daughter jumped at the chance and chose to live in France. As you can imagine, during that year the daughter discovered there is so much to the world and she was in no way ready for the commitment of marriage. She broke up with the boyfriend and decided to continue with her fulltime education. Although this was extremely expensive for average income parents, I'd say they got a great return on their investment. Several years later, when their daughter was about 28, she met a different man and is now happily married.

I thought this was a great story about a set of parents who definitely didn't fail their child when it came to relationships. They put some thought (and money) into the problem, and now they get to see their daughter live in a happy marriage. It's clear her chances of divorce would have been much greater if they'd simply folded and supported her marriage at 19.

Also, the money they spent on their daughter's year abroad was well worth it. Now her chances of getting divorced (and possibly moving back home with one or more of her own kids) have been greatly reduced. I don't know about you, but I'd hate it if my golden years were impacted by my son moving back home with a few kids of his own following a divorce!

I was recently discussing this complicated concept with my good buddy, Miguel, when he shared some relevant stories about his parents. Miguel's parents have been married for over 50 years. They are both Hispanic immigrants who, to this day, speak mostly Spanish. His dad is one of those hard-working guys who raised six kids working 14 hours a day while his mom stayed home and managed everything else.

Miguel's dad was the oldest of 13 kids raised in the 1930s in a very poor village in Mexico. His dad actually had to leave home when he was 17, not because his mom and dad kicked him out, but because there just was not enough room. Miguel's dad worked his way north until he could save enough money to enter the US legally a few years later. I give Miguel's dad so much credit as a "tough guy."

Just imagine being 17-years-old in the mid-1940s and traveling to an entirely new country where you don't speak the language. There's only one word for this—"balls!" Yet with all this life experience, neither of Miguel's parents ever once talked with him about women and relationships.

I also remember another story Miguel told me about his family. One day, when Miguel was in his early thirties, he was having a beer with his dad's brother, Uncle Chuy. They began chatting about the family, and Uncle Chuy started naming all the kids trying to remember the exact order in which they were born. All of sudden, Uncle Chuy named a child that Miguel had never heard of, Arturo.

Miguel replied to Uncle Chuy, *"I've never heard of an Uncle Arturo."*

Uncle Chuy calmly replied, *"He died when he was about nine. Arturo was two years older than me. I remember one day we were playing, and the next day Arturo started acting sick. Two days later he was dead. We cried for a day or two, but life just went on. We were too busy finding food to cry."*

Wow, what an amazing story! The generations that came before us were made up of survivors. It was all about the basics, and only the strong truly survived. It was the same for one of my grandfathers; he lost a little sister to some kind of illness during the depression. Grandpa also had to live in a Catholic Seminary for three years when he 17 because his house was just too crowded and food was scarce in the Italian community of East Boston.

Many of you can relate to these kinds of stories. Even if you are one of the few exceptions that had a dad who talked with you about women and relationships, I guarantee most of your guy friends had dads who were emotionally unavailable. I have nothing against these men of years past. They were certainly much tougher than me. I'm just being honest so we can hope for a clearer level of understanding.

So now that we've briefly talked about the tough guys who came before us, let's shift gears to us younger folk, commonly referred to as "Generation X." A late 80s article in *Time Magazine* once described "Generation X" like this:

> *". . . They possess only a hazy sense of their own identity but a monumental preoccupation with all the problems the preceding generation will leave for them to fix. This is the twenty-something generation, those 48 million young Americans ages 18 through 29 who fall between the famous baby boomers and the boomlet of children the baby boomers are producing. Since today's young adults were born during a period when the U.S. birthrate decreased to half the level of its postwar peak, in the wake of the great baby boom, they are sometimes called the baby busters. By whatever name, so far they are an unsung generation, hardly recognized as a social force or even noticed much at all... By and large, the 18-to-29 group scornfully rejects the habits and values of the baby boomers, viewing that group as self-centered, fickle and impractical. While the baby boomers had a placid childhood in the 1950s, which helped inspire them to start their revolution, today's twenty-something generation grew up in a time of drugs, divorce and economic strain... They feel influenced and changed by the social problems they see as their inheritance: racial strife, homelessness, AIDS, fractured families and federal deficits."*

Below is another excerpt about "Generation X" from Wikipedia:

> *"Generation Xers were brought up on television, Atari 2600s and personal computers. They are the generation that was raised in the 1970s and 1980s, and saw this country undergo a selfish phase that they do not want to repeat. "Generation X grew up in the 'me generation' of the 1980s, and now they are able to see that it is not all it is cracked up to be," said Jackie Shelton, 31, vice president of Minor Advertising in Reno. The term Generation X came from a book written in 1991 by Douglas Coupland by the same name. It is a fictional book about three strangers who decide to distance themselves from society to get a better sense of who they are. He describes the characters as 'underemployed, overeducated, intensely private and unpredictable.' Coupland took his book's title from another book Class, by Paul Fussell. Fussell used 'X' to describe a group of people who want to pull away from class, status and money in society. Because the characters in Coupland's book fit that description, he decided on the title 'Generation X.' The media found elements of Coupland's characters' lives in America's youth and labeled them Generation X. This stereotypical definition leads society to believe that Generation X is made up of cynical, hopeless, frustrated and unmotivated slackers who wear grunge clothing, listen to alternative music and still live at home because they cannot get real jobs. It is a label that has stuck, stereotypes and all."*

I hope you're seeing how the title "Our Fathers Failed Us" is a very broad statement that speaks to the extremely rapid evolutions throughout our society, along with how relationship mentoring has never quite made it to the forefront. Past generations didn't have the time, the inclination, or the luxury of being like the Generation Xers. On the other hand, Generation Xers may be a little too self-absorbed.

TV, movies, and the media are also major contributors to these problems. In fact, I'm a firm believer that the media is responsible for about 80% of our societal problems, but that's a whole other book. But just think about TV and the media. Most of our dads were raised on "Leave it to Beaver" and "The Mickey Mouse Club." Although that crap is entertaining, what did it really teach them about healthy relationships?

Some other examples are shows like "The Honeymooners" and "All in the Family." Oh, Jackie Gleason and Carol O'Connor talked a big talk, but their wives were queens of the hill. We kids even had our own animated versions of these shows in cartoons like "The Flintstones."

Fred Flintstone tried to be the boss, but we all know Wilma wore the pants in Bedrock! Although I watch religiously when I was a kid, all of these shows certainly didn't give us young men great examples of healthy relationships.

Here is another of my favorite examples—the 60s cartoon "The Jetsons." I'm sure most of you remember this cartoon. At the beginning of each episode, George Jetson dropped his family off one-by-one as they flew through the sky in their floating car.

As George dropped off his wife last at the Space Mall, he opens his wallet and hands his wife a few bills. But she quickly snatches George's wallet from his hands, leaving him with only the few bills he was trying to give to her. This very scene symbolizes the pussification of the modern man within the home.

Author Phillip Wylie coined the term "Momism" in his 1955 book <u>Generation of Vipers</u>. He defined this phenomenon as: "An excessive attachment and devotion of children to their mothers, resulting in a child's dependence and failure to achieve emotional emancipation." I personally prefer the term "Pussification," but Wylie's title of "Momism" is the clinically accepted norm.

Momism continued through the 60's and then on into the 1970's. And speaking of the 70s, do I even need to comment on Mike Brady? I mean, was there ever a bigger pussy in the history of modern mankind than the dad from "The Brady Bunch?"

Furthermore, what did we really learn about relationships from "The Brady Bunch?" The parents never fought; money problems were never discussed; none of the kids ever ended up on drugs and/or pregnant; the kids never had issues with the apparent deaths of their biological parents and the marriage of Mike and Carroll, etc.

I couldn't even imagine the real life problems of bringing a widow and widower together, each with three kids, and trying to make life run even half as smoothly as that TV family. I know many of you are probably thinking, "Chill out Joey. They're just mindless TV shows."

I completely agree with you. However, understanding TV, movies, and the media is essential when following societal mindsets and the evolving cultural norms of varying time periods. We must consciously comprehend what has been engrained into our psyche.

Here's another example; how about Ray Romano? Tell me that "Everybody loves Raymond" is not the most sissy show to ever air on primetime TV. Now that I'm actually divorced and have finished my journey, I can see this ever-so-clearly. When I was married, I actually used to love the show. However, after getting divorced and moving forward, I began to see what an absolute weakling Ray Romano portrays on his show.

I guess I found Ray funny when I was married because I could relate to how his wife ran their life. But now I absolutely hate the show. Seriously, next time you come across the re-runs on TV watch closely for what I'm saying. Deborah is an absolute bitch to Ray, but he just takes it like a little child. A classic example of Momism!

I was flipping channels a few days ago when I stopped on an episode. Ray was talking to his brother Robert about how Robert needed to leave because Ray "might get sex later." Ray was acting like a groveling little kid as he explained to Robert how he had gotten a babysitter and set everything in motion to get Deborah "in the mood." Ray insisted this was a very delicate process that could be disrupted by the slightest interference.

Just then, Ray's mother entered the scene and began insulting Deborah about something trivial. So of course, Deborah became so angry that Ray's chances of getting even a goodnight kiss went right out the window.

And then there's Ray's dad, another classic example of a guy who has thrown in the towel and submitted to his bitchy wife. Although Ray's dad is a funny and sarcastic son-of-a-bitch, his whole attitude and demeanor toward Ray's mom is one of detachment and indifference. Whenever Ray's mom asks his dad anything, Ray's dad simply brushes her off by saying as little as possible. Ray's dad then ends almost every conversation by telling Ray's mom, *"Now make me somethin' ta eat!"*

I remember discussing this very topic with an older friend, Norman, at his retirement party. Norman actually reminds me a lot of Ray Romano's TV dad. Norman was retiring after working over 35 years for the same company. I was very surprised when Norman told me he had already secured a retirement job.

I asked why he was so eager to work when he had just retired. To this Norman replied, *"What da hell am I gonna do, stay home with da wife all day? Kid, we've been married 38 years. I've pretty much said everythin we need ta say ta each-otha."*

Although there was a bit of humor meant by my Norman's comments, I also know there was a lot of sincerity in his words.

As I've said, I hold no ill feelings for any role model I ever had. I'm a firm believer that society and the masses have shaped what our fathers were able to share with us about relationships.

But as you read this book, I hope you feel empowered to discover your weaknesses and overcome what societal norms have been instilled within you. And if you're not a good communicator, there're countless books, programs, classes, therapy, etc., available to you. In 2009, there are simply no excuses for not confronting what we know to be incorrect perspectives.

Furthermore, it's now our turn. I cannot help but wonder what our sons (and daughters) will say about us. Will they also be saying, "Our fathers failed us?" I intend to do all I can to help my son in this area. I will discuss his feelings, share emotions, and help him understand his wants and desires.

I know the very sound of these words make me seem like a "girly man." So be it. I want to give my son a fighting chance to have successful relationships. In fact, I have already found myself providing very calculated and age-appropriate responses to his inquiries about boy/girl relationships, along with his relatively advanced curiosity about my divorce.

I know this is not a book about parenting, but I go off on this brief tangent for a reason—to remind you once more that your divorce is very much about becoming a better person. As we learn during this amazing experience, we become better men, better lovers, better friends, and, most importantly, better fathers. I've learned to find joy in being able to help others from my experiences and enlightenment about divorce, having children, relationship issues, etc.

For example, whenever I find out that a friend or acquaintance has a wife/girlfriend pregnant with their first child, I feel strongly obligated to tell him the truth about the challenges of having a baby. I obviously stress how he will feel an instant love and connection with his child, but I also comment on the lack of sleep, the constant strain on marriage, the lack of personal time, and the utter and complete change to every single aspect of his life.

Although this may sound harsh, many of you with children know exactly what I'm saying. I know you love your children and would die for them without hesitation. But I'm referring to the absolute and total change to your life that you would have never imagined was possible.

And not surprisingly, almost every man I've said this to has later thanked me as the only person who told them the truth about having kids. Each of these guys said that, other men had tried to tell them how difficult childcare would be, but the others essentially sugarcoated the total lifestyle impact.

Most men seem afraid or embarrassed to actually say how difficult it was with their very own children. Since becoming a father myself, I have never held back when advising future dads about the challenges of their first child.

Now that my son is eight, I truly enjoy him more each and every day. However, until he was about two, becoming a dad was just as much of a culture shock as getting divorced. The change to my life was total and complete.

I'm now a firm believer that we must begin to be honest with one another. As men, we must talk to each other about our feelings, our relationships, and our mistakes. Obviously, we must tailor the conversations to the individual age and emotional maturity of whomever we're speaking; however, it's essential we do our best to limit the future failings of our children. We must take this responsibility seriously.

That is why I stress the need for each man to truly embrace his divorce and learn all he can from the experience. The best practitioners in any field are those who're both educated and experienced. You now have the opportunity to become an expert in divorce and relationships. It's obvious that, if your divorce just began last week, you have a long road ahead of you and won't have all the answers for months to come. But the first step in gaining this knowledge is to open your mind and heart to the total experience.

Relationship author Daphne Rose Kingma writes, *"While we'd like to think that time heals all wounds, the fact is time doesn't heal—time passes. Insight heals. We can't get better until we understand what happened."*

And don't make the mistake of thinking that becoming a "divorce expert and scholar" means you must turn into a bookworm who spends all your time reading and researching at the library and bookstore. It may sound strange coming from a guy who wrote a book, but I actually hate reading—it puts me to sleep.

But I do love learning, and I became obsessed with the topic of divorce. I actually learned to scan books for relevant topics and ideas. Some days I would read for five minutes, the next day for 30 minutes, the following for 10 minutes, etc.

Some weeks (especially in the beginning months) I was so messed up I didn't read anything for the entire week because I was too busy crying and watching sappy movies on Lifetime. But knowledge is cumulative, and time is your friend.

Soon into my quest I began going to bookstores and buying all kinds of literature about divorce. However, I quickly learned most books contained bits and pieces of information relevant to my situation, along with a bunch of other wordy and boring crap that meant nothing to me.

Also, buying a lot of books didn't fit well with my limited divorce budget. Not to mention, I really didn't have room in my little divorce pad to store volumes of books. My place actually was so small my son and I were sharing the one and only bedroom, so where the hell was I going to store a bunch of divorce books?

I subsequently decided to get reacquainted with the public libraries. I got a city and county library card (both free by the way) and began checking out several books about every two weeks. I would scan through each book when I had a few minutes to spare, write down the applicable notes, and then move to the next book.

Going to the library was also one more fun thing to do with my son. Our regular trips became one of his favorite things to do. As soon as we entered he'd say, *"Ok dad, I'm going to the kid's section."* It got him excited about books and reading while saving me from having to spend money at the book store.

And we all know that kids get bored with things quickly. When my son was done with a particular book, it didn't sit collecting dust; we would just return it and get some more.

In short, becoming educated and well informed about divorce does not mean you need a big extravagant study in your house where you sit each evening sipping Brandy by the fire while wearing your silk robe and smoking a pipe.

You can be the same old you while researching divorce sitting on your back porch drinking a beer from the bottle and covered in dirt from a hard day's work at your concrete pumping business. You don't need to be a "scholar" and attend conventions, lectures, and poetry readings or to be an expert in anything—especially divorce and relationships.

On a side note, there're often hot chicks at libraries. I would hit various libraries around town at differing days and times, and I quickly learned when the eye candy was best at each site. This made doing my research very easy on the eyes.

In closing, I would like to share that the entire time I worked on this book I kept a picture of my son on the desk next to my computer. I frequently looked at this picture and reflected on the opportunity my divorce has afforded me to properly mentor my son about relationships.

I'm not naïve enough to believe my son will never have his heart broken, never make a mistake, or never experience confusion and feel lost. But I hope I can be a pillar of strength for him when he needs guidance. (or a swift kick in the ass! Ha!) I've done all this research and written a book just as much for him as I have for me. He is my boy and deserves more than to be raised by Ray Romano, Al Bundy, or Mike Brady.

CHAPTER 7

LET'S DO IT BETTER; DON'T REPEAT THE SAME MISTAKES

Up to this point, I've made references about the absolute importance of not repeating the same mistakes. But this chapter focuses specifically on helping you better understand what you screwed up, along with some of the reasons you may have done what you did. I firmly believe that learning from your mistakes is one of the most essential aspects of any man's journey through divorce.

Even if you're a man who is mostly concerned about the financial troubles of divorce (and could not care less about the emotional crap), it's still essential you take time to concentrate on learning from your mistakes. I once interviewed a man, Glen, who fit this mold.

Glen initiated his divorce, and it was essentially based on his ex's horrible spending and financial habits. Glen really didn't feel upset about the emotional aspects of his failed marriage; for him it was mostly about the money.

Tragically, several years later, Glen got remarried to a woman with the exact same spending problems as his first wife. Glen is now almost 62 and unsure if he will need to get a post-retirement job. He is confident he could live very comfortably on his pension. However, Glen's second wife has such expensive taste that he is seriously wondering if he'll need to continue working after retirement. It's painfully obvious Glen didn't spend the time necessary to understand why he married two women with very similar personality traits.

I share this story because so often we think of learning from our divorce in the context of strictly emotional or personal choices. It's essential we remember to think globally when it comes to learning from divorce. No matter what you think were the issues in your marriage, you must look at yourself and take the time to understand the totality of failures.

Although it may be very painful to arrive at the root cause of your mistakes, please devote the time necessary to ensure you truly understand everything. Your divorce is a rebirth—a chance to do things better next time around. You'll only have you to blame if you disregard these opportunities for immense growth and continue making similar mistakes.

It's such a tragedy most of us never fully realize the amazing opportunities afforded by divorce. Like clockwork, most men begin divorce moping around and feeling very depressed; this is generally followed by a type of rebirth that leads men to either become a "man whore" or to quickly "shack up" with another woman who is frighteningly similar to the last.

Or, guys often jump to the opposite extreme of their ex-wife. These are the men who get divorced from a woman who never wanted to have sex, so they run out and find the nastiest, dirtiest stripper with more issues than *Time Magazine*—but she is crazy in bed so they're like blind puppies. Remember, fellas, we're after balance here, not insanity.

So again; we rarely spend time focusing on the opportunities afforded to us from divorce. Could this be a symptom of our increasingly chaotic lifestyles? After all, we're busier than ever these days. Taking our time with anything is becoming an obsolete concept. Divorce is no different; inevitably our divorce becomes one more wave battering us in the storm of life as we simply try to come up for air. Subsequently, we often do the bare minimum to just get through divorce without really benefiting from the experience.

There is another really great scene from the 1991 movie *City Slickers* that helps illustrate this point. Billy Crystal and his friends had just fought off the drunken cowboys and taken away their guns. Phil (Daniel Stern) held the pistol as he yelled at the cowboys to go sleep off their drunken binge. Phil then entered his tent, followed by Billy Crystal and Bruno Kirby.

A conversation followed in which Phil began crying over his recent divorce, losing his job, and the fact that he may never see his kids again.

Billy Crystal looks at Phil and says, *"Remember when we were kids and somebody messed up a game and we'd yell, 'Do-Over!' Well that's it; your life's a Do-Over… "*

This is exactly how I think men should view divorce. It gives us a chance to "do over" what we may have done wrong in the past. And don't think just because you are in your 40s, 50s, or even 60s that it's to late for a do over.

When I was a kid, being in your 40s was OLD! I know some of you are laughing right now. (or maybe crying? Ha!) I remember how I looked at my dad when he turned 40—he was almost dead! But now that I'm approaching 40, I really don't feel that old. (funny how things change!)

But in all seriousness, I have many retired friends and family who live in Arizona, so I've spent a lot of time there over the years. It's a great place for a lot of reasons, one of which is the active old people. There're so many people well into their 80s (and even 90s) who're living healthy and active lives.

It's funny to watch these crazy older folks so full of vigor and life. They ride their bicycles, go on long walks, sip their margaritas, and just enjoy life. So never think you're too old to start over. As I repeat, you can learn to control your thoughts and perspective (including your feelings about your own age), it just takes a conscious effort to get started.

But back to the problem at hand; why is it just so tough for many of us to do something positive with our divorces? Is it because people in general seem to gravitate toward the negatives rather than the positives? After all, it's a hell of a lot easier to just say, "My ex is a bitch! Fuck her! I'm gonna find a cool chick now!"

Well, unfortunately, living in this kind of denial will just not work too well. If it did, divorce rates for second marriages wouldn't be 25% higher than those for first marriages.

On the other hand, I'm in no way inferring you should swing to the other extreme uttered by self-help cults that chant, "Just think happy, happy, happy thoughts" and ignore all the bullshit in your life.

As I've mentioned, I have read dozens of self-help and positive thinking books and they often drive me nuts. Although there is a definite place for such advice during a divorce, it can often be a bit much for most men, a little too touchy-feely for us big macho men, right?

For some reason, when I think of self-help authors, I picture a big-hair smooth talker with a spray-on tan and lacquer white veneer teeth telling me, "Use your inner strength to move into a deeper state of positive living…" Or I visualize a long-haired monk with a full gray beard wearing a silky robe and a purple sash to one side. My response to their happy thoughts; screw you, pal, and your happy thoughts! This divorce shit sucks!

Divorce is really an amazing balancing act of confronting the negatives while reaching for the positives. It would be nice to just think happy thoughts; however, too many men are bombarded with debilitating emotional stress while at the same time being sent to the poorhouse.

The added stresses of the unknowns are enough to drive you nuts. "How will my life eventually turn out? Will I get enough time with my kids? Will my ex have some asshole move in and try to replace me as dad to my kids?"

But the bright side is that learning from your divorce is not restricted to a one semester course at a community college. There is no time-set final examination that gets you a pass or fail grade in "Divorce 101." You can proceed through the process at your own pace while doing things that work best for you.

I have even got one friend, Richard, who separated from his wife (at her request) over 18 months ago. Richard is still all messed up and hasn't had sex since. (Holy cow! You think he still knows how to do it?) Now, my personal opinion is that this is way too long to grieve over any woman (and even Snow White herself doesn't deserve such emotional devotion), but it's not my place to judge. That's Richard's journey and only he can travel his road.

But using Richard as an example, based on the extended time he has taken to obsess over his wife, can we honestly say he has committed himself to learning from the mistakes of his marriage? Although I certainly have a great deal of respect for Richard's overwhelming commitment to his ex, at what cost is he delaying the inevitable and his own personal growth?

It appears to me that he is hiding from reality and living as a victim. At some point it becomes essential for those of us getting dumped to accept the truth so we can begin a transition into the learning process.

And this transition between grief and growth is far from a seamless and sterile process. Although there're exceptions to every rule, most of us make the transition very gradually. One day you'll suddenly realize you're crying less and analyzing more. But this usually doesn't mean the crying and sadness is completely over. A moment of clarity should simply be used as a point of reference, a time to reflect on one's progress through the journey.

I personally didn't begin to examine and understand my culpability in the failure of my marriage until I got to the point of crying less and thinking more. Then, and only then, was I able to begin the painful but rewarding process of learning about myself and how I was going to do things better.

Unfortunately, too many of us never get to this point of self-growth. The divorce stats clearly reflect that most men would rather spend their divorce running out and "getting laid" than taking the time to learn from their mistakes. Don't get me wrong, running out and getting laid is completely your business. You just need to schedule the time and effort for some analytical self-reflection.

I'm sure you can think of several people who just keep repeating the same poor choices when selecting romantic partners. I have several friends on their fourth marriage and counting. If you're one of these guys competing for the *Guinness Book of World Records* in the number of marriages, it's not too late for you, either. At any point you can choose to spend the time necessary to learn and grow.

You will probably think this is pretty stupid, but last night I was flipping channels when I came across, "The Real Housewives of Orange County." (But please don't tell anyone I was watching that shit—seriously!) For those who don't know, this is a cable reality show profiling ten women from Orange County, California. They're all rich, spoiled, and bitchy women who have more drama in their lives than a primetime soap opera (guess that's why they have a TV show!) Last night they were focusing on one of the housewives who had just split with her filthy rich boyfriend.

At one point, they showed the sad woman and her friends standing around the kitchen talking about the breakup. As this girl got teary-eyed about her ex, one of her friends said, *"Don't be sad. We're going out to find you a man!"*

What the hell! Did I miss something here? If these chicks were friends with any common sense, they would take her to a movie, go to the spa, do chick stuff like getting massages and facials, or just stay home and cook dinner having "Chick Night" doing each other's toes or some other crap like that!

But nooooooo! These female rocket scientists are planning to run right out and play heavenly matchmakers at a night club occupied by guys who are on the prowl for a quickie! That sure sounds like a great plan to me.

I can't see this particular Orange County Housewife really learning what went wrong in her relationship by shaking her ass in a sleazy dress with some 8-inch stripper shoes and no panties. (Okay, so maybe that's not such a bad thing for us guys, but I digress…)

The reality is that before you can seriously consider dating anyone, you must understand two things—the relationship mistakes you made in the past and the warning signs you missed or chose to ignore when you began dating your previous spouse.

Yup, I'm talking to you. You made mistakes; it was by no means all her fault your marriage failed. Even if she had an affair and you remained faithful, there were things you did to contribute to the problems. Of course I'm not condoning infidelity, but we're talking about you, not her. Your personal growth following the separation is completely separate from hers—you're on your own now!

After all, don't you want to learn what you did wrong and the warning signs you missed so you never go through this crap again? I mean, here you are in the middle of probably the most difficult experience of your entire life, and you aren't going to learn from your mistakes? If that is you, then you are a true dumb ass!

Maybe you're not a good communicator; maybe you're too sensitive; maybe you're a drunk; maybe you're a cocky asshole; maybe you need to stop being a pussy and letting women boss you around; maybe, maybe, maybe… There are simply so many endless examples of what we can learn from our failed marriages. Finding out what went wrong and taking corrective action is one of the most important things one can do to stack the cards in favor of future relationship success.

I direct your attention back to the book Coming Apart: Why Relationships End and How to Live Through the Ending of Yours. The author, Daphne Rose Kingma, really opened my eyes to the reasons we select romantic partners. Of all the readings I recommend to you, Kingma's book is at the top of my list. I cannot stress enough how her words guided me during the beginning (and most painful) part of my divorce.

She also really helped me understand what I could do better. I actually liked Kingma's book so much that I bought a second copy after I loaned my first to a friend who never gave it back.

I found Kingma's book to be a very easy read that is also emotionally soothing. She pushes you to confront the truth behind your past relationships; to peal back the façade and understand the reality. Chapter 3 of Kingma's book is titled, "Exploding the Love Myths: Why Are We Really in Relationships?" This chapter contains a great explanation about why we fall in love, but then also why we fall out of love. In this chapter, Kingma writes:

> *"In our lifetime, we are each trying to do a single thing: to create ourselves. We are tying to solve our basic psychological problem—which is to answer in depth and to our own satisfaction the question; 'Who am I?' What this means is that as we proceed through our lives, we are all trying to get a sense of our own identity. In order to do that, we create a series of life experiences that either help us discover who we really are or confirm who we have discovered ourselves to be. This process of self definition or self discovery occurs through what I call "Developmental Tasks," and it is our relationships, more that anything else in our lives, that help us accomplish the way through which we define ourselves. That's why we choose the people we do and that's why they choose us. That's also why relationships begin and why they end."*

Furthermore, as Kingma examines how developmental tasks affect our relationships, she actually speculates that maybe we're not always meant to be together forever. I know that is a really deep and unorthodox concept, but it certainly peaked my interest.

Here is one of Kingma's examples:

> *"Deborah, an immigrant, grew up in deprivation. Her father was an alcoholic, and, as a result, her mother had to become the bread-winner of the family. Her mother, feeling guilty about her husband's alcoholism and her own continual absence, indulged her children materially, giving them everything they wanted. With gifts she tried to make up for what she was unable to give by being home and present to her children's emotional needs. As a result, Deborah grew up thinking that, materially at least, she'd get whatever she wanted, and so in spite of the severe emotional deprivation of living with an absent mother and an alcoholic father, she was a spoiled child. When she met John, she was immediately attracted to 'his grown-upness.' A traveling furniture salesman, he seemed to know a lot about life and how to function in the outside world, things she had never learned because her mother had been too busy and her father had been too drunk. She had goals, education goals in particular, that she had been too unfocused to pursue, and when she told John about them, he encouraged her…*
>
> *…In this relationship, Deborah was growing up; that was her developmental task. She was learning the skills she would need as a grown up, so she could function in the world. John was also fulfilling some defects from his early life. Finally he experienced what it was to be appreciated and loved, to have some attention directed towards him."*

Both John and Deborah fulfilled needs within each other; they helped the other in developmental tasks that were necessary at certain points in their lives. But then, as John and Deborah each grew individually, their developmental tasks changed—causing them to actually grow apart. So maybe your relationship/marriage was not a failure; maybe it just outlived its purpose in your life.

Using Kingma's theory, I have been able to look back at every relationship in my life and identify the reasons why it began, how it evolved, and why it ended. Although it's not as clinical and absolute as it sounds because emotions are deeply involved, Kingma's analytical process is a great tool for individual self-discovery.

With over 250,000 copies of her book sold, Kingma should be considered a real expert in this field. After reading Kingma's book, I had a much more profound understanding of the mistakes I made. More importantly, I especially knew a lot more about why I had made those mistakes.

It's not enough to simply assert you were an asshole during a particular incident. You must seek to understand why you were an asshole. On the other hand, maybe you're a really thoughtful guy who simply married a bitch that brought out the worst in you. Or, maybe you're a selfish prick and your ex was the sweet one. Or, maybe it was a little of both? This is something only you can decide.

Taking this further, let's examine another major problem for a lot of us guys; we marry our mothers. That's not intended to be some sick incest joke, but rather a statement about what men are often looking for when we marry—especially when we marry young. The best way for me to elaborate is to tell you the story of Ross.

Ross first met his ex-wife when he was 22 and she was 25. Ross was in the military and had been stationed in a city halfway across the country. Ross opened an account at a local movie rental business when he met his future wife, Michelle, who worked there. Ross became a frequent customer renting a lot of movies. Ross and Michelle quickly formed a mutual attraction. They exchanged numbers and began meeting for coffee. (Ah… innocent coffee. Isn't that how it all starts?)

Over the next few months, Ross' trips to the movie rental place became increasingly frequent, and his coffee meetings with Michelle also increased. Ross quickly learned Michelle was a very strong woman who was good at controlling money, bills, and everything else in a modern American household. There was just one teeny-tiny catch. You guessed it—Michelle was married. But regardless, Ross and Michelle began having and affair.

A quick side note: never get serious with any woman you begin seeing while she is in another relationship. 99% of the time it will end for you in just the same way. But that's another topic to be covered later.

So, shortly thereafter, Michelle left her husband and moved in with Ross. Two years later, Michelle's divorce was final and she got re-married to Ross. Remember, Ross was 22 when he moved in with Michelle. Other than living in barracks-style military housing, moving in with Michelle was Ross' first experience living outside of his parents' house. Ross was basically 22 and going from his parents' house directly to living with Michelle.

Ross was very honest with me when he said:

> *"I hate to admit it, but Michelle quickly became Mommy. She took care of everything; she cleaned; cooked; did the shopping; the laundry; etc. I think she did everything but cut the grass, and that's only because it was military housing and we had a gardener."*

In short, Ross missed some major warning signs. First and foremost, I think we all agree that Ross was way too young to move in with a woman and get that serious. (and we already covered getting married too young in the previous chapter, "Our Fathers Failed Us") Ross also never had the chance to live on his own as a grown man.

This caused a big problem when Ross and Michelle moved in together because it was just too easy for him to remain a kid at home. Michelle did everything around the house, just as Ross' mom had done back home. This started a tragically negative spiral; Michelle looked at Ross more-and-more as a young goof-off, and Ross looked at her as a nagging mom.

I'm sure you can imagine how things evolved. They had less sex because Michelle was simply not attracted to do a guy she viewed as a little boy, and Ross would pressure Michelle and give her "the sex talk." You know, fellas, this is when we basically beg for sex like groveling little kids whining to our parents about wanting the "GI Joe with the Kung Fu Grip" for Christmas.

Although most guys never actually get on their hands and knees and grovel for sex, we might as well with some of the begging we do. We act as though they hold all the cards and we have nothing. You know, "Power to the pussy!"

And then, when we beg for sex, we transition into the next problem a lot of us guys need to correct—we become wimps! I'm so glad to say that I will never, as long as I live, make a woman feel like I'm pleading for her to have sex with me.

After going through the emotional trauma of divorce, having to go without sex because a woman is being difficult (or just flat-out bitchy) is not even an option for me. My pride and respect for myself has become much more important than getting laid or gaining the favor of a woman. It's actually a great place to be, and I truly hope you get there. (if you're not there already)

So, back to Ross. He now sees things very clearly, and he holds no ill feelings toward his ex, Michelle. He understands how his relationship outlived the development tasks for both himself and his ex.

Even if your situation is completely different than Ross', I hope you can use this as a guide to evaluate the dynamics that brought you and your ex together. Most of the men I have interviewed already knew these reasons in their heart, it just takes them a while to admit. And that's okay; again, there're no time limits here.

Another very big mistake we make when entering relationships is to not accept our partners for who they really are. We all know that relationships are fun and exciting in the beginning. Hell, it's actually really easy in the beginning. Most of us men bathe well and watch our language, while most women hide what can often be a bossy and overbearing personality.

But then, when the newness wears off and things settle into bliss and boredom, most men start doing stupid stuff like playing "pull my finger" and pissing on the toilet seat. I even had one buddy, Archie, who used to purposely pee on the toilet seat when his wife was mean to him. Archie is now divorced (thank God) and I'm proud to say he learned from his mistakes and has matured (he is now a reformed "toilet seat urinator!")

One thing women do frequently is to get with a man who is not a communicator and "try to change him!" I have had numerous conversations with women about how their guy doesn't express himself well; he never sends flowers; he never wants to talk about their relationship, etc.

Yet, if these ladies were to think back to the beginning, their man never did those things. It was all a self-created fantasy on the woman's part. But these women were so eager to sink their claws into a man that they disregarded things they absolutely should not have overlooked.

Dr. Laura can be a real bitch about this topic, but she is so right. (What, so I listen to Dr. Laura. It's only to help me with this book! So shut up!) Women constantly call Dr. Laura complaining about their man who never wants to do anything romantic or have heart-to-heart talks about their relationships. Dr. Laura always interrupts these ladies to ask, *"Was the guy always this way?"*

After a few seconds of dodging the question, almost all the women say, *"Yeah, I guess he never was a good communicator."*

Dr. Laura assertively insists that the women must accept things the way they are and stop complaining! The moral of the story is that, if a guy or girl is not a certain way when you're dating, they are not going to suddenly become this magic person you want them to be after you get married.

For example, I have a really good friend, Tommy, who loves to hang out at the bar with his buddies. I can honestly say Tommy is not an alcoholic, but he is close. Truthfully, Tommy is just a really social person who loves chatting over drinks—and he is funny, too. I can totally see Tommy as a regular on the TV sitcom "Cheers."

One day, not too long ago, Tommy's wife kind of nagged him because she thought he was spending too much time at the bar. Tommy immediately reminded his wife that he has been exactly the same way since they met, 15 years ago. In fact, Tommy said to his wife, *"This is me. You know that. After all, we met in a fucking bar!"*

To her credit, Tommy's wife quickly saw the message and ended her attempts at convincing Tommy to reduce his time at the pub.

Here's another example that I'm sure most men can easily relate to—a woman's weight. It's no secret most of us want a woman that is hot. Come on, this is a guy book. You can be honest. Remember, I'm writing this to say all the crap men would love to say but often can't. In short, if you're dating a woman you can tell will have a weight problem in years to come, but you're a fitness nut, chances are pretty darn good you're not going to be happy.

It's not so much that you're an insensitive and superficial bastard (okay, well maybe just a little), but rather that you two have very differing priorities in this area. If she goes to the gym in the beginning with you, but you can tell she's just not all that into it, chances are when the relationship bliss settles in, you'll be doing "the Hibbidy-Dibbidy" with Mrs. Potato Head!

Again, you can't change a person. She may show a different face in the beginning, but you need to dig deep to discover who she is when not trying to impress you.

However, the weight example does work both ways. A woman could just as easily be into staying active and healthy while her man remains contender for "Beer Belly of the Year."

For example, I know a woman, Catie, who divorced her high school sweetheart after 26 years because he was a real "fuddy-duddy," and she was a very happy-go-lucky and active person. Catie was in her early 50s and still very energetic. Catie frequently walked, jogged, swam, hiked, worked-out with weights, etc., while her husband was a boring guy who mostly sat around and complained a lot.

The year Catie separated from her husband she was so energized that she developed the stamina to complete "The Death March." This is a 48-mile hike through the Grand Canyon that must be completed in 24 hours. It runs from one rim to the other, and then back. You go up-and-down a total of 11,000 feet in elevation during the event.

It was great to see Catie truly blossom after her separation. It was clear she had emotionally detached herself years before. She was now free to be herself and couldn't stop smiling from ear to ear. Catie's adult children were also very supportive of her leaving her husband. They basically said, "What took you so long, mom?"

Another good example of trying to change a person can be found in the differences over the way each person handles money. If you're so tight with money that you can scrape the Lincoln head off a penny, then you shouldn't be getting serious with "Ms. Super Shopper." But be warned, the money example also works both ways—just like the weight/fitness scenario.

I've known too many wives who work their asses off trying to balance the family budget in spite of their motor-head husband buying every new toy that comes along. Think of all the guys you know with an endless money pit in the garage. (like a dune buggy or a classic car) If this is you, maybe it's time for some serious self-reflection.

I'm only being this harsh because I was one of these guys when I was married. I always had a dirt bike, a boat, a dune buggy (God, both dune buggies were literal money pits!), etc. My ex would try to balance the family budget despite me constantly upgrading toys and accessories.

I now see why I tried to be the toy master, and actually it's pretty simple; I was compensating for the unhappiness in my life. But it still doesn't make it right. Does this sound familiar to any of you?

Of course, there's nothing wrong with having a toy or two. Some guys love their fishing boat, while others need a fixed-up Jeep to climb the biggest hill they can find. I'm simply stressing that you look at the real reasons for your purchases. Is it partially because you're unhappy at home? Or, could it be you're compensating for something?

I mean, if you're a grown man and you need a truck lifted 8" with Gumbo Monster Mudder tires, maybe you should honestly examine the real reasons you have "Big Foot" in the driveway. I'm not gonna even stoop to the small penis jokes. It would be so unprofessional to infer that guys with big, lifted trucks have small genitalia. So I'm not even gonna go there…

But seriously, if you're a fellow toy master, ask yourself why you strain (or strained) your family's budget. I have a friend named Rick who's a regular guy living on an average middle class income, just like me. Rick has a small two-bedroom house with a wife and two toddlers. It's a nice house, but it's kind of small for his family.

However, Rick also has a 38-foot long diesel motor home that cost $110,000. And when he bought it, it was already 10 years old! Rick also has a $35,000 sand car (a dune buggy) plus a few dirt bikes and quads. I think he may have recently bought a boat, too. It's tough to keep up. But man, it freaks me out just thinking about all that debt!

Again, there's not a darn thing wrong with having toys. I'm just stressing the need to really understand the reasons you do what you do. I now consider myself a "Recovering Toy Master" and have since downgraded to having only a Jeep (which is also my one and only car), several plastic kayaks, and one mountain bike.

What's amazing is that, although I now have fewer toys, I spend much more quality time with my son and my friends. It's so great to go paddling on the kayaks or off-roading with my son sitting in my lap steering the Jeep through the scenic outdoors.

I'm actually having way more fun doing these things with my son than I ever did on my motorcycle or my jet ski without him. In fact, when I had a dirt bike, I always felt bad because I had to leave my son at camp during anything other than a little 10 minute putt-putt.

But back to the task at hand, identifying the warning signs of a possible bad relationship fit. Here's an easy example that so many of us completely ignore—physical violence. It seems so simple, but it's not. If you and a woman engage in physical violence, there're two things you absolutely must do. First, break up with the chick and enter the Witness Relocation Program. I'm dead serious!

Every guy I've ever known who was in a volatile relationship (either verbally abusive or physically violent) never had a successful long-term marriage. Although a few have remained married, they're more miserable than a cow getting a cattle prod stuck up its ass twice a day. (ouch!) And secondly, you need to get some serious counseling!

If you stay with a woman a moment after she hits you, and/or you hit her back (or you hit her first), it's essential that you two separate. I'm not saying this to be mean; you just really need to realize how serious violence is. If you've ever engaged in physical, mental, or emotional abuse with a woman, and you don't get help to understand the reasons why, all of the research data (and just common sense) indicates you'll be doomed to this hellish cycle of love and hate.

Maybe you were abused as a child, or maybe you saw your dad smack the shit out of your mom; either way, please seek-out help so you can once and for all break the cycle. I have a friend I used to work with, Simon, who got himself involved with a woman like this about 15 years ago.

Things were great at first, just like most other relationships—nice, sweet, supportive, fun, etc. Then, about a year into the relationship, her psycho side started to rear its ugly head. She began to display the violent mood swings and mentally unstable rants one would expect from your average crazy princess.

And, as with most guys who tolerate this kind of crap, Simon also has a bit of a temper, and he gave it right back to her. Simon ignored all the warning signs and married the woman. One night, shortly after they married, she took things to a physical level and popped Simon a good one right in the nose. Simon ended up with two black eyes and had to call in sick to work for over a week after making up a story about falling off a ladder. (or something stupid like that)

Shortly thereafter, Simon and his wife reconciled and she begged him not to leave. They continued with their ups-and-downs while also having two kids back-to-back. A few more years passed, and things got even worse.

On one occasion the cops were called and Simon got arrested for domestic violence. After some lengthy court crap, Simon was forced to plead guilty to a misdemeanor. Luckily, Simon had already retired from police work on a medical injury so he didn't lose his job. But guess what? Even after all that, they still stayed together. Finally, after about 11 years of marriage, all that violence and drama (along with a few affairs on her part), they finally got to the point of divorce.

I wish I could tell you how it turned out, but as I write this book he's in the middle of some lengthy court battles. I can share that Simon is probably going to be screwed. With a domestic violence conviction Simon will have a tough time convincing a judge he's a good dad. (even though I can honestly say he's an awesome dad and she's a crappy mom) Simon's attorney has braced him for the worst. We're all doing our best to support Simon, but there's not much we can do other than listen and be there for him.

As crazy as this situation sounds, it's tragically all too common. I bet almost every guy can think of a friend who's had a similarly volatile relationship. Maybe you're one of them; maybe you're a guy who's just like Simon and you missed all the warning signs to remain within the confines of a violent relationship.

If this is you, I'm not even going to begin to try to analyze why you stay in such a harmful situation. I can only urge you to find the right therapist to truly help you resolve the issues. This is almost the worst of the worst when it comes to needing professional help.

And a little side note: when Simon met his ex-wife she already had three kids from her first marriage. She had gotten pregnant at 15 with the first child and they married a few years later. This is by no means a slam against dating a woman with children, but it's simply a little red flag deserving of attention. Simon's wife's first husband also turned-out to be a methamphetamine addict who was physically abusive.

In Simon's case, the red flag should have been for him to honestly ask if his ex had learned from the mistakes of her youth. If the answer would have been, "yes," than she may have actually presented an awesome partner who'd grown beyond the errors of her ways into a powerful partner prepared to do things right the second time around. (but we now know this wasn't the case) In some instances, it can be great to get with someone who's made mistakes; the key is whether or not they've learned from them.

When speaking of red flags, I'm just stressing you to keep count of the number that surface. We've *All* carry some type of emotional baggage. In the correct context this baggage is much of what shapes us into ourselves—they're the bricks that fill-in the construction of our individuality.

But, before I rag on Simon too much, let me share a really shitty psycho story of my own. Talk about missing the warning signs and the red flags—this one is nuts. It's actually just about the worst experience of my entire life!

About seven years ago, my ex and I were having some issues, so we chose to separate for a while—not that uncommon in today's married world. I've met so many couples who've taken a break throughout their marriage. I'm not saying it's good or bad; I'm just saying it seems to be pretty common.

Our son was about 10 months old and we agreed on a mutual separation. I moved back into my parents' spare room and brought a crib for my baby. Talk about feeling like a loser. I felt like a teenage boy who had knocked-up my girlfriend and had to bring home the baby.

About a month after moving back into my folks' house, I began talking to this tall and gorgeous 21-year-old girl I'd met through a co-worker. (I was 28 at the time) I'm not kidding you when I say she looked like a taller version of Anna Kornakova, the professional tennis player. So we decide to hang out one night.

At this time it had been probably over eight years since I'd dated, and I was pretty surprised at how easy it was to meet a very attractive woman and begin a pre-dating friendship. Hell, maybe that should have been the first clue; a smoking-hot girl wanting to go out with a guy separated for only a month and living back at his parents' house. But on with my story...

I arrived at her house one evening to have dinner and a few drinks. I had my little boy with me. It was not unusual for me to take him. I've always been the kind of dad who's taken him everywhere. It was actually a very nice few hours of chatting and getting to know one another. She began to tell me about her family, including the fact that her dad was rich but had tried to commit suicide several times. (okay, another clue)

She'd also dropped some hints about eating disorders. But again, it wasn't anything I clued in on; either because I was just so dumbfounded about being out so soon with a really hot chick, or because my psycho radar was down as a result of my recent separation. Either way, if I'd been in a healthy state of mind, I probably would have run out of that place faster than a rocket headed for the moon.

At about 7:00 p.m. I gave my little guy a bath at her house. Shortly thereafter, he fell asleep and we proceed to make out. Some other cool stuff happened, but not sex. I grabbed my son and headed home at about 9:30 p.m. Needless to say, I was feeling pretty good when I left. It had only been about a month since separating, and already I got to make out with a hot, young chick.

The next day I called her and left a message. However, a few days passed before I got a return call. When she finally did call me, it was like a nuclear bomb went off. She proceeded to tell me how upset she was because she couldn't remember what had happened, and she accused me of drugging her.

I can't even tell you how I felt. This woman had gone completely crazy on me and was throwing around some unbelievable allegations.

After about 20 minutes on the phone, she just told me to never call her again. I gladly complied.

About three months went by and this story became the talk of happy hours among my friends. It was one big joke how so many of my married buddies cheat on their wives with anything that breaths and has a vagina, yet nothing bad ever happens to them. But I don't even have sex with a woman and she goes completely nuts-o! But unfortunately, the story doesn't end there.

Several months later, I got a call from a sex crimes detective. I first thought nothing of it. I was a cop, and she was probably calling about a preliminary report I had taken on patrol. It was not until I returned her call that I learned this psycho bitch had actually filed a criminal complaint against me alleging I had drugged her and that she had no recollection of anything that occurred the night we made out. After making an appointment for me to come and meet the detective (as a suspect in a sex crime), I hung up the phone and promptly ran to the bathroom to puke my guts out!

A few days later, I arrived at her office and we went into the interview room; you know, just like the ones you see on TV with the mirror someone on the other side watches you through. I can't tell you how I felt. I was usually the one doing the interviews in rooms just like that, but that time I was the interviewee. And forget any thoughts that the detective going easy on me because I was a cop.

I think she may have actually been tougher on me simply to prove she was doing an unbiased investigation. At the end of the interview she insisted that I take a lie detector if I wanted to prove my innocence. "Un-fuckin-believable," I remember thinking. But, I had no choice. I had to put my faith in the polygraph machine and take the test.

The next day I arrived for my lie detector test. I was hooked-up to that machine for 2 hours and 37 minutes of the most grueling questions I'd ever been asked. The guy doing the test was one tough dude who was ruthless in his questioning. At one point I even remember getting light-headed and dizzy as I sat strapped to the machine.

At the end of the test, he asked me if there was anything else I wanted to add before he stepped out to grab the detective working my case. *"Anything to add,"* I thought. This guy had just given me the biggest mental ass-whopping in the history of modern civilization, and then he asked if I had anything to add!

I sat dumbfounded in the chair waiting for them to return. Prior to stepping out, the polygraph guy had given me no indication about what the machine had told him. I was fully ready for them to swoop into the room *Apocalypse Now* style and slap on the cuffs. About 10 minutes later, the polygraph guy and the detective officiously entered the room, sat down directly across from me, and stared me right in the eye.

Suddenly, the polygraph guy looked away from me and turned his head toward the detective as he said, *"He didn't put anything in her drink, they didn't have sex, and whatever happened in that apartment was completely consensual."*

I actually got a bit misty-eyed as I felt the stress release surge through my body. I quickly asked him, *"Could you please repeat that?"* I just had to hear it once more to make sure I wasn't dreaming.

He again looked me dead in the eye and said the polygraph clearly indicated I was telling the absolute truth.

Then the detective completely changed her tone and became very nice to me. She explained that, from the initial complaint, both she and her supervisor were certain the girl was crazy and lying. However, because I was a cop, it was essential they conducted the most thorough investigation strictly by the book. I immediately understood their point and was actually thankful they did such a good job.

To this day, I'm confident that anyone viewing those interview tapes would be assured I got absolutely zero special treatment. Even though I was completely cleared of all allegations, it still doesn't change the unbelievable stress of the entire experience.

A few weeks later, I met with a mutual friend who had known the girl for several years prior to us meeting. When I told the story about the false allegations, this friend began to tell me all kinds of crap about how crazy the chick was. She had even been institutionalized for some type of mental issues and eating disorders. I yelled at my friend about not telling me this sooner, to which my friend replied, *"I didn't think you were actually stupid enough to go out with her!"* I couldn't believe it. I wanted to punch my friend!

To this day, I have no idea why this girl went crazy. It was literally like she had multiple personalities. One moment she was sweet and nice, and the very next moment she lost her mind.

I simply share this story to help illustrate just how easy it is to get hooked up with an absolutely crazy bitch. This story is exactly why no one should ever fall madly in love and spontaneously get married in an all-night Vegas drive through staffed by Elvis.

Most of you're laughing right now. But admit it, there's been at least one time in your life where you've been stricken by a condition commonly referred to as "pussy blindness!" Hopefully, you didn't stay blind long enough to get married within a few months of dating. At the very least, I'm sure you know one guy stupid enough to fall victim to his gonads! I've heard from so many men, "But I love her! I've never met anyone who makes me feel this way!"

No kidding she makes you feel so good; it's called chemical endorphins being released that are flooding your body with actual physical pleasure feelings. My therapist once told me the physical feeling of "newness" that are so good generally last between 12 and 24 months. After that, the body limits the amounts of these good-feeling chemicals and reality of longevity sets in. This is when things seem to become more work and the relationship requires effort.

Don't rush to get remarried before you feel the lull of relationship bliss. Just like you should never get a tattoo when you're drunk, don't get hitched while you're on the "crack high" of a new relationship. If you'd like to learn more about this physical release of lust chemicals, read The Alchemy of Love and Lust, by Theresa Crenshaw.

You might be asking, "When is it time to get serious with a woman after divorce?" This question (as with everything else related to divorce) is such an individual concept that it doesn't have a textbook answer. I believe the question of when to get serious is less about time and more about whether you're emotionally ready and you've learned from prior mistakes.

Many people leave a marriage and wait several years before entering their next serious one, yet they still repeat the same mistakes. They select the same type of woman as their ex and conduct themselves in the same damaging manner that helped to destroy their previous marriage. Although they waited a long time, they learned nothing from the failure of their marriage.

So you need to ask yourself, "Have I truly accepted responsibility for what I did wrong in my failed marriage and can I be confident I'm not going to repeat my mistakes?" And your response cannot be, "I'm gonna do it better next time because I won't get with such a bitch!" Nice try, but if you want something serious and successful in the future, you must learn from the last one.

"Emotional healing" is a phrase I didn't think would ever happen to me. Although it's common sense to believe you'll feel and live better some day, it's just such an intangible concept to grasp when you're knee-deep in your divorce bullshit.

For many men, the idea they'll someday be happy is buried so far under all the other physical, mental, emotional, and spiritual stress that it's just too intangible. I remember trying to be happy over the constant stomachache—it was virtually impossible for several months.

Remember, boys, this is a time in your life when you must be selfish. I know that sounds strange, especially if your ex said you were selfish when you were together. But I'm talking about being emotionally selfish. This is a time for you to put your needs before almost anything else. How you heal—or fail to heal—will have a profound impact on the quality of the rest of your life.

It's sad, but we all know at least one person (probably more than one) who ended up getting married two or three times and having the same troubles over and over. Maybe they get bored too easy; maybe they have commitment issues; maybe it's a woman who keeps selecting abusive men; maybe they pick a controlling partner who is not supportive of their dreams, etc.

The stories are endless, but they all have one common theme—one must choose to grow from an emotionally challenging event. It's not an easy thing, but it sure is easier than the pain of living a life poisoned by repeating bad patterns.

Here's a quick summary to help:

- First and foremost, you must form a realistic picture in your head of the woman you want. If you don't yet know, that's quite all right. As you shop (a.k.a. "date"), you'll learn.

- At the same time, you should begin to be honest with yourself about who you are. If you're a computer dork and you hate the gym, don't try and become a body builder. It's okay, just be you. It makes life so much easier.

- You must ask yourself if the women you're attracted to would want to date you. In short, you must project what you hope to attract. I'll ask you this question in a later chapter, "Would you date you?" If not, it's time to do some more soul searching.

- Don't settle and overlook things in a potential partner that are essential to you. Remember, there's bullshit everywhere. The key is knowing what flavor of bullshit you like. If you're a workaholic, don't get with a 9-5 woman who bitches at you everyday because you own your own business and thrive on working 80 hours a week. If you're a poet who likes to take long walks in flower gardens, just accept you're gay! (sorry, just kidding) But seriously, if this is you, don't get with a chick who hates long walks and has season tickets to her favorite hockey team simply because she loves the fights and seeing blood on the ice. She isn't going to change and this isn't going to work!

In closing, I'd like to remind you of the two quotes I listed at the beginning of this book...

"Tomorrow is the most important thing in life. Comes into us at midnight very clean. It's perfect when it arrives and it puts itself in our hands. It hopes we've learned something from yesterday."

—John Wayne, 1981

"While we'd like to think that time heals all wounds, the fact is time doesn't heal—time passes. Insight heals. We can't get better until we understand what happened."

—Daphne Rose-Kingma, 2000

CHAPTER 8

OH GREAT, MY BODY TURNED AGAINST ME, TOO... (THE STRESS MANAGEMENT CHAPTER)

I titled this Chapter "Oh Great, My Body Turned Against Me, Too" because that's exactly how I felt. While I was dealing with my crazy emotions and an out of control imagination, the physical stress of divorce inflicted sheer havoc upon my body. I couldn't believe how being stressed out made me feel so bad. My entire body ached 24/7 for over four months. No matter what I did, I couldn't physically feel better. My constant stomachache was the worst; it never stopped. As a result, I lost close to 30 pounds in just over three months.

Prior to my divorce, I thought I knew about physical pain. I was wrong. I actually had a painful nose and sinus surgery several years before my divorce. Getting my nose broken and reset, along with having my sinus cavities scraped, put me on my ass for over three weeks. (Stay with me—there's a lesson following this brief story...)

I have suffered from bad allergies and sinus trouble since I was a kid. By my late twenties, the mucous membranes throughout my sinus cavities had become scarred and callused—much like the calluses one develops on the palm of their hands. This scar tissue trapped dust and bacteria, and I was getting serious sinus infections about three to four times a year. I also had a deviated septum. (one side of my nose was open too much, while the other side was almost closed)

I needed to have my sinuses "Roto-Rootered" and my nose broken so it could be set straight. As you can imagine, it sucked when I awoke after surgery with my nose and sinuses packed completely closed with gauze. I also had splints sewn into my nose to keep the septum straight. The pain was unbelievable. It took me three weeks before I could breathe through my nose and another week before I could go back to work.

I rambled with this story to make a point. We've all endured some kind of physical pain in our lives. Maybe you lived through a devastating car crash; maybe you lost some fingers working construction; or maybe you're a cancer survivor and endured the torture of chemotherapy and radiation. It's tough to make it to adulthood without feeling some type of pain. It's just a fact of life.

But reality shows us a divorce is completely different from almost any other common stressor in our daily lives. Divorce stress is that serious, fellas, and you'd better take a moment to recognize it. Based on the Holmes-Rahe Scale, divorce is the second most stressful event a person can face in their entire life. Only the death of one's spouse is listed as more stressful than divorce.

I strongly encourage you to rate yourself on the following Holmes-Rahe Scale…

The Holmes-Rahe Life Stress Inventory
The Social Readjustment Rating Scale
INSTRUCTIONS: Mark down the point value of each of these life events that has happened to you during the previous year. Total these associated points.

Life Event	Mean Value
1. Death of spouse	100
2. Divorce	73
3. Marital separation from mate	65
4. Detention in jail or other institution	63
5. Death of a close family member	63
6. Major personal injury or illness	53
7. Marriage	50
8. Being fired at work	47
9. Marital reconciliation with mate	45

10. Retirement from work	45
11. Major change in the health or behavior of a family member	44
12. Pregnancy	40
13. Sexual difficulties	39
14. Gaining a new family member (i.e. birth, adoption, older adult moving in, etc)	39
15. Major business readjustment	39
16. Major change in financial state (i.e. a lot worse or better off than usual)	38
17. Death of a close friend	37
18. Changing to a different line of work	36
19. Major change in the number of arguments w/ spouse (i.e.. either a lot more or less than usual regarding child rearing, personal habits, etc.)	35
20. Taking on a mortgage (for home, business, etc.)	31
21. Foreclosure on a mortgage or loan 30	
22. Major change in responsibilities at work (i.e., promotion, demotion, etc.)	29
23. Son or daughter leaving home (marriage, attending college, joined mil.)	29
24 In-law troubles	29
25. Outstanding personal achievement 28	
26. Spouse beginning or ceasing work outside the home	26
27. Beginning or ceasing formal schooling	26
28. Major change in living condition (new home, remodeling, deterioration of neighborhood or home etc.)	25
29. Revision of personal habits (dress manners, associations, quitting smoking)	24
30. Troubles with the boss	23
31. Major changes in working hours or conditions	20

32. Changes in residence	20
33. Changing to a new school	20
34. Major change in usual type and/or amount of recreation	19
35. Major change in church activity (i.e., a lot more or less than usual)	19
36. Major change in social activities (clubs, movies, visiting, etc)	18
37. Taking on a loan (house, car, rental, etc)	17
38. Major change in sleeping habits (a lot more or a lot less than usual)	16
39. Major change in number of family get-togethers	15
40. Major change in eating habits (a lot more or less food intake, or very different meal hours or surroundings)	15
41. Vacation	13
42. Major holidays	12
43. Minor violations of the law (traffic tickets, jaywalking, disturbing the peace, etc)	11

Now, add up all the points you have to find your score.

150pts or less:
A relatively low amount of life change and a low susceptibility to stress-induced health breakdown.

150 to 300 pts:
Implies about a 50% chance of a major health breakdown in the next 2 years.

300 pts or more:
Raises the odds to about 80%, according to the Holmes-Rahe statistical prediction model.

Sources: Adapted from Thomas Holmes and Richard Rahe. Homes-Rahe Social Readjustment Rating Scale, Journal of Psychosomatic Research. Vol II, 1967.

Where do you rate on the scale? During my divorce and the following 18 months, I was well over 300. I was a stress case but was completely unaware of exactly what I was facing. That's because (as I've said repeatedly) divorce is not just one single stressful event. The journey through divorce truly affects every aspect of your life.

I once interviewed a divorced Iraq War veteran, Coy, who'd lost a lower leg to a land mine. I was dumbfounded to hear Coy say the pain of having his leg blown-off was not nearly as bad as the ill feelings he felt during his divorce.

Coy briefly remembers the explosion and being thrown through the air. However, he passed out as soon as he hit the ground. He never felt any pain in his leg at the scene of the incident, and he remembers nothing about being medivacked.

Coy awoke three days later on a Navy hospital ship and saw that his leg was gone below the knee. The physical pain was confined to his stump and the phantom pains of the missing limb. But in comparison, during Coy's divorce, his entire body ached all the time. If Coy wasn't throwing up, he had a migraine headache or he would break-out in hives all over his body.

And as I interviewed more divorced men, I quickly discovered this to be a common theme. They all agree that the physical stress of divorce was like nothing they had experienced before, or since. This is why it's so essential to recognize and understand the physical stress of divorce.

Tragically, most men simply try to "tough it out" as they do with most other difficult things in life. Maybe we do this because we're guys, and guys aren't supposed to show emotion or that we're hurting. Whatever the reason, the "bury your head in the sand" tactic can have dire health consequences. By the end of a divorce many men find themselves dealing with hypertension, high blood pressure, stomach ulcers, depression, anxiety, panic disorders, and much, much more.

Look at the list below. Are you having some or all of the following physical symptoms?

- Not being able to eat and suffering weight loss at an unhealthy rate
- Overeating with excessive weight gain
- Constant stomach problems
- Headaches
- Bowel troubles (Oh, I just loved having "the squirts" for three straight months!)
- Chest pains
- Anxiety
- Panic Attacks
- Sleeping problems (What's good sleep when you're getting divorced?)
- Dental problems as a result of grinding your teeth
- Frequent colds, flu, and infections caused by a weakened immune system

And if that's not bad enough, much of the physical stress response to divorce is striking similar to the phenomena of Post Traumatic Stress Disorder (PTSD). I know it sounds strange to speak of PTSD and divorce in the same sentence. But, side-by-side, their similarities are all too clear.

The excerpt below is quoted directly from the United States Department of Veterans Affairs:

"Posttraumatic Stress Disorder (PTSD) is an anxiety disorder that can occur after you have been through a traumatic event. A traumatic event is something horrible and scary that you see or that happens to you. During this type of event, you think that your life or others' lives are in danger. You may feel afraid or feel that you have no control over what is happening. Anyone who has gone through a life-threatening event can develop PTSD. These events can include:

- *Combat or military exposure*
- *Child sexual or physical abuse*
- *Terrorist attacks*
- *Sexual or physical assault*
- *Serious accidents, such as a car wreck*
- *Natural disasters, such as a fire, tornado, hurricane, flood, or earthquake.*

After the event, you may feel scared, confused, or angry. If these feelings don't go away or they get worse, you may have PTSD. These symptoms may disrupt your life, making it hard to continue with your daily activities."

This excerpt eerily describes much of the way I felt throughout my divorce. And remember, emotional trauma can be just as damaging as physical trauma. Much of what we fear in divorce is just as real in our mind as what we'd feel if a robber were holding a gun to our face.

Your mind does not interpret physical stress any differently than it does mental and emotional stress. Each day of your divorce, your body physically reacts to your emotional fears in the same way it would react to someone pointing a gun at you, a car about to run you over, or a lion about to eat your ass (Ha!), etc.

Here's an example of what I mean. Have you every been really startled, like when someone sneaks up behind you with a scary mask or touches you on the shoulder from behind when you're in deep thought and not expecting it? When that happens to me, I jump out of my seat and I can feel my heart skip a beat.

I actually experienced this same intense feeling at least 20 to 30 times a day when living through the worst part of divorce. My physical safety was never in jeopardy during my divorce, but my body's negative reaction to the emotional stress was far greater than anything I'd ever felt.

I'd be doing something completely unrelated to the divorce (playing with my kid, typing something at work, etc.) when suddenly a scary thought about the divorce would race through my head. My heart felt like it would skip a beat. Quite often, I'd have to run to the bathroom because I was suddenly going to mess my shorts. This is why it's so important that we talk about taking care of our physical health and not ignoring the stress of divorce.

You must also understand that pain is not a relative concept. We all have different pain tolerances, just like we all have different tolerances to cold, heat, alcohol, etc. I once discussed this issue with my therapist. The conversation went something like this:

Me	*"I just feel like such a pussy. I'm a real history buff and I can tell you countless incidents in history where people have been tortured, murdered, had their kids raped in front of them, etc. and here I am getting all sappy over a divorce!"*
Therapist	*"Joey, pain is a very individual, abstract and intangible concept. You can't compare your suffering to someone else's experience and how they deal with it. There are so many variations that go into each of us to make us individuals, so you can't possibly begin to compare how you feel to someone else."*

So don't get hung up on the additional guilt trip about feeling bad during your divorce. There're always others who've had it worse than you, but I'm sure there're a lot who've had it far better, too.

How your divorce affects you emotionally and physically is a very individual and personal experience. You must not concern yourself with how divorce affects others. It's smart to look at how other people handle things so you have a good point of reference for an overall perspective, but make sure you don't get hung up with comparing your divorce responses to anyone else's.

For example, as I mentioned in Chapter 4, "Your Ex is Datin' Someone Else," so many men have a real problem with the idea that their ex may be dating another man following their separation. We've already discussed how many of these guys talk about this issue with their friends, family, and counselors, but they simply can't get the images out of their head.

These men often experience an actual physical stress response when thinking of their ex "doing it" with another man. Their mind literally creates a physical response to the emotional trauma of their ex possibly having sex with another man.

Many of you could not care less who your ex is dating, and the situation elicits absolutely no type of stress or worry. But you could very well have emotional stress from something completely different. (e.g., the money problems, kid issues, etc.)

Another example of how we all deal differently with stress can be found in the age old concept of "fight, flight, or freeze." Just follow me for a minute—I'll try to keep it simple... This is an idea that goes all the way back to the caveman days.

When our ancestor, Mr. Caveman, was being chased by a saber tooth tiger, his stress response told him to do one of three things.

1. FIGHT: He would stand his ground and fight the tiger
2. FLIGHT: He would run away from the tiger
3. FREEZE: He may be so paralyzed with terror that he was just plain frozen stiff

The Caveman chose one of these three responses based on a million different factors that would require a physiologist to explain.

The following is an excerpt from www.helpguide.org.

> *"The 'fight-or-flight' stress response involves a cascade of biological changes that prepare us for emergency action. When danger is sensed, a small part of the brain called the hypothalamus sets off a chemical alarm. The sympathetic*

> *nervous system responds by releasing a flood of stress hormones, including adrenaline, norepinephrine, and cortisol. These stress hormones race through the bloodstream, readying us to either flee the scene or battle it out.*
>
> *Heart rate and blood flow to the large muscles increase so we can run faster and fight harder. Blood vessels under the skin constrict to prevent blood loss in case of injury, pupils dilate so we can see better, and our blood sugar ramps up, giving us an energy boost and speeding up reaction time. At the same time, body processes not essential to immediate survival are suppressed. The digestive and reproductive systems slow down, growth hormones are switched off, and the immune response is inhibited."*

I'm truly dumbfounded by all things that occur within our bodies when we're under stress. It's no wonder our heart doesn't jump from our chest and we don't puke our guts out. Further complicating things, divorce is the first time many men will experience things like Generalized Anxiety, Chemical Depression, Obsessive Compulsive Disorder (OCD), and/or Panic Attacks. Some of you don't even know what these things mean, yet you could be suffering from one or more at this very moment.

One day during my pending divorce, I was walking through a large indoor shopping mall with my son. Suddenly, within about three minutes, I went from my normal uneasy divorce feeling into a full blown panic attack. I began sweating profusely, my chest became so tight I couldn't breath, and it was a miracle I was able to keep from puking. It sucked!

You're probably asking how to recognize these conditions and what you can do about them. This is a tough question because the majority of men will resist my suggestions. As I've said repeatedly (and most of you know), men are generally "tough guys" and not willing to do the things required for emotional growth.

Learning to communicate your feelings better, going to therapy, and taking medications are generally considered "for pussies." Men seem to hide behind the fear of being labeled as "weak" or "gay." Nothing is further from the truth, and it's time that men open our minds to things that can really help us!

Below is a brief overview of several of the common mental and physical disorders that can result from divorce stress. It's essential you don't get stuck on the word "disorder." You're not crazy!

For many years, therapy was reserved for the loons in straight jackets. I think Jack Nicholson's performance in *One Flew Over the Cuckoo's Nest* sums up people we picture as needing therapy. As a society, we must change this stereotype, especially for those suffering through divorce.

Most of the following information was obtained easily from websites. All you have to do is Google any of the below-listed conditions and you'll be inundated with more information than you'll ever be able to read.

1. **Generalized Anxiety Disorder (GAD):**

   I'm telling you about GAD first because it is a condition that's near-and-dear to my heart. I personally suffer from GAD. My anxiety started in childhood and was simply compounded during my divorce, so I feel very qualified to speak about GAD. A one word summary for GAD is "worry." This is why I believe GAD is so common for people getting divorced. Also, GAD is almost twice as likely to occur in men than in women. (Oh joy!)

   The real key with GAD is "irrational worry." As I've said, there're a lot of legitimate things a man has to be concerned with during divorce. I wish I could tell you that instability in many aspects of your life is not part of the divorce package, but you know I'd be full of shit. When you're smack dab in the middle of your divorce, there're just so many unanswered questions. This results in the aforementioned "runaway imagination" that leads to constant irrational worry.

If you feel you're suffering from GAD, a great self-help book is Anxiety and Panic Attacks, Their Cause and Cure, by Robert Handly. Handly presents a simple-to-follow explanation of anxiety causes, along with a five-step program to help you conquer your fears and much more. I really appreciate that Handly himself suffered from extreme anxiety (Agoraphobia), so he speaks from experience. He conveys a real sympathy for anxiety sufferers and his passion to help is very clear.

Don't be too hard on yourself if you may be suffering from GAD as a result of your divorce. Nothing in any book is going to take away all your worries about finances, child custody, the emotional well-being of your children, etc. This is divorce, and you're supposed to feel uneasy about all of the open-ended questions. Just make sure you do what's necessary to maintain perspective.

2. **Clinical depression (also called major-depressive disorder or unipolar depression):**

The term "depression" is something that can be very confusing. The very word is used to describe so many different and varying types and degrees of sadness. The mildest form of depression is quite normal and happens to everyone. It's our mind and body's natural response to a sad event, such as the death of a loved one, a severe or debilitating injury, serious financial problems, etc.

But there's a much more serious side of depression. This occurs when there is an actual chemical imbalance within the brain. The chemical process in the brain malfunctions and causes the depressive condition. Professional treatment (often including medication) is a must to overcome the condition. Furthermore, this severe aspect of depression may never truly go away and may require treatment for the rest of one's life.

I cannot even begin to diagnose your degree of depression. I've already stressed the need to seek professional help during your divorce. Once you find the right therapist for you, I strongly encourage you to discuss your sad feelings in great detail. A good therapist will be able to translate your feelings and diagnose your level of depression.

Your therapist may tell you that your feelings are normal for your current situation. Remember, you're not getting through divorce without some level of sadness. But the therapist will be of greater assistant in helping you navigate away from a more serious type of depression. I'll talk more about medication later in this chapter. I'm simply asking you to keep an open mind.

I've found www.depression.com to be a great introductory site about depression. It's extremely easy to follow and has a lot of great resources and links. It may also help you better describe and communicate your feelings to your therapist. Good therapists will not need you to speak their *clinical language* of psychology. But the more you already know about describing your feelings, the sooner your therapist may be able to help.

Don't just walk into a therapist's office, plop your pathetic ass on the couch and say, *"Doc, I'm getting divorced and I feel like shit!"* Well, no fucking kidding you feel like shit. Thank you, Captain Obvious! The more you can educate yourself to accurately describe your feelings, the better help you'll receive.

3) Obsessive Compulsive Disorder (OCD):

Prior to divorce, my very limited knowledge of OCD came from watching Leonardo Dicaprio's portrayal of Howard Hughes in 2004 film *The Aviator*. I include information about this disorder because I felt like I had OCD about my marriage and divorce. As I've mentioned, the first two months following my separation are a literal blur. I felt trapped by the repetitive thoughts of my divorce—it was all I thought about 24/7. Everything else was inconsequential during that time. The experts may say that I never had OCD, but I share information about this disorder because I sure felt like I did.

According to WebMD (http://www.webmd.com/anxiety-panic/guide/obsessive-compulsive-disorder) OCD is described as:

"Obsessive Compulsive Disorder (OCD), a type of anxiety disorder, is a potentially disabling illness that traps people in endless cycles of repetitive thoughts and behaviors. People with OCD are plagued by recurring and distressing thoughts, fears or images (obsessions) that they cannot control. The anxiety (nervousness) produced by these thoughts leads to an urgent need to perform certain rituals or routines (compulsions). The compulsive rituals are performed in an attempt to prevent the obsessive thoughts or make them go away.

Although the ritual may make the anxiety go away temporarily, the person must perform the ritual again when the obsessive thoughts return. This OCD cycle can progress to the point of taking up hours of the person's day and significantly interfering with normal activities. People with OCD may be aware that their obsessions and compulsions are senseless or unrealistic, but they cannot stop themselves."

This excerpt perfectly describes me. I was all of those things. My obsessive thoughts about my divorce were repetitive, distressing, and fearful. I even suffered from the idea that ritual fighting with my ex would make my pains go away and somehow end my divorce. I may not have been the classic clinical example of OCD, but I share this because it may help some of you. If you even suspect you could be developing this condition, share these concerns with your therapist.

4) **Panic Attacks:**

Based on my experience and research, this is a very common condition suffered by men living through divorce. Just read the below excerpt from the Mayo Clinic —it is exactly how I felt at numerous points throughout my journey:

"Panic attacks are sudden, discrete periods of intense anxiety, mounting physiological arousal, fear, stomach problems and discomfort that are associated with a variety of somatic and cognitive symptoms. The onset of these episodes is typically abrupt, and may have no obvious triggers. Although these episodes may appear random, they are a subset of an evolutionary response commonly referred to as fight or flight that occur out of context. This response floods the body with hormones, particularly epinephrine (adrenaline), that aid in defending itself from harm. Experiencing a panic attack is said to be one of the most intensely frightening, upsetting and uncomfortable experiences of a person's life.

According to the American Psychological Association the symptoms of a panic attack commonly last approximately thirty minutes. However, panic attacks can be as short as 15 minutes, while sometimes panic attacks may form a cyclic series of episodes, lasting for an extended period, sometimes hours. Often those afflicted will experience significant anticipatory anxiety and limited symptom attacks in between attacks, in situations where attacks have previously occurred, and in situations where they feel 'trapped.' That is, where escape would be obvious and/or embarrassing.

Panic attacks also affect people differently. Experienced sufferers may be able to completely 'ride out' a panic attack with little to no obvious symptoms or external manifestations. Others, notably first-time sufferers, may even call for emergency services; many who experience a panic attack for the first time fear they are having a heart attack or a nervous breakdown."

Need I say more? I've had panic attacks and they suck. I've also spoken with some pretty big and strong guys who've described how panic attacks literally brought them to their knees.

5) **Post Traumatic Stress Disorder (PTSD):**

According to the National Institute of Mental Health (http://www.nimh.nih.gov/) Post Traumatic Stress Disorder (PTSD) is described as:

"Post Traumatic Stress Disorder (PTSD) develops after a terrifying ordeal that involved physical harm or the threat of physical harm. The person who develops PTSD may have been the one who was harmed, the harm may have happened to a loved one, or the person may have witnessed a harmful event that happened to loved ones or strangers.

PTSD was first brought to public attention in relation to war veterans, but it can result from a variety of traumatic incidents, such as mugging, rape, torture, being kidnapped or held captive, child abuse, car accidents, train wrecks,

> *plane crashes, bombings, or natural disasters such as floods or earthquakes."*
>
> I don't know about you, but give me a car crash, train wreak, bombing, flood, earthquake, nuclear war, the end of the world, dogs and cats living together, mass hysteria, etc. rather than divorce. Again, I don't have the training or experience to even begin to diagnose you with PTSD. Also, I don't believe most men digress to the level of such a debilitating mental condition such as PTSD. I only share this information as an extreme example of how some men may feel during divorce.

I hope you are helped by these brief explanations of some of the more common conditions. Maybe you completely identified with one of these examples. If so, you now have a place to start with your quest to care for your health. Either way, you must accept that you're emotional and truly sensitive and believe that it's okay. Again, if you weren't sensitive and hurting over your divorce, you wouldn't be reading this book.

And what are you going to do if the physical manifestations of your emotional sufferings are affecting your ability to go to work, parent your kids, and maintain relationships with family and friends? Remember some of the stories I shared in Chapter 2, "Pick Yourself Up, You Big Bumbling Idiot," and Chapter 3, "Fake it Till You Make it." Those are examples of guys who let stress and their lack of ability to properly deal with stress make their situations even worse.

But there's good news. The topic of "stress management" is very well studied, and there is tons of information available to us. But you're going to have to take some action. You can't manage your divorce stress by simply ignoring it and hoping things will get better.

I've known many men who end up having to still deal with the physical stress of divorce long after their journey is over. Some impacts of stress, such as hypertension and PSTD, can have lasting effects on your physical and emotional well-being long after the conclusion of the actual event.

One friend of mine suffered from anxiety-provoked chest pains years after his divorce ended. The pains began about a month into his divorce, and they persisted for about six years. At several points throughout the day, my friend would suddenly feel a sharp pain in his chest. It lasted about five to ten minutes and would then subside. We all pushed him to seek treatment, but he never did. Eventually the pains would appear less frequently; however, I wonder what lasting damage was done to his body.

So what can you do to help your body and take better care of your physical health? First, you need a healthy diet. I know it sounds stupid and belittling, especially since many of you can't even bring yourself to eat anything.

I remember one afternoon, about two months into my divorce, I was having lunch with several friends. I ordered a very light cobb salad since nothing sounded good. It was actually pretty strange. I felt hungry, but my stomach hurt and I had to force myself to eat. When my food arrived, it was all I could do to get a few bites down. I'll forever remember this as one of the strangest experiences. I was hungry and the food was good, but I couldn't eat.

This problem with eating was a very common issue for me day-in/day-out for months. A side benefit was losing 30 pounds in four months. (Although I'm sure there're much healthier ways to lose weight.) The main way I tried to offset my inability to eat was by making smoothies and shakes.

Usually twice a day (once for breakfast and again for dinner), I'd blend some oatmeal, protein powder, egg whites, yogurt, and milk. Sometimes I'd throw in various frozen fruit. This was easy to drink and kept my body nourished. If it wasn't for my shakes, I'm positive I'd have been far worse off physically. Soups are also a good substitute if you can't eat.

But then there's the other extreme, which is overeating as a result of stress. If you eat for comfort, there're a lot of things you can do. First and foremost, you need to substitute trail mix and fresh/dried fruits for stuff like cinnamon rolls and cookies.

There are also different prepackaged low-fat puddings, yogurts, pizza pockets, etc. that are sold in bulk. It only takes five to ten minutes to pack a lunch, and you'll feel so much better. You may not know it because you already feel so shitty, but I'm confident you'd feel a million times worse if you overeat unhealthy food.

I also began taking large doses of Vitamin C and Vitamin E to help maintain my immune system. I'll never know just how much this helped because I still got sick more than usual. But I have to think it at least helped prevent some colds and flues when I was at my weakest point with stress and anxiety.

Therapy—which I've frequently alluded to—is the next thing that can really help during your divorce. I believe therapy is a must if you truly want to grow from this experience while simultaneously limiting the hurt. I've been a big fan of therapy for many years.

The key is finding the right therapist. It's my duty to warn you that seeing a therapist is not always as easy as just making an appointment, showing up, and then spilling your guts out. Unfortunately, in my humble opinion, a large number of therapists are more screwed up than their patients.

For example, I used to work with a girl who eventually became a therapist. We'll call her Lori. I first met Lori when she was about 23. She held a clerical position at the department where I worked. Shortly thereafter, Lori began dating a guy a few years older. It quickly became one of those on-again/off-again relationships.

Every few months, Lori and her man would break up and reconcile. This pattern continued for over eight years—that's right, eight years! Some of their breakups lasted a few months, during which time Lori and her ex would date others. But they'd always end up back together only to break up again a few months later.

Lori eventually earned a Master's degree in Psychology and became a marriage and family counselor. I still hear about her through a mutual friend, and she continues going back-and-forth within that tumultuous relationship. Yet Lori is now a professional counselor advising men, women, and children about relationship issues. What the hell? That's as crazy as getting marriage and divorce advice from a priest.

Don't laugh, but I actually went to see a priest once during my divorce. He was a nice guy and a trusted friend of the family. Although he gave me spiritual guidance, he wasn't able to offer much in the way of relationship advice. I'm not saying there's no priest who can give good relationship advice. A lot of men are very faith-based, so seeing a spiritual mentor could really help. You must simply do whatever works for you.

I'm just hesitant to seek relationship guidance from a person sworn to celibacy. The same can be said about the value I'd place on advice from Lori. Here you have a woman who's completely trapped in an unhealthy relationship, yet she is in a position to dispense daily advice to people living through very dark times.

As you can see, the process of finding the right therapist can be extremely challenging for someone in the middle of a tough time. After all, you're already struggling with emotional hell, and the last thing you want is to wade through therapists to find the right one.

Unfortunately, that's the name of the game. Just be a little resilient. When you find the right therapist it can truly change your life. I personally saw five therapists before I found one that I loved and has been my saving grace for years.

In his book, Anxiety and Panic Attacks, Their Causes and Cure, Author Robert Handly writes the following about finding a good therapist:

> *"Let me warn you, however, that some professionals do not understand phobias or anxiety symptoms. You could wind up with a bunch of tranquilizers, as I did. They make you numb without ever overcoming your feeling that you are on the verge of exploding with anxiety. Other anxious people spend several years in analysis seeking to find the 'missing link' between a traumatic childhood event and their present emotional problems. I'm not knocking psychiatry of psychology. In fact, I went to a psychologist myself to learn some techniques for dealing with my phobia. And when I used these behavioral tools, I recovered fairly quickly. I'm simply urging you to be aware of what you may encounter when you seek help."*

Although Handly speaks of therapy specifically as it pertains to his issue—anxiety and panic—the process for any man living through divorce is the same. You could have the same challenges finding the right counselor to fit your specific needs, emotions, and issues.

I remember the first therapist I ever saw—a woman who seemed nice enough in the beginning. But about ten minutes into the one-hour session, I noticed her eyes drifting over my shoulder. It was as if she was daydreaming or just unengaged with what I was saying. I couldn't wait to complete the session. As I was leaving, I looked on the wall behind my seat and saw a big clock just about my head. It became clear she was watching the clock each time I caught her looking above me.

My second therapist was a man, and he was great. He gave me really good advice and was obviously interested in helping me. However, I quickly realized I wasn't comfortable talking with a man about emotional issues. It was nothing more than that. I needed to see a woman to really open up. Therapist numbers three and four were okay, but again I just didn't feel comfortable for a variety of reasons.

It wasn't until I got to therapist number five that I hit the jackpot. I found a woman a few years older than me who was very informed and a real straight shooter. I appreciated the way she told me exactly what I needed to hear, not just what I wanted to hear. She would even cuss as needed to stress a point. I loved her style and I could talk with her about anything and everything.

Over the years, I've referred many people to her. Most said they got a lot from her style and the advice she gave. But even as great as she is, no one is perfect for everyone. I remember a buddy of mine and his wife went to her for marriage counseling. The wife did not like my therapist because she was too direct and not soft enough in her approach. So, what works for some may not work for you, and vice versa.

One final word about therapy—"Garbage in, garbage out." In order to get some good personal growth from therapy, you must be willing to bare your soul when you find the right therapist. I've known too many people who've tried a few sessions of counseling only to say the therapist insisted nothing was wrong with them. Well, no shit—nothing's wrong with you if you tell the therapist everything is hunky-dory!

For example, I have a good friend whose wife was mentally and emotionally abused by her parents as a child. There were four kids in the family and mom and dad stayed married and in the home. The problem was primarily with dad; he was an alcoholic who believed his kids were house slaves. The kids were assigned so many chores you'd have thought slavery was reinstated. From laundry to cleaning, the kids did it all and had very little time to play. Dad frequently got drunk and was emotionally and mentally abusive. He said stuff to his kids I wouldn't say to a dog.

As you can imagine, my buddy's wife suffered immensely from a variety of issues as she grew to adulthood. Unfortunately, she never sought help, she gained a lot of weight and complained and nagged more than anyone I'd ever met.

All of us guys did our very best to stay clear of her. We all dreaded when she would come over for get-togethers. On a good note, she was so anti-social that she would usually just sit in the living room alone and watch sports or reality TV shows.

But guess what? This chick had actually gone to a few sessions of therapy and bragged about how the counselor said nothing was wrong with her. As I've described, you know that's a bunch of bullshit. She either got a bad therapist, or she told him superficial crap about herself which caused him to say she was fine. (or both)

So you see, you just can't go to therapy and not put forth some emotional effort. I remember many times being extremely anxious before a therapy appointment. This was because I knew I had some real shit to discuss and it was going to be painful. But, I almost always felt better after leaving one of these stressful appointments.

Think of this analogy. You can't just go to the gym and half-ass your way through the workout if you really want to get into shape. Working out takes effort, concentration, thought, and commitment. The same must be said for therapy—it takes personal commitment and effort.

My therapist once told me counseling is like physical therapy for the mind. You must work your mind over and over for you to feel better and improve your thought process. When you have knee surgery, it's almost always followed by extensive physical therapy that involves working the knee extensively. It takes the exact same effort and focus when it comes to mental and emotional therapy.

But what if you're so upset that therapy alone is not working? Let's say you've found a great therapist but you're still so distraught you're not able to adequately function throughout the day. Maybe your work is suffering and you're so sad and stressed that you're getting in trouble. Maybe you can't get focused and your kids are starting to feel your stress. What do you do? There's another option I highly recommend, which is to explore some of the many anti-anxiety and anti-depressant medications currently on the market.

Now don't freak out! As I've said before, you're not crazy. Before we go further, let's keep things in perspective. If you were a "normal" guy before your divorce, but it's the separation that's messing you up, you're not a Loony Toon. The stress and emotions from your divorce will eventually go away, and so should the need for medications. So if you even suspect you could benefit from a mild dose of medication, please listen up.

Here's a situation that exemplifies the way medication can be used to help a person through a very tough time. A good friend of mine, Travis, was married to a nice lady and they were very happy with two small boys. Tragically, at the young age of 32, Travis' wife discovered a lump on her breast. She went to the doctor who promptly ordered a biopsy.

During the biopsy, the doctors discovered she had a very aggressive form of cancer and were forced to conduct a radical mastectomy. (they cut off her breast right there!) Over the next year, Travis stood by his wife as she endured chemo, radiation, and numerous reconstructive surgeries.

Needless to say, this took a real toll on Travis. He couldn't sleep and developed several stress-related illnesses. To help him cope during this crazy time, Travis saw a therapist who prescribed him a low dose of Efexor. (a very mild anti-depressant/anti-anxiety medication)

This story does have a happy ending. Travis' wife recovered and has been cancer free for over five years. I'm telling you this story to make a point. You may need some type of medication as you endure the process of divorce. A good physiologist/psychiatrist will also provide you with a plan to ease off the medication as soon as you begin feeling better.

The website for the antidepressant medication Pristiq (www.pristiq.com) lists the following information describing depression and antidepressants:

> *"There are several types of prescription antidepressant medications that are divided into different classes. Each antidepressant class affects the levels of chemicals in the*

> *brain called neurotransmitters, which are thought to be involved in regulating mood.*
>
> *The most commonly prescribed prescription antidepressant classes are SSRIs (selective serotonin reuptake inhibitors) and SNRIs (serotonin-norepinephrine reuptake inhibitors). SSRIs are believed to treat depression by affecting the levels of a neurotransmitter called* serotonin.
>
> *It's important to know that it could take as many as 6 to 8 weeks for the full therapeutic effect to occur. It is important to give the medication a chance to work and to take it exactly as directed by your health care professional."*

The Mayo Clinic (www.mayoclinic.com) has this to say about finding the right medication:

> *"Finding the right antidepressant for your situation might take time. Each antidepressant has its own pros and cons, and until you try one, you won't know exactly how it'll affect you or how well it'll work. You may need to try several antidepressants before finding the one, or the combination, that works best for you.*
>
> *In general, most antidepressants work pretty well for most people. So which antidepressant you and your doctor choose depends largely on:*
>
> - *Anticipated side effects*
> - *Your ability to tolerate these side effects and stick with the treatment*
> - *Cost and health insurance coverage*
> - *Previous experiences you or family members have had with antidepressants*
> - *Whether you're pregnant or breast-feeding*
> - *Your age*
> - *Your other medical and psychiatric conditions"*

According to the Royal College of Psychiatrists, below is a list of some of the most common antidepressant medications:

Medication	Trade name
Amitriptyline	Tryptizol
Clomipramine	Anafranil
Citalopram	Cipramil
Dosulepin	Prothiaden
Doxepin	Sinequan
Fluoxetine	Prozac
Imipramine	Tofranil
Lofepramine	Gamanil
Mirtazapine	Zispin
Moclobemide	Manerix
Nortriptyline	Allegron
Paroxetine	Seroxat
Phenelzine	Nardil
Reboxetine	Edronax
Sertraline	Lustral
Tranylcypromine	Parnate
Trazodone	Molipaxin
Venlafaxine	Efexor

All I ask is that you remain open to the idea of medications. Believe me, nowadays there are far more people taking meds than you possibly know. I'd bet a paycheck that someone you're working with today is taking a psychological medication and you don't even know it. It's okay. It won't get tattooed on your forehead when you pick up the pills at the pharmacy.

Any record of you receiving physiological counseling or taking medications are protected by the 2003 Health Insurance Portability and Accountability Act (HIPAA). I've known many guys who've undergone very extensive background/security clearance checks for high level jobs, and it never came out that they took medications of this type.

As I keep telling you, you're not crazy. You're simply seeking treatment to assist you in moving through one of the darkest periods of your life. I believe those who go to therapy and take medication should be commended rather than ridiculed.

Someone taking a mental health medication is no different than someone taking high blood pressure medication or insulin for diabetes. People would actually look at you funny if you had diabetes but refused to take medication and monitor your diet. The same should be said for a chemically depressed person refusing to take the appropriate medication—it's just plain stupid and prolongs suffering.

Also, be weary of trying to quit certain bad habits, such as smoking or drinking, while you're right in the middle of your divorce. Although I cannot advocate smoking or heavy drinking (and I strongly encourage you to develop a plan to quit both if they're some of your vices), timing is everything. If you're so stressed out with of your divorce that the only thing literally helping you through the day are your cigarette breaks, you may want to consider delaying quitting.

The same is true for drinking alcoholic beverages. During my divorce, I found myself having a rum and Coke about four nights a week. It just really took the edge off at the end of a long day plagued by my thoughts working overtime. But, I can honestly say I kept this stress relief in check. I never had more than one per night and never got "smashed." (Okay, so maybe I got smashed once; or maybe twice? Ha!)

In today's age of political correctness, it may sound odd to hear an author speak of smoking and drinking in this fashion. As I said, my goal is to be as honest with you as possible about all aspects of divorce—the good, the bad, and the ugly. Just remember, when you find yourself drinking each night until you pass out, you've gone overboard.

Of course it's a million times better to live through your divorce training for a marathon, going to the gym each day, or writing a book (like yours truly); however, that's a somewhat unrealistic expectation for most of us. I went through a few weeks spending a lot of time at the gym, but working out was a very on-again/off-again activity throughout the toughest part of my divorce. I'd often just have to come home and have a drink. Again, not too many, just one would do the trick.

After reading this chapter, you still may have a huge stomachache and feel like shit, but trust me when I tell you it will get better. Just don't simply wait for time to ease the pain. You can be doing so many things right now to help you get started.

Therapy, diet, and possibly medications are all essential aspects of moving through the physical suffering of divorce. If you can't eat, try making shakes. If you can't stop eating, substitute some fresh/dried fruits, trail mix, beef jerky, etc., for the fast food and sweets. And not to mention, grocery stores are great places to meet women—just a little bonus.

CHAPTER 9

DIVORCE, THE LAW, AND THE MONEY

It's no secret that the legal and financial aspects of divorce are two of the biggest issues facing a man. We all know money makes the world go round, and divorce has left many-a-man in the poor house. I often thought how much easier divorce would have been if I were rich and money wasn't an issue. But the reality for most of us is that every penny does matter, and financial issues are clearly one of the biggest (if not the biggest) frustration brought on by divorce.

Furthermore, most of us have little to no experience in legal matters. As a cop, I probably had far more exposure to the legal system than most men; however, even I was terrified at the legal prospects related to divorce. That's because divorce law (the legal process) is constantly changing. In short, the legal part of divorce just sucks!

So you're probably asking where you could even begin to decipher and navigate the legal complications of divorce. In this chapter, I'll do my best to give you the most solid advice possible. You must understand that almost all divorce laws are governed by individual states. This makes it very difficult to write something that is definitive for every man living in America. My goal here is to help you understand the general process of divorce and provide resources to better support you.

Below is a long list of things I'd like you to really think about as you ask yourself, *"Does this specific issue pertain to me?"* If the answer is *"Yes"* or *"I don't know,"* I highly recommend putting a check mark by it. This is one of the most essential aspects of your entire journey through divorce.

You must identify each and every legal aspect that may require your attention. It only makes sense that you cannot work out a problem without really knowing what the problem is, right? If you're like most guys, you haven't yet identified all the things that must be decided upon during your legal divorce process.

Too many men are also far too eager to give in during divorce. I can't tell you how many times I've heard some drunken dumb shit slurring, *"Fuck it! She can have it all…"* This is the rest of your life we're talking about. Although I'm certainly not a fan of lengthy court battles, you must assert yourself to ensure a fair and equitable split.

Remember, not all of the things listed below are going to apply to you. (If they all do, you're truly screwed! Sorry, just busting your balls, again!)

- Will you need an attorney?
- How to select and attorney
- Attorney's fees and expenses
- Are there alternatives to an attorney depending on varying circumstances?
- What is mediation?
- What is "discovery?"
- Child custody issues
- "Legal" child custody as opposed to "physical" child custody
- Child support
- Visitation with non-custodial parent
- Grandparent visitation
- Visitation with stepchildren
- Health insurance for children
- Dental insurance for children
- Uninsured health care costs
- College education
- Residence in the marital homestead
- Beneficiaries of life insurance policies
- Claiming children as dependents for income tax purposes
- Religious upbringing of children
- Division of real estate holdings
- Home furnishings

- Business assets
- Division of retirement benefits (pensions, IRAs, 401(k) plans)
- Motor vehicles
- Personal property
- Savings accounts
- Stocks, bonds, and funds
- Compensation for contributions as homemaker (What the hell?)
- Hidden assets
- Debts
- Domestic violence
- Order for protection
- Child abuse
- Parental kidnapping
- Restoration of maiden name
- Post divorce non-financial support

I'm really sorry there's not some scale indicating just how screwed you are based on the number of issues that specifically pertain to you. Just because you may have highlighted over half the list doesn't mean you should put your head between your legs and kiss your ass goodbye! You could still have a fairly smooth divorce from a legal perspective.

Maybe you were married for over 20 years, but the divorce is mutual and mostly civil. It's only natural that after that length of time there may be many things requiring attention and discussion. But this in no way sentences you to a long and drawn out courtroom drama.

And, just a little side note—stay away from movies like *Kramer vs. Kramer* while you're getting divorced. I like Dustin Hoffman, but why the hell did he have to make a movie like that? That kind of courtroom drama is very rare; 90% of divorces are generally settled without either party ever having to make a courtroom appearance.

If you want to read a very good and thorough book about the legal aspects of divorce, check out The Divorce Source Book, written by Attorney Dawn Bradley. The book is very long (and sometimes a bit dry); however, Bradley does great with the relatively sterile topic of divorce legalities. Bradley shares interesting stories and uses relevant examples from personal experiences representing divorcing parties.

Bradley actually says it's often the simpler divorces that can turn complicated. The ones that seem very labor intensive are often the easiest of all. Bradley explained how she once represented a divorcing party and things were going quite well. Each and every issue (child custody and support, property divisions, spousal support, etc.) had all been amicably agreed upon, and the divorce was going through without any court appearances. However, there was a strong disagreement about a very inexpensive family heirloom, and both parties adamantly wanted the item.

The disagreement led to hostile feelings that escalated into an insane battle. As the fighting intensified, the couple began recanting on their already agreed upon settlements. Lengthy courtroom confrontations ensued, costing each party tens of thousands in unnecessary legal fees, not to mention the added stress.

I'm in no way insinuating you should just cave on an issue that is important to you. I just strongly caution you about developing "tunnel vision." It's essential you maintain proper perspective and remember what's really important. I'm just speculating, but the situation I just described probably went something like this…

> Both the man and woman were going with the flow of their divorce and working well through their attorneys. However, there were still some very unresolved feelings (maybe even slight hatred) hidden between the couple. When this one little issue surfaced about a relative insignificant object, the fighting began and all the ill feelings boiled to the surface. The resulting lack of mental and emotional clarity made a simple situation explode into chaos.

We're all sitting here thinking that guy was a dumb shit! He should have just given the bitch the stupid item and been done with it! But again, we can't be too hard on the man because we're not feeling his emotions and living his life or experiencing his tunnel vision.

Let me share another tunnel vision story from Larry. You probably know this as "the drive-by." This situation is very common and happens to a lot of men and women—maybe it's even happened to you. Larry's story doesn't have anything to with the legal and financial aspects of divorce, but I'm sure you'll see my point. Larry said:

> *"I was working the evening shift one night during the beginning stages of my divorce. This was a time when I was very emotional and angry, and I was not always thinking very clearly. I was on my way home from work at about 11:00 p.m. About ten minutes from arriving home, I began thinking about my ex and how I suspected she left me for someone else. Although I had minimal proof, my emotions [and his tunnel vision] began to run away with my imagination. I decided I was gonna drive by my ex's house and see if this guy's car was parked in front. I remember feeling angrier and angrier as I approached her condo. My heart was pounding and the adrenaline was hot as it surged through my body. I even became nauseous and shaky as I turned down her street. Fortunately for me, there was no car in her spot at the complex and her unit was dark."*

I'm sure you can imagine ways things could have gone bad for Larry. What if there was a guy's car there; would Larry have done something stupid like knock on the door and cause a scene? This is exactly how those love-triangle murder suicides happen—no shit!

I know you're thinking, "What a dumb ass!" But before we judge Larry too harshly, consider that I know so many men and women who've done something similar, or worse.

Larry then added:

> *"A few minutes later, I arrived home and realized what a total and complete stupid ass I'd just been. I truly felt some divine intervention from up above. I realized I needed to ensure I never again got such 'tunnel vision.' Thank God*

the entire incident never materialized into anything. This was a real wake up call for me. I really learned from that experience and never lost sight of keeping my thoughts and emotions in check."

The bottom line is that if you want to lose your composure, do it in therapy or do it in private with a close friend and a good bottle of booze. But you must keep things together when you're dealing with the legal matters.

One of the best ways to keep focused is to know your rights. It sounds cliché, but education and knowledge are power. Knowing as much as possible about the legal aspects of your divorce can really ease your worries and your runaway imagination.

Consulting an attorney is the best way to educate yourself. A good divorce attorney handles this bullshit for a living. As I mentioned before, the laws can vary greatly from state to state. Also, various mediators and judges can handle things differently from county to county. A seasoned attorney may even know what to expect when he/she finds out which judge will be presiding over your case.

By now you're probably wondering about the proper way to select an attorney and what services you'll require. My experience leads me to believe most people pick their divorce attorney based on referrals and word of mouth. Although this is good because the person making the referral should be able to give you some honest feedback, this selection method can sometimes be faulty.

The circumstances of your friend's divorce may have been totally different from yours. For example, the primary disagreements surrounding your friend's divorce may have been financial, while your divorce problems may center on a child custody dispute.

I recommend you first make a list of what you think you'll need from your attorney and then begin shopping. As you then talk with friends and associates about an attorney they used, you can ask more specific and informed questions. Remember, you're looking for an attorney to fit your needs. Don't just go with a friend's attorney because they say, *"My divorce attorney was great!"*

I highly recommend retaining an attorney who specializes specifically in family law. Many attorneys practice within several fields of law. Family law is so complicated (and changes so frequently) that one should really choose a specialist in the field.

Also, be extremely leery of any attorney who promises the world. Your life is in turmoil and you know it. Don't get lured into a false sense of security by an attorney who promises you everything. It's okay to retain a lawyer who is positive and provides an appropriate level of support. Just remember the very old saying: if something is too good to be true, it probably is!

And don't forget to ask about a particular attorney's track record of returning phone calls. It's essential you find a lawyer who has a history of promptly returning messages. You've probably known more than one person who, at times, had problems getting in touch with their attorney. *"He won't return my calls. He's being a dick. He's not fighting for me like I need…"*

Next, you really need to think long and hard about just how much you'll actually need from an attorney. If you and your ex are getting along, it may not be very smart for you both to retain expensive attorneys.

My ex retained an attorney, but I did not. (okay, don't call me a dumb ass until you hear the rest of the story) I had a very amicable divorce. She and I worked out everything on our own and came to a solid agreement, so why should I have wasted thousands on an attorney?

We only needed the attorney to prepare the proper paperwork and guide it through the courts. Our initial thought was to find an attorney to represent both of us; however, I learned this wasn't possible in California.

My ex found a highly recommended local attorney and explained our situation. This attorney took her case for only $1,500 total, with the stipulation that we continue to agree on everything. If she and I began fighting about our divorce, the attorney would revert back to the normal $3,000 retainer with additional cost accruals.

Her attorney then drafted the initial Marriage Settlement Agreement (MSA) and gave it to her for our review. We went back and forth a few times over slight verbiage changes, but overall it went smoothly.

Once my ex and I agreed on the final MSA, I then paid a separate attorney to review the document strictly on my behalf. Several of my good friends, with similar situations to me, had all used one particular attorney and were very happy with his services. I did not retain this attorney, but I paid him $300 to review the final MSA just to ensure there was no legal bullshit that I missed. Remember what Ronald Regan said about the Russians during the Cold War? *"Trust but verify!"*

The attorney who drafted the MSA was working for my ex. Although I never once felt like she was trying to screw me financially or with child custody, I wasn't sure about her attorney. $300 was a cheap price to pay for that necessary piece of mind.

Some states actually allow you to draft your own MSA. This may be a route that works well for you if you or your ex are good with legal documents. As I've said, I live in California where things are very complicated, and I just didn't feel comfortable drafting my own documents. But this may be easier in states that are a lot less litigious.

In some states attorneys can also be family law "Board Certified." These attorneys specialize in divorce cases and family law issues. This is good because it means the attorneys are required to have extensive experience and participate in ongoing education.

Family Law is a legal field that is constantly changing, so it's great to have a specialist. If you'd like to know whether your state has something similar to a "Family Law Board Certification," you first need to find out what government entity certifies attorneys. It may take a bit of work on your part, but it will be well worth it in the end.

Try to stay away from attorneys who talk in legal mumbo-jumbo. You're not interested in the fact that they have a superstar vocabulary. You want someone who can work with you, put your mind at ease, and educate you throughout this long process.

You should also select an attorney with whom you feel comfortable. We all have people we "just click with." This doesn't mean your attorney needs to be your next best friend, just someone you feel will take care of your legal issues.

But a strong word of caution—your attorney is not your therapist! Don't expect your attorney to hold your hand and wipe your ass. Your attorney is there to handle the business aspect of your divorce, only! Think about it; would you really want an attorney who cried with you? Hell no!

Don't be afraid to interview potential attorneys. Many people are intimidated by lawyers simply because of their education, title, and debate skills. It's impossible to be a good attorney without being able to confront, convince, and demean others.

But just because someone's a good talker doesn't negate your need to do further research. I don't believe anyone should ever retain the first attorney with whom they meet. Take some time and really examine the qualifications and expertise of any potential attorney before you sign.

The next issue deals with affordability. If you don't have a lot of money for your legal assistance, you may be forced to go with a lawyer who doesn't have a lot of experience. But this doesn't automatically mean your divorce will go bad.

A newer lawyer does have some advantage—namely if you get one who seems really motivated to build a successful practice. He/she may in turn work even harder for you and welcome the challenges of a confrontational divorce. Again, it will all come down to how much work you devote to interviewing and selecting your attorney.

Another thing that can sometimes help you save money, along with resolving disagreements, is something called "mediation." According to www.divorcemediationfl.com, benefits of divorce mediation can consist of:

- **Affordable:** Mediation can cost considerably less than litigation.
- **Efficient:** The meditation process can usually settle a dispute within a few sessions. Most mediations conclude or settle within thirty days from initiating the process.
- **Effective**: Mediation statistically settles over 80% of initiated disputes.
- **Informal:** The process of Mediation is flexible and informal. It is not necessary to have an attorney represent you during the mediation process. However, some individuals feel more comfortable with attorney representation.
- **Empowering:** Disputing parties are directly engaged in the negotiation of their settlement. Parties also enhance the

likelihood of continuing their relationships by utilizing mediation.

- **Confidential:** Information disclosed during mediation may not be divulged as evidence in any trial or judicial proceeding.

According to www.divorceinfo.com:

> *"Divorce mediation still feels like a new idea in some parts of the country, but it's increasingly well known and widely accepted. Mediation means different things to different people. In the form I recommend, you and your spouse would sit down in the same room with each other and with a neutral mediator. With the mediator's help, you would work through all the issues you need to resolve so the two of you can get through your divorce."*

An important aspect of mediation is that it allows you and your ex to maintain joint control, as long as you can remain somewhat civil. Rather than relinquishing the outcome of your divorce to a judge, mediation has the goal of mutual agreement. Many experts also agree this can help foster a more cordial and even friendly relationship after the divorce is final. But to clarify, there is a difference between "mediation" and "arbitration."

www.divorceinfo.com provides additional clarification on the difference:

> *"Both mediation and arbitration are ways you and your spouse can resolve any differences between you without going to court. And many of us tend to merge them in our minds. Don't. Mediation and arbitration are very different ways of resolving differences.*
>
> *A mediator has no power to impose a decision on the husband and the wife. He or she is there solely to help the husband and wife find a resolution that both of them will find acceptable. If they cannot agree, that's as far as the mediator can go.*

> *An arbitrator, on the other hand, has the power to impose a settlement. The arbitrator listens to the arguments in favor of the husband and the arguments in favor of the wife, and then renders a ruling. Typically, the husband and the wife will agree in writing to submit to arbitration before the process begins. They will agree in advance to be bound by the arbitrator's decision, whatever it is."*

Mediation can especially help with one of the biggest issues facing divorced couples, child custody and child support. I'll never understand why so many couples fight over the kids. The kids are not pawns to be use as a tool for getting back at your ex, yet so many people use their babies as leverage against their exes. I absolutely hate people like that. This type of behavior is truly one of the most tragic examples of the evil side of divorce.

With that being said, what if you're a guy facing an ex who wants to keep your children from you? We've already established how little control a man may actually have over a crazy ex who becomes a total and complete bitch during a divorce.

Therefore, the first thing you must do is understand your rights. Although the Internet has revolutionized the ways in which we obtain information, it's no secret that navigating the net can be extremely confusing.

One of the best sites I found related to child custody is http://family.findlaw.com/child-custody/state-divorce-laws.html. It provides a link to each and every state's specific laws related to child custody and child support. Although I caution you to verify any information through formal legal council, this site is definitely a great place to begin your own research.

As I've said, the child custody issue was one of my biggest concerns during my divorce. Although my ex and I always had my son's best interests at heart, I wanted to ensure I was covered for the future; to ensure all legal documents reflected equal parenting rights and responsibilities. In California, the term for equal parenting is often referred to as "co-parenting" or "shared parenting." This verbiage in your divorce settlements provides the best protection for each parent.

For example, what if your ex remarries several years later and she wants to move away with the children and her new hubby? If you have a custody agreement that dictates 50/50 custody, shared parenting, co-parenting, etc., you should have a much greater chance of fighting such attempts. If your children are a priority to you (and I pray they are), you'll want to ensure you do everything in your power to stack the cards in your favor.

I'm not trying to make you paranoid. If you currently have a great relationship with your ex and things are going well with the children, consider yourself lucky and embrace your situation. I'm simply cautioning you to always have a plan for the worst. You don't know what turns your ex's life will take, whether she'll later desire a job out of town or meet the love of her life who may want her to move away with your kids, etc.

And it's not simply enough to have the legal agreement; it should go without saying that you must also follow through with all mandates. I've known several men who regularly neglected their parental responsibilities and didn't pick up their kids during designated times. Not only is this tragic for the children's emotions, you can be setting yourself up for your ex to take you back to court for revised child custody and child support.

Your ex could present calendars she's kept about the actual times you each had the children, along with her records of times she claims you neglected your parental responsibilities. There's no guarantee a judge will allow personal records into future custody proceedings, but I wouldn't want to face that chance. I also encourage you to maintain your own records to show that you always adhere to your custody orders.

The more you do for your children, such as providing health insurance, financial support, savings accounts for college, etc., the better it could look for you in future proceedings. This is not sound legal advice—that's what attorneys are for. I'm simply sharing things that I've been told from many-a-man about their individual courtroom experiences.

As for child support, that's another story. You may have 50/50 custody of your children and be the most involved super-dad ever and still have to pay child support. Based on my experience and research, most child support decisions are based primarily on income.

Take a man named Gus for example. Even though Gus has complete 50/50 co-parenting with his ex, he still pays $578.00 a month in child support. This is strictly because Gus makes more than she does.

The San Diego County Superior Court lists the below information on the website about child support:

1. A parent's first and principal obligation is to support his/her minor children.
2. A parent shall pay the court-ordered child support payment as the first priority before payment of any debts owed to creditors.
3. Each parent has equal responsibility to support the child.
4. The state uniform child support guidelines consider each parent's actual income and level of responsibility for the children.
5. Courts are required to add to basic child support payments the costs for child care related to work, reasonable and necessary education/training, and reasonable child's uninsured health care costs.
6. Courts may also include as additional child support the costs of a child's special education and visitation travel expenses.
7. Court must order health insurance be maintained by either or both parents if health insurance is available at no cost or at nominal cost.
8. Child support is determined by income of the parties, number of children, tax filing status, share of physical responsibility for child.
9. Court may allow income deductions for extreme financial hardship due to justifiable expenses, such as, extraordinary health expenses, uninsured catastrophic losses, minimum basic living expenses of natural or adopted children who reside with the parent. (No hardship deduction if other supported child receives AFDC).

10. Support continues until age 19 while still in high school, completion of high school and over 18, or self-supporting. A disabled adult child is entitled to child support beyond this period.

Simply Google "child support calculators" and you'll be linked to dozens (if not hundreds) of various calculators. The below calculator comes from www.alllaw.com.

Number of children who are the subject of the pending action:	1
Monthly Net Income of Non-Custodial Parent:	0
Monthly amount of court ordered child support and/or alimony from prior relationships paid by non-custodial parent:	0
Monthly amount of health insurance premiums paid by non-custodial parent:	0
% of time that non-custodial parent has physical responsibility for children:	0
Monthly Net Income of Custodial Parent:	0
Monthly amount of court ordered child support and/or alimony from prior relationships paid by custodial parent:	0
Monthly amount of health insurance premiums paid by custodial parent:	0
Calculate Reset	

As you can see, it requires a relatively simple amount of information. Although you'd be a fool to simply base your numbers on an online calculator, it gives you a place to start.

Once again, I cannot stress enough the need to properly research and educate yourself about all aspects of your divorce, especially the legal implications and your options. One of the best sites I've ever found is www.divorcemag.com. It has links to just about every aspect of divorce.

Be a student of your divorce, especially as is relates to the financial and legal aspects. Don't ever take anything on face value when dealing with the legality of divorce. It may suck and be the worst part of divorce, but you could really find yourself up shit creek for years to come if you half-ass this aspect of the process...

CHAPTER 10

EMOTIONALLY GETTING OVER DIVORCE—WHAT'S THE KEY?

This chapter is about the good side of divorce. It's time to understand how to make things better and move your life forward. You may not be ready for this yet—that's okay. Maybe you're still "faking it" and it's a major effort to even get out of bed in the morning—again, that's okay. No matter where you are in your journey, take a deep breath and open your mind and heart. Allow yourself a break from the worries and anxieties of divorce. I want you to see that you do have a future, and it can be very bright.

If you're at all like I was, you're spending endless nights asking yourself two questions:

> When will it finally start to get better?
> What's the secret to divorce?

I personally anguished over these questions for months following my separation. I would repeatedly ask my friends, my therapist (at the cost of $120 an hour), and just about anyone else who would listen, to please share the secret of moving through divorce toward a better life.

Unfortunately, no one could really give me an answer. It was the great allusive treasure to which no one had a map. Maybe it's because divorce is such an individual experience that no one has ever really tried to nail down a "one size fits all" explanation. Whatever the reason, I couldn't find peace.

Let me stress that, this chapter is strictly about the emotional aspects of divorce. If you're stressed about the legal and financial aspects, this can only be relieved when the court battling is over or you discover a way to improve your income.

But regarding the emotional aspects of divorce, how does a man move forward? How does he see the light shining from the good that divorce can bring? I've spent the last 18 months pondering, researching, and living the experience of divorce, and I think I've finally figured out a two-part answer to this question.

I hope these answers give you the freedom to finally feel the burden of divorce being lifted from your heart. I know I sound a little sappy, but just go with it. Again, you're reading this book because you're sappy, too. Just accept it. I won't tell anyone if you don't.

So here goes. First and foremost when moving past divorce, <u>you must reinvent yourself without her and completely separate yourself from the former relationship</u>. I know, I know, you're probably cussing at me right now and ready to burn my book. You're saying, *"Reinvent myself! No shit! Tell me something I don't know!"* Before you start dreaming of running me down with a city bus, just follow me for a bit.

When a couple gets married, it's obvious they combine their lives. But I don't think we consciously comprehend to what extent the other person becomes such an intricate part of our true identity. Most married couples join their lives at the very core of their existence. Everything you both hold important becomes intertwined.

When we get married, we truly grow into one entity that cannot be separated with a single stroke of the divorce pen. Although many of us maintain our own interests and hobbies while married, these generally remain small and insignificant when compared to the important stuff.

Take me for example. During the majority of my marriage, my favorite hobby was riding off-road Enduro motorcycles. I had a group of friends with whom I rode extensively throughout the mountains and deserts of Southern California. Although this was an activity I did without my wife, in the grand scheme of things it was just a hobby. Everything else in my life (my son, my home, my finances, my evenings and weekends, vacations, dreams, etc.) included my wife in one form or another.

I'm not saying this to belittle you. I know it's obvious your married life was completely intertwined with your ex. I'm simply asking you to examine just how much it will take to separate everything and truly become your own person. When talking about getting over the pain and stress of divorce, you must first ask yourself how invested and attached you were in your marriage.

Here are a few questions to consider:

- How long were you married?
- How passionate was the marriage at one or all phases (e.g. were you high school sweethearts, etc.)?
- How many children do you have and what are their ages?
- How will the children react to the divorce?
- Will you both look out for the best interests of the kids, or will they be used as pawns?
- How many properties, investments, and financial commitments join you together?
- Will the divorce be amicable?
- Will you actually be able to maintain a friendship afterwards?
- Will the divorce go relatively smooth and uncontested, or will you be like Kim Basinger and Alec Baldwin, or Brad Pitt and Jennifer Aniston, with their never-ending battles from hell?

There are many other things to be considered—these are just a few to get you thinking. As you begin to reinvent yourself absent of your married self, you should start to see the positive side of divorce. Remember the analogy of cutting the fibers of a rope in Chapter 3, "Fake it Till You Make it."

I wrote this particular chapter about 18 months after my separation (and six months after my divorce was final), so I obviously benefit from hindsight. I can look back at my process and the detailed notes I kept and see it took me about five to six months before I really started to feel like a new me. I began looking in the mirror and liking what I saw—the "new Joey." I no longer felt I was "Faking it 'Til I Make it." I had really begun living better and feeling good about myself.

I also discovered the process of divorce seems to start slow and sluggish, but then picks-up speed and feeds on its own momentum as it begins moving faster. Here's as analogy:

As boys, I'm sure most of you did things like riding in an unpowered go-cart down a big hill. Or, maybe you would lie on a skateboard and cost down a long and sloping street in your neighborhood.

At first, you move kind of slow. Even if someone gave you a push, it still takes a while for gravity to build up your speed. But then, as you get moving, you go faster and faster and the speed and momentum compounds. My divorce was very similar. Once I arrived at the point of beginning growth, it just seemed to really take off.

In your current state you may not believe me, but there is a very positive side to divorce. Even if you're emerging from a 20 or 30 year marriage, you can't cave to the common tendencies of depression, regret, self-pity, and what-ifs.

After all, if you're just going to mope around like a big bumbling idiot, then why not just give up? Why work on this at all? I'll tell you why; because you know deep down in your heart that there's much to enjoy about divorce.

You may not as of yet be at the point of truly enjoying this chapter. But I hope it will bring you some comfort to know the good that's ahead. You may be in the pits of depression, but there is still a little fight left in you, and you know it.

It's also important to note that this chapter is about the good side of divorce apart from dating new women. Contrary to popular belief, a man's world does not simply revolve around his penis. Yes, it's true. There's more to life than getting laid.

Okay, well maybe not much more, but there are a few things. Maybe that's why this chapter is so much shorter than the dating chapter (coming up next). But either way, it's still important, so shut up and read on…

I found the personal freedoms of divorce to be absolutely amazing. Being able to be yourself is probably the best benefit of getting divorced. Take a moment to ask yourself, *"Do I really know me?"*

If you were at all like me, you got married at a young age and developed into a mature man while existing within the confines and restrictions of your marriage. Ten years later, I found myself single, in my mid-thirties, and having a limited idea about who I truly was outside of my marriage. Well guess what? After months of deeply painful soul searching I met the real me, and I really like the guy.

I once interviewed Josh, who said:

> *"Ever since I was a kid, I always liked myself. I was even kind of cocky about it. But when I was married my ex made me question myself. She made me feel bad about liking myself. She beat me down like a dog…"*

My friend Bill has a story very applicable to this topic. Let me first describe the "married Bill." In one single word, the married Bill was "miserable!" He was one of those guys whose wife just beat him down until he was a shell of a man.

Bill began dating his wife when they were both 16. At 19, Bill knocked-up his wife. He wanted to *Do The Right Thing,* so they got married. Bill thought things were going okay, so they decided to have a second kid. Eighteen months later, Bill's daughter was born.

I remember visiting Bill at his house when he was married. I'd knock on the door and his "evil wife" would open up and just glare at me without saying one single word. As soon as I made eye contact with Bill's wife through the screen door, I felt just like a little kid standing on my friend's porch asking his mom if my friend could come out and play.

I shit you not! I pictured myself groveling to Bill's wife as I begged, *"Can Bill come out and play?"* She would immediately turn her head into the house and yell to Bill, *"It's for you!"*

Moments later, Bill slouched as he walked past "the wicked stepmother." (aka Bill's wife) Bill opened the screen door and stepped outside onto the porch. With his head down and shoulders drooped forward, Bill continued walking away from the front door without saying a word as he passed me. I'm not exaggerating, he really looked that pathetic. Bill finally stopped walking about halfway into the driveway, just out of his wife's earshot.

It was so amazingly tense as we would talk quietly in the driveway just like two little kids getting a momentary reprieve from a serious restriction over a bad report card. All the while, Bill's evil wife stood at the door staring at us to ensure we had not one moment of fun. Bill won't admit it, but I'm certain he would have gotten flogged in the basement after I left if he so much as cracked a smile while we talked!

Okay, so you get the picture. His wife was the "C-word" for sure. In fact, if it wasn't for Bill's kids, we all worried he might have taken a long fall with a short drop.

After he divorced, Bill started coming around little-by-little and hanging out with his friends. He seemed like a turtle cautiously poking his head out to see the grand world beyond his shell. (his shell of course was his marriage)

At first, Bill wouldn't stay at gatherings more than an hour or two, and he remained very quiet. But after a few months we noticed Bill becoming more social—he even looked happy. Since then, Bill has continued to grow socially.

Learning to really like yourself is one of the greatest gifts afforded by divorce. I'm not saying you don't already like yourself, but divorce provides the freedom to truly rediscover you. Just like Bill, we all make personal sacrifices when we get married.

In a healthy marriage these sacrifices are well worth it and the benefits far outweigh anything we give up. But when you're in a marriage like Bill's, you literally become another person—you lose a part of yourself.

I personally grew into far more of a man as part of my divorce. I took control of my life, my finances, and my home in a far better and more mature way. As I began to meet the new me throughout the ongoing process of my journey, I liked myself more and more. I felt an increasing amount of pride and respect for myself that improved the quality of my life.

I remember one day I was riding my brand new $1,200 mountain bike—my divorce present to myself. By the way, I didn't have to ask permission to buy the bike. I needed only to consult my new *solo checking account.* I set out one hot Sunday morning in early May for about a 25-mile ride along some of San Diego's prettiest coastlines. Much of the ride was actually directly on the sandy beaches.

I realized about halfway through the ride that no one knew where I was. My son was with his great aunt and I had my cell phone for emergencies. But I hadn't bothered to tell anyone where I was going, nor did I need to.

I spent the remainder of the day reflecting about my newfound freedom. I didn't tell anyone about my ride until it was all over, and even then I only told others because I wanted to, not because I had to.

This story is but one small example of the extreme freedom I began to enjoy as I grew past the initial pain and emotional shock of divorce. I'm living proof that divorce can be a good thing.

I'm now a much better parent, friend, brother, uncle, lover, employee at work, etc. I'm much more liked by the most important person of all—me. I truly love myself and who I've become as a result of my divorce.

Another thing that really helped was moving from my initial divorce pad (the little place I describe in the Introduction) back into my house. I actually ended up with our family house in the divorce. Although the payment was a bit steep for my divorce budget and there was not much equity in the house, it felt good to have a real home to invite family and friends over.

I began hanging pictures everywhere and got into decorating and painting. I quickly learned I had a flair for decorating and really enjoyed discovering my own style. (and once again, no I'm not gay, so stop thinking that)

I remember one day when my ex stopped by to pick up our son. It was about six months since I'd moved back into the house and had been doing a lot of work, both inside and out. My ex commented on what a clean freak I'd become and how impressively I had decorated. She jokingly said, *"This is really nice. Why didn't you take this kind of care of the house when we were married?"*

I replied, *"Because I never felt like it was my house. It was your house and I just lived here."*

She quickly said, *"That's because it wasn't your house."*

She actually said it with a smile on her face, and we both kind of laughed. But she was right and we both knew it. While we were married, she controlled everything on the walls, the colors, the furniture, everything. (primarily because I was just too lazy about that stuff) But after the divorce I had the chance to reinvent me as a man who likes his home and enjoys fixing it up.

Again, this doesn't mean you need to have a lot of money to spruce up your home. I moved back into a relatively empty four-bedroom house, but within about four months I had it nicely furnished while spending little money. I was just patient.

I put out the word to all my female friends and family. (women love to help us guys—remember, the wounded dove thing) Almost immediately I began getting calls from people giving away pretty nice stuff. You can also find relatively nice furniture at thrift stores and no-name local places for reasonable prices.

My son also helped me find the new me. Just last week, he and I were talking about divorce in general. It was an interesting conversation, and he was asking some fairly advanced questions. (it still amazes me how smart kids are nowadays) We were talking about how divorce could be a good thing as long as both the mommy and daddy can remain friends and make sure the children are put first.

My son said he's happy about the divorce because he and I spend a lot more time together. That hit me hard to hear my son say he sees a difference in the amount of time we spent together before and after the divorce. I immediately knew what he was talking about.

When I was married, I thought like a lot of other parents. I assumed because my kid had his mom and dad in the home, along with enough money for a solid middle class lifestyle, that he was well cared for.

I'm sorry to say I didn't generally put my son first from an emotional standpoint. I didn't lay with him each and every night before he went to bed; I didn't read to him as much as I should have; we didn't play a lot of games together; and he often seemed like a burden to me.

I was simply busy doing things I thought were important. But as soon as his mom and I separated, I quickly made my son the foremost priority in my life. During that process I discovered something wonderful, I was a far better divorced dad than I was a married one.

I know I comment extensively about parenting throughout this book. Therefore, I won't bore you with more regurgitated information about my kid. I share this story to stress that becoming a better father was one of the most essential parts of me reinventing me. I found a joy in parenting that I never would have experienced had I stayed married.

I was recently discussing this very subject with a good friend, Jason, who is still married. Jason agreed with me and knew exactly what I meant. I really commend his honesty. Jason reluctantly admitted to sometimes putting off his kids because he feels they have everything since he and his wife are still married.

I was actually surprised to hear these words because Jason appears to everyone to be the true "super-dad." Jason is a guy who coaches, cooks, takes his kids to school everyday before work, spends quality time with them, etc. But I guess we can all improve.

This brings to mind a funny story about my son. A few months ago my son asked for a tetherball court in the backyard. Tetherball is a big deal at his school—it's all they play at recess and lunch.

First off, it was really cool not to have to consult anyone about cementing a tetherball pole in the back yard. Not like my ex would have said "no" to something like that, but it was just one more bit of freedom to not have to ask. I installed the tetherball and my boy became the instant star of the neighborhood. Kids always came to our house to play.

One day shortly thereafter, my ex came by to pick up our son. Before she could exit the car my son grabbed her hand and began pulling her to the backyard to show off his talents on the new tetherball court. Once in the backyard, my son began displaying his moves while my ex and I chatted and watched.

But then, my son suddenly pulled down his pants and began peeing on the backyard grass. My ex sternly looked at me and said, *"Look at your son!"*

His comeback was perfect; my son was in midstream as he overheard her concerned comments. He promptly looked back at her and replied, *"Mommy, it's okay, this is The Man House!"*

I then looked at my ex and said, *"He is right, this is now The Man House."*

To her credit, my ex just laughed it off. I know she enjoyed watching her son getting to be a dirty little boy while thinking he was cool because he could pee in the backyard of The Man House.

Another time my son said he wanted a hammock in his bedroom, *"just like the Pirates of the Caribbean have on their ships."* Again, who was going to say no to a pirate hammock in The Man House?

We immediately got a big net hammock that took up most of the bedroom. I drilled holes in the wall for the anchor bolts and hung it from wall-to-wall. My son thought he was the coolest kid ever because he had a real pirate hammock inside his bedroom.

The point of these two stories is to enjoy your children. Comfort their fears and help them grow strong. Move forward with them as a team. I once heard a great quote by an unknown author. *"Life is like riding a bicycle, you must keep moving forward to maintain your balance. When you look back you'll fall every time."* Moving forward with my son has been one of the happiest aspects of my post-married life.

I'm not saying I felt like a bad dad when I was married. I'm just a super-dad now. (if I may toot my own horn!) I remember one night when I was still living in my little divorce pad. My son was spending the night and I could tell he felt a little sick. It didn't seem that bad so I put him to bed as usual. I then proceeded to doze on the couch while watching TV.

Holy shit! About 30 minutes later I was startled by the sound of him crying while I felt something warm and wet gushing over my legs. (thank God it wasn't on my face) I opened my eyes to see my son standing over me puking his guts out. I'm not exaggerating—it was that projectile kid vomit! It reminded me of that scene in *The Exorcist* where Linda Blair was puking that green shit all over her room, the priest and her mother!

I scooped him up and ran to the bathroom as he continued to spray vomit all over everything. We both got undressed and jumped in a warm shower for about 15 minutes. I got out first and let him sit with the soothing water as I cleaned, and cleaned, and cleaned, and cleaned.

I then made him a bed on the couch. (because his bed was soaked in "Exorcist Puke") I slept with one eye open on the floor near him, ever mindful of gurgling sounds coming from the couch above.

I called my ex to tell her about our boy being sick. She had plans to go out of town with him the following day to visit her folks. She immediately uttered, *"Oh my God! Do you want me to come get him and bring him home?"*

I was startled by her words. Obviously she meant no insult to me; she was speaking out of serious concern for her son. I remember quickly replying, *"He'll be fine, and he is home."* This especially meant a lot to me because my ex is a great mom to our son, yet I was doing well enough to take care of him.

It was such a pivotal moment for me. When I was married she was the one who cared for our son when he was sick. After all, I was the dad, and dads don't do sick. As I shared in "Our Fathers Failed Us," it just wasn't the thing when I was raised in the 70s and 80s.

But there I was, taking care of my son. And the best part about the whole thing was that he never asked for his mom that entire night. He felt so comfortable with the tender way I was caring for him. I was all he needed.

Some of you who may already be super-dads might be thinking this was no big deal, but for many of us this is a common theme. And if this story doesn't apply to you because you don't have kids, I'm sure you still see my point. You'll become the new you as you grow into a better person than you were before—as you improve and make right the mistakes of your past.

This is also time for you to begin to plan for your financial future as well. Maybe you never finished high school or college. Maybe you would like to open your own business but your ex never supported you taking such a risk.

If you want to get a second job to save money to open a business, it's your time. If you want to work out a lot, it's your time. If you want to go back to school, it's your time. You do what you want with your new found freedoms and spare time.

Maybe you always wanted to go to law school but never had the motivation. Maybe you used your bad marriage as a crutch or an excuse. Were you lazy, scared, or both? Is that why you never took the leap for your dreams?

Please don't think it will be easy. Chasing any dream is always a challenge. It should go without saying that this is why achievement is such a reward. If personal and professional success were easy, everyone would be doing it.

A lot of getting over your divorce has to also do with perspective. Remember Big-Brother-Carlos from the Introduction? He's the guy who helped me find the title of this book. Carlos got taken to the cleaners in his divorce. Half of his entire take-home pay went to his ex for the first five years following his divorce. It was so bad he had to move into his parent's house and couldn't leave for years. But his attitude made all the difference in the world.

Carlos said, *"When I was married, I used to get $200 a month for everything—gas, food, booze, everything. But after I got divorced, I got a $1,600 a month raise. Who cares if she got half of my check? I considered myself rich."*

Many of us would have let that situation get us down. I know I would have if I had to move back into my parents' house and stay there for years. I'd have been bummed out and pissed off, but not Carlos.

Carlos was literally the happiest man ever. His perspective made all the difference in the world. Every time I saw Carlos he was with one or more of his kids going on ride bikes, swimming at the beach, watching a movie, etc. Carlos is just an amazingly positive person.

Perspective is everything. How you view your newfound freedoms and what you do with it is completely up to you. Although it may take time, don't become obsessed with the destination. Stop and live the journey. Besides, there's a new you out there who I'm sure is just dying to meet you…

Chapter 11

Getting Back in the Saddle (The Dating Chapter)

The first thing you may notice is that this chapter is one of the longest in the entire book. That's because the topic of post divorce dating is essential and must be really understood. So many men don't take their time and become trapped in another horrible relationship following divorce. I'm not trying to scare you or paint some dooms day scenario. I'm just stressing the need to give this subject some serious thought. Take your time and make sure you have a clear picture of what you're doing when you re-enter the dating world.

For a lot of men, this part of divorce will be a blast. You may be excited about actually having a chance to do (and DO!) what was never possible during your marriage. This new freedom affords an opportunity to discover what you really want from a woman and in a relationship.

On the other hand, there're so many guys literally terrified of dating. I'm not kidding—dating can be shear torture for a large number of recently divorced men. Many of you were married for a long time and you're scared to death of new and unknown social norms. Maybe you're wondering where to begin, what to say, how to act. I was one of these guys when I began dating. I literally felt like a fish out of water.

There're actually so many different ways a man can react to dating that it's difficult to find the right words to support everyone. My goal is to share some of my dating experiences, along with a bunch of information I learned from doing a lot of research. After reading this chapter you should at least have a very good place to start. I also hope you'll enjoy a good laugh, too.

I quickly learned dating wasn't actually that bad. It really came down to developing the right attitude and perspective, along with taking the time to understand the process and what to expect.

Let me put it in guy terms. You'd never play on an organized sports team without first understanding the rules and going to practice. Dating is exactly the same way. You need to understand it (and even practice a little) to get it right.

But first let me give you the all-important disclaimer. Never (no matter how clean and wholesome you think a woman may be) should you engage in intercourse without protection! I don't care if you're about to bed-down with Snow White herself, NEVER assume she's "clean."

This is even more critical for those of you who were married for over 15 years and haven't had sex with anyone other than your ex during that time. Sexually transmitted diseases are on the rise, little boys, and it's no laughing matter.

The excerpt below was taken directly from womenshealth.com:

> *"The rise in divorce is being blamed for increases in sexually transmitted infections among the over 50's. More older men and women are returning to the dating scene, experts say. But many fail to follow the recommendation to use CONDOMS, assuming medical warnings about safe sex is aimed mainly at the young. As a result rates of diseases such as chlamydia and gonorrhea are increasing among middle age and elderly as well as the young.*
>
> *Between 2002 and 2006, cases of chlamydia among those aged 45 to 64 rose 51 percent from 1,276 to 1,933. Among the over 65's there was a 37 percent rise in gonorrhea among those aged 45 to 64 fell over the period. But among the over 65's there was an 11 percent rise!*
>
> *Meanwhile, cases of genital warts went up 22 percent for the younger age group and 17 percent for pensioners. While first attacks of genital herpes rose by 13 percent among those aged 45 to 64 with cases totaling 1,563 there was*

a 10 percent rise for pensioners. Syphilis cases rose among those aged 45 - 64 rose 139 percent from 172 in 2002 to 411 in 2006.

Statistics show more than 42 percent of British marriages end in divorce, the highest in Europe. There is a rising trend for break up among marriages which have lasted 30 and 40 years.

Last month, the LANCET medical journal warned of an upsurge of syphilis cases in developed countries. Most syphilis is found in men, but the rates have been rising in women. The disease is affecting young heterosexuals as well as mature women in 'particular sex circles.'

The overall trend for the last decade is rising among all age groups with 1,500 percent increase since the mid Nineties according to health protection agency. The elderly were being left out of official campaigns to tackle STI.

Most people think that STI ONLY affect young people but this is clearly not the case. Too often, campaigns against STI are solely aimed at teenagers and people in their twenties!"

Okay, so now that you've been reminded you can actually die from this dating stuff (holy shit that really sucks), let's move on…

I really, really want to stress the idea that dating can be very difficult for a lot of newly single men. If you're having anxiety and feel like dating could very well suck, you're not alone. So many men just don't feel confident in the dating scene.

Tragically, far too many men submit to their dating fears and end up settling for the first or second woman who comes along after their separation; they basically buy the very first piece of ass they get after divorce. And quite often this new woman is strikingly similar to their ex-wife. Some men would simply rather settle for the quick stability than conquer their dating fears.

Let's stop and really think about this. You're getting divorced because you were in a shitty marriage. Come-on, you know it's true. As we already said repeatedly, even if you got dumped and didn't want the divorce, I'm sure you weren't as happy as you could be.

But the fear of being "Alone" is often more powerful than the misery of a bad relationship. Therefore, thousands of men are far too eager to pacify their lonely fears by hooking the first or second woman to come along after their separation.

Being happy in any aspect of your life takes courage. It means you must be patient and often requires effort to make *active choices* that adhere to goals. Don't get lost in your fears of being alone. If you don't yet know what you want from a woman and a relationship, that's great. You're just getting divorced. You're not supposed to know it all yet—dummy!

I even interviewed a divorced man, Eugene, who talked about computer porn and how it had taken the place of his dating life. This is so important to address because I believe the availability of mass Internet pornography has become a real problem.

Now don't get me wrong; I'm not some anti-porn crusader. I subscribe to the "live and let live" philosophy, and watching a dirty movie once and a while is no big deal. But my research has led me to believe the issue of extremes is the problem.

As I spoke with Eugene, I noticed him becoming increasingly down on himself. He was a normal guy in his late thirties with a good job, but he was embarrassed that his dating life had deteriorated to such a low point. He'd been divorced for over two years, but he hadn't gone on a single date, let alone had sex with a woman.

I began to see a man who'd been really messed up by his bad marriage, and that computer pornography had become his very unhealthy outlet. Eugene was in no way crazy, but his circumstances had brought him to a very low place. During our conversation Eugene finally gave me the typical line, *"I just don't know where or how to begin dating."*

I know many of you may be reading this and thinking, *"I see a lot of similarities between Eugene and me."* That's perfectly fine. True self-realization is exactly what I hope you'll get from reading this—to open your eyes and stimulate your thoughts. I really hope I can put a different spin on dating because so many of us are completely uninformed and haven't a clue where to begin.

Think of it this way. Your dating life is now the dark desert in the middle of the night. As you walk along you can't see any of the bumps, holes, rocks, cactus, snakes, scorpions, lions, tigers, bears, etc. But as you gain more knowledge and experience, the sun begins to rise over the desert horizon and your vision becomes clearer. You increasingly see the bigger picture. The sun will eventually fly high in the sky and you'll be able see the entire desert, both good and bad. But until then, you must be cautions.

Dating is exactly the same way. It takes time to see the big picture, and if you're not cautious in the beginning, you may very well end up in a "rebound relationship." The rebound is actually something we hear about so much that it can often sound just like the little boy who cried wolf. "The rebound, the rebound, the rebound…" It's drilled into our heads so much we can easily become desensitized to it.

I suppose you're wondering how to tell when it is, or is not, a rebound relationship. Well, I recommend you don't get too serious with a woman until you truly feel comfortable with your divorce and being on your own. (until the sun is shining and you can see the entire "dating desert") I know that may suck for many of you, but I strongly caution you about getting too serious with any woman until you're confident you've moved on.

Now of course there're exceptions to every rule, and you may find "Mrs. Right" shortly after your separation, but do you want to risk your future (and maybe the chance of another divorce) on such slim odds? The goal here is healthy dating, not an insecure rebound relationship.

I was once discussing the rebound concept with my therapist, and she offered me the following advice:

> *"Remember, Joey, you generally aren't going to find your Mrs. Right until you're completely over your divorce. It's okay to date, but be very cautious about getting too serious with anyone before you can look in the mirror and HONESTLY say you're through most of this. This doesn't mean there aren't exceptions to every rule and a very small number of people do meet their soul mate while in the middle of their divorce; however, this is certainly the exception and not the rule. If you suddenly think you may have met your Mrs. Right, just get your ass back in here right away and we'll talk. Don't try to figure it out alone!"*

From this discussion I also realized another important fact—it's perfectly acceptable to remain single indefinitely. (or even forever) This may sound a bit patronizing, but it needs to be said. Don't ever let anyone say you *need* a girlfriend or a wife. Many men and women are increasingly discovering that marriage may just not be for them within their foreseeable future. (or maybe forever)

So whatever you want to call it—getting back in the saddle, finding your balls, getting your groove back, etc.—dating is an important part of the healing process after an emotionally difficult separation.

I once heard an analogy that really helped me during the dating process. Look at dating this way: you would never buy a car without test driving a lot of different makes and models to find the one that feels just right to you. Well, what makes dating any different?

After all, a romantic partner has a much greater effect on a man's life than a car. Yet so many of us spend much more time finding the right car than we do finding the right woman. I know, I know, a car can be a lot more fun than a chick, but let's stick to the task at hand. (I can just see *Tool Time* Tim Allen doing his grunting right now as we talk about cars.)

Let me also stress that test-driving a woman does not automatically mean you must have sex with the entire world in order to clear your head and understand what you want. Although sex is a big part of dating, it doesn't have to be the one and only thing you're after.

You may just want to get your feet wet (but not your pecker! Ha!) until you feel comfortable having sex. That's completely up to you. Or, you can also run out and be the "man whore" you've always wanted to be—it's all your call. Again, that's the beauty of this process. It can be custom-tailored to you depending on what you're after and where you're at in your own personal divorce journey.

I even spoke with a recent divorcee who was forced to confront Erectile Dysfunction during his first sexual encounter following his separation. (holy shit!) I really felt bad for this guy—what an experience.

His name is Phil. He was 39 at the time of his divorce and had been married for 18 years. Phil never had sexual problems during his marriage. (that was, when his wife would actually have sex with him)

But about six months into his separation, Phil began casually dating a woman. One thing led to another and they ended up naked in the sack, but Phil was unable to "perform."

Phil described a feeling of shear panic as he was stark naked with this woman but couldn't get a "boner!" Phil finally worked up the nerve to date a woman and have sex, but he couldn't take care of business. I can't even imagine what Phil must have felt.

But this story does have a happy ending. I ran into Phil several months later and we began talking about divorce and his E.D. experience. Phil actually took the initiative to see his doctor shortly after the incident. Phil's doctor was very sympathetic and he provided a prescription of "Cialas."

Surprisingly, the doctor explained to Phil that he'd seen several recently divorced men experiencing similar problems. The stress and anxiety of new sex for the first time after getting divorced can be very difficult for a lot of men.

But, of course, we macho men never talk about stuff like this. After all, every man is a sexual dynamo. Sex comes ever-so-naturally for each one of us. We never have problems in this department—right!

Obviously, you can sense my sarcasm. But this is a prime example of what I mean when speaking of men having a tough time with dating. So many guys are just really out of practice and it can cause some real blows to our fragile male egos!

As for Phil, the next time he was about to hit a home run with a chick, he was able to *slide* right into home base! It was so great to see the smile on Phil's face as he explained his sexual triumph. It was the look of a man who'd really made it through some tough times. But he would have never overcome this issue had he not sought-out help from his doctor and really opened-up about the problem.

And that's actually one of the great things about writing this book and interviewing so many men. I've had the honor and pleasure of seeing a lot of men go from being down-and-out to rising from the ashes of divorce. I'm not being overdramatic. That's exactly what most men experience during their journey through divorce, and I was certainly one of them.

This is also why it's so important we as men talk about divorce. We need to study everything so we truly feel we're not alone in our fears, our worries, or even our "boner problems."

The individuality of divorce is exactly why it's essential for a man to cautiously ease into dating. It's perfectly okay to date a woman and not have a lot of sex (or any at all) if you're not so inclined because of personal beliefs, religious commitments, or you're simply just not ready.

But if you really do feel ready to go the route of "conquer and screw" as many lovely ladies as possible, that's fine too. I'll share some great resources with you later in this chapter about being all you can be in that department.

There're some really intelligent fellas who've done years of research (including thousands of nights of trial and error) to develop tried-and-true techniques when it comes to dating and having lots and lots of sex. I've read a lot of this material, and I must say one would be a fool to disregard the years of experience of these modern-day pick-up artists. Most of these authors also present some really funny material that's good for a great laugh, too!

On the other hand, please be cautious about friends and what I call the "pity set-up." I coined this phrase because that's what it seemed to become in my life. Soon after my separation I learned everyone had "a really nice girl" they wanted me to meet.

I quickly began to wonder, if she's so nice, so pretty, and so smart, then why does she need to be set-up with a guy just getting out of a marriage? I'm not saying that being set-up can never grow into the absolute love of your life. I'm just relaying some serious words of warning.

I remember one of the first times a buddy tried to set me up shortly after my separation. One afternoon, a good friend I work with came to me extremely excited about a woman I just had to meet! In his words she was, *"A guaranteed lay!"*

My response? I immediately told him *"No!"*

This was only about two months after my separation, and I knew I was in no condition to be dating anyone. As another friend put it, I was *"one big vagina."* I was crying all the time and still picking fights with my ex about the divorce. You tell me what healthy, attractive, and "normal" lady would have wanted to go out with me. Well, after about 10 minutes of convincing, my buddy talked me into having lunch with this girl in a group setting.

The entire time I was driving to the restaurant, I remember having a knot in my stomach. Was she gonna be pretty, or pretty ugly? Was she gonna be nice, talkative, friendly—what, what, what? My mind was spinning like a cheap carnival ride. (you know, the shitty ones that make you puke)

I arrived a few minutes late and everyone had already taken a seat. You guessed it; my good friend made sure I had a seat waiting for me right next to the nice young lady he wanted me to meet.

Okay, so I know you're wondering about my first impression. Well… she was okay-looking. A bit heavy set with an okay face. But I made myself keep an open mind. I just took a deep breath, sat down, and joined the group with a smile on my face.

After all, maybe she would be a really great girl, right? Well she immediately began to talk, and talk, and talk, and talk… After five minutes I wanted to shoot myself. (which was bad because I was on-duty and had a gun on my side)

Have you ever met a woman who talked so much you couldn't get in one single word? That was this chick. It was all I could do to sit there for 40 minutes. But then, as if listening to the chick wasn't bad enough, my body began making things much worse, I had a full-blown panic attack!

My chest suddenly became extremely tight, and my stomach had the worst case of butterflies ever. (and these were not the good butterflies, either) I was feeling sick to my stomach and began sweating. I remember thinking, *"So this is dating! This is what it's gonna be like." My life has been reduced to women like this!"* The anxiety and panic train came speeding by and I jumped onboard and let it take me for a ride!

Lunch was finally over and we said our goodbyes. My buddy walked the girl to her car as I waited a few aisles over. They talked for a few minutes and she got in her car and drove away.

He walked over to me with a huge smile on his face. To this day I remember his exact words, *"Dude, you're in. You're going out with her Friday night. She's a guaranteed lay!"* To which I quickly replied, *"NO!"*

My buddy was shocked and insulted as he asked me why. I replied:

> *"So I'm gonna go out with her Friday night. I'm then gonna have to sit with her for three or four hours, spend 60 to 80 bucks on drinks and food while listening to her talk my ear off about things I could give a shit about, all so I can bang a chick I really don't want to bang in the first place. And lets not forget that she's gonna wanna 'cuddle' afterwards and go out again! So call her and say I'm not interested. I'll just stay home, save the money, and play with myself!"*

My friend was totally shocked and spent 30 minutes telling me how he had gotten over his divorce by banging every chick who came along—both attractive and ugly. If that worked for him, I was happy for him.

But I insisted banging chicks just for the conquest was not my thing. And no, I'm not gay! I know some of you may be thinking that right now, but I'm not. So shut the hell up!

The overall point of my story is to be *very cautious* of everyone who has that one "great girl" you just have to meet. Although it's a cool gesture and really nice to have friends who want to help, there're much better ways—in my humble opinion—that friends can help during this time of emotional transition.

I recommend making it very clear to your friends that you just want to hangout and begin the process of reinventing yourself with women. Tell them you'd like to be invited to social events where you can mingle, but where you're in no way, shape, or form the center of attention.

Stress to friends that you may need to cancel at the last minute, depending on how you feel at any particular moment. True friends (especially those who've been through a divorce) will understand and support you.

Reality is that there may be numerous times you'll make plans, but need to cancel at the last minute because something upsets you. Remember, fellas, this is completely normal. I remind you that you're reading this book because you're not the cold-hearted bastard society makes you out to be. You're being affected by your divorce and that's okay—in fact, it's actually a really good thing!

Now, if a year has gone by and you're still an unreliable blubbering piece of "emotionally distraught vaginal tissue," I highly recommend finding a good shrink. (and I'm dead serious about that!) However, there's nothing wrong with taking six months or so to be a flake. In fact, if you didn't need that time to heal then I'd really think there's something wrong with you. Just don't drag out your divorce too long and use it as a dating crutch.

Once again, the name of the game here is "healthy dating." You have to do what's right for you at the time. This will, of course, evolve as you navigate through the complicated maze we call the wonderful world of divorce. One day you may feel like hopping on a plane to Vegas with the boys (or maybe a nice young lady), while the next day you'll be huddled in bed with the blinds drawn shut and a box of kleenex.

As we talk about how ready you are to date, and how far you should go emotionally, I'd like to share a great question I once heard from a dating expert appearing on an afternoon talk show. (okay, so I was watching Oprah and it was a guest on her show. So what!) I actually wish I could remember the person's name because it's such a poignant and direct question that really meant a lot to me. The question she posed to the audience was, *"Would you date you?"*

Wow! *"Would I date me?"* I really had to think about that. I never thought of it that way. After a few minutes of racking my brain over the question, I was forced to admit to myself, *"No, I wouldn't date me."* Not because I was a crazy bastard who needed to be committed in a straight jacket. I was simply in no position at that time to give my love to any woman.

I was still distraught and crying on a regular basis. There was no way any woman in her right mind would get involved with me. I would have ended up with some other emotionally distraught woman who shouldn't be dating, either.

This concept is also important because many women love to care for "the wounded dove." They can smell your bleeding heart like a shark can smell blood in the water. When you're oozing with sorrow and pain, there's many-a-woman who'll be ready to sink their claws into your pained soul. Sorry if I'm being melodramatic, but it's true!

Most women are nurturers by their very nature, and they love to play "caregiver" and even "mommy." And if you're in the range of women from their mid-twenties to early forties, you could easily fall victim to the "my biological clock is ticking" syndrome.

This is a quote from one of my favorite scenes in the 1992 movie *My Cousin Vinny*, when Marissa Tomie was rambling about her biological clock while attempting to convince Joe Pesci of the urgency for them to marry. That was a funny scene with her stomping on the wooden porch screaming about how her time was running out. (Boy she was hot, too!) If you've never seen the movie, put it on your divorced movie list.

And to help clarify this issue, here's one of my personal example that epitomizes exactly what I mean. I had a vasectomy at age 27 when my son was about 6 months old. My wife and I were 100% certain we wanted no more children. I really was extremely content having only one kid.

But as I re-entered the dating world shortly after the start of my divorce, I learned that most of the adult female population of San Diego was not too happy about me having been neutered. I can't tell you the number of first dates when the woman blatantly told me she wanted to find a man to marry and have children with.

Have you ever experienced this, boys? Holy shit! Some women all but prick your finger to obtain a DNA sample for examination under an electron microscope to see if you'd produce good offspring! They're on a mission—it's ridiculous.

One particular time, I remember being in a happy-hour group setting with my brother, my sister, a few friends, and a girl with whom I shared a mutual attraction. A few hours into it, I began a side-bar conversation with my brother about my vasectomy. Suddenly, from across the rather large table in a noise bar, this lovely 31-year-old young lady zeroed-in on our conversation and promptly injected, *"You're fixed? Oh, well that can be reversed!"*

I remember my brother and I immediately looked at each other and, without saying a word, both communicated to one another that this chick was a "stage-4 clinger." (a term from 2006's *Wedding Crashers*—a great dating flick by the way)

I hope that story illustrates my point. So many women are just itching to find a man who can spread his seed in them and make little babies! Tragically, you vulnerable men just out of a relationship represent such an easy target for the Huntress Black Widow who wants nothing more than to biologically steal your seed and then discard you into her jaws of misery!

Hey, while we're talking about relationship misery, here're three marriage jokes for you:

1. You know why divorce costs so much? Because it's worth it!

2. You know why a woman smiles when walking down the aisle? It's because she just gave her last blowjob!

3. You know what's the most fattening female food ever? Wedding cake! Haaaa!!!

Alright, so maybe I shouldn't quit my day job to become stand up comedian. But now that I've hopefully scared the living crap out of you about "the rebound," let me transition to something that can actually ease the pain of divorce and help you have some fun—ever heard the terms "friends with benefits" or "F-buddies?"

This concept is something that is becoming really common in the dating world. (thank God for social evolution) The arrangement can work extremely well for those in a transitional divorce situation. It also works very well for the super-busy career-minded people who just don't have the time required for a serious relationship.

I personally see absolutely nothing wrong with having a good female friend who can also satisfy your lustful needs. I discussed this at length with my therapist, and she said it can be a very healthy and normal way of easing back into the dating scene.

There's just one thing that almost always sucks about this type of situation; one person will generally develop feelings and want to further the relationship when the other does not. Or, one person will decide to begin dating other people and it usually spells the end of any platonic friendship that existed prior to the two of you jumping into bed. For a lot of people (especially women), sex translates into the development of feelings that will almost certainly be destroyed during the severing of intimate relations.

However, don't let this deter you from dating in this fashion. I believe that as long as you are 100% up-front with a woman, creating a friends-with-benefits situation is more than acceptable. I'm not at all a fan of lying or misleading women just to get laid. This only leads to drama and is really a dishonorable way to live. Besides, YOU DON'T NEED TO LIE TO WOMEN to get laid.

That may have been true years ago, but it's just not that way anymore. I'm speaking primarily to those of you re-entering the dating scene after more than 15 or 20 years. The rules have really changed since you last pounded the pavement of love. Society in general has accepted the sexual needs of women. Many ladies are now more than willing to "get theirs." I know it sounds very bold and direct, but it really is the truth in 2009 and beyond.

So by now you're probably wondering where you can go to meet some nice young ladies, especially the sexually liberated ones I just described. After all, if you were faithful during your marriage, it's probably been years since you've had to approach a woman in a romantic or sexual way, and you may be a bit rusty, to say the least.

It's obvious there're many ways to meet women. First off, there's always the good old bar scene. You may very well be a guy who prefers sitting at the pub enjoying a cold one (or two) while striking up conversations with a friendly new lady. If this describes you, then you're probably a pretty social person and talking with new chicks shouldn't be a big problem.

But what if you're not a bar guy? What if you're like most divorced men who work 50 to 70 hours a week mixed-in with little league, soccer, night school, working a second job to pay off the ex-wife, etc.? On top of all that, you may just be a guy who doesn't like spending hours on a bar stool. I personally hate the bar scene, so I was forced to learn other ways to meet women.

You can always meet women just doing things you like. There're women everywhere in all activities. Maybe you're a rock climber. So, join a club and keep your eyes open for ladies in the group. The gym is always filled with women. It's easy to tell the women who're open to meeting men, too. They're the talkative ones on the machine next to you. But just stay clear of the women with their head phones on who never look at you. Many women are simply at the gym for a workout only. (how dare they! Ha!).

The list is endless of things to do that women will also enjoy: sporting events, bike clubs, 4x4 groups, kayaking clubs, poetry readings (for you sensitive fellas), runners groups, skydiving clubs, surfing, hiking, etc, etc, etc… Don't do activities strictly to meet women—that will certainly come across and you probably end up looking desperate. Just have fun doing the things you like doing and keep your eyes open.

Now don't laugh, but I actually took a leap and tried the online dating thing. (Shut up! Stop laughing!) At first I was very hesitant. It happened like this…

My sister and I were sitting around one night getting shit-faced when she suggested going online. She had done it years earlier and said it was fun. I was initially like most men. I adamantly asserted, *"There's no fuckin' way I'm doing that stupid online bullshit!"* But after a bit more convincing from my sister (and a few more rum and Cokes), I signed up and posted a profile on a few sites.

It was actually pretty easy. All of the reputable dating sites walk you through the process step-by-step. And just a friendly reminder: be accurate and honest in your profile. You've got to be yourself in the dating world. Once again, this is your chance to be you and meet someone who likes the real you, and vice versa.

The very next day (after I sobered up), I went ahead and checked the sites. Holy cow if my little sister wasn't right! I had several replies from women interested in me based on the real profile and pictures I'd posted about myself. This began about a five-month stint of me having a real blast with online dating.

In retrospect, the best thing about meeting women online was that it simply got me talking to many different girls. It was a way to get my feet wet and learn about what to say, and what not to say, as a "new dater." It afforded me a great way to learn about women in 2009.

It was also convenient because being online allowed me to talk with women at my leisure and without spending 60 bucks a night at a bar. (money I didn't have on my divorce budget) As I said before, I truly hate the bar scene—it's just not my thing. Furthermore, going out a lot would have taken precious time away from my son.

I repeatedly get asked the blanket argument of, *"aren't chicks online psycho and don't they lie in their profiles?"* My response to that; aren't there both crazy and dishonest men and women everywhere? My experience shows me that there're more psycho chicks in bars than anywhere else. You just have to be willing to stand your ground and really go after what you're looking for. Don't let your gonads take over and you'll be okay.

I would often type back and forth with a woman for several weeks before even getting a phone number. Then, depending on how the telephone conversations went, I would arrange to meet her for coffee or drinks.

However, if I didn't like the phone conversations, it was very easy to simply get busy and let the phone calls fade away. Most of the time, I'd just be up front with the girl and tell her on the phone that it wasn't a good match. Many of the women I met online were equally honest, and it was often pretty easy for us to both admit it wasn't a good connection.

And if you have kids and would embrace a woman who also has her own, going online can be great for that, too. It's perfectly acceptable to put on your profile that you don't want any more kids. Obviously, this will limit your available field, but if you're serious about finding a woman with whom you can have a real connection and relationship, you have to be honest.

I was once complaining to a good buddy about the difficulties of finding a good woman. My friend replied, *"Well, you just went through a couple more bad ones over the past month. Now, you're statistically closer to a woman that will work out."*

He was so right. Dating is a numbers game. It's also a game of trial and error. Don't be super sensitive; just keep plowing ahead while having a stern conviction about your true identity and what you want from (and can give to) a woman.

Online communicating also got me very comfortable with experiencing rejection. Yup, I said it, "rejection!" Get used to it fellas, and please don't take it personally.

In his book, Double You Dating, author David DeAngelo cites statistics about the percentages of woman who're actually available:

> *"My guess is that in a random group of 100 women, only about 30 of them might be open to meeting someone new right now (in a romantic sense). What that means is that 70 percent aren't interested in meeting someone new. And of the 30 who are interested in meeting someone new, maybe only 15 are nice, friendly, happy people. Do you see where I'm going? If you want to be successful at meeting women, you have to understand that many of the women you talk to aren't interested. Most people take things like this personally. Instead of just moving on to the next woman, they get all uptight and feel bad about it."*

I highly recommend DeAngelo's book. When I read it, it was an Internet-based book that you could download after paying a very reasonable fee. (I think I paid about 20 bucks a year ago) DeAngelo's style is really great.

His entire book focuses on what women truly want and how to shape you into that person without compromising yourself in the process. A lot of his suggestions also have a real bearing on your overall self-confidence. I've even applied much of his guidance to my professional life and the way I interact with others at work.

And don't think you'll be the only one getting dumped—you should also get equally comfortable being the one doing the rejecting. This goes hand-in-hand with developing a sound sense of post-divorce self-confidence. It also goes back to "the rebound" discussion. I beg you to not get roped into anything before you're ready. Don't ever be afraid to tell a woman if you need some space or want to stop dating completely.

Remember, anyone who has ever been successful in just about any endeavor has crashed and burned a bunch of times before they got it right. For example, the most successful businessmen I know have all had more than one business fail before they found their winner.

Take Donald Trump for example. The man has made and lost millions over the course of his life. I once went to a leadership conference where Trump spoke. It was actually pretty cool to see. At one point he was speaking on the topic of pushing through the bad times and believing in yourself. He then told a story about one evening in the early 1990s.

Trump was walking down a street in New York with his girlfriend. (I can't remember her name, but I'm sure it was some hot model) He pointed to a homeless guy sleeping on the street and said to his girl, *"See that bum, he's worth $900,000,000 more than me."*

Trump then explained how, at that time, he was upside-down $900,000,000 in crashed real estate deals. But the man is a Pit Bull and kept fighting, and years later he's once again one of the richest men in America.

Dealing with divorce and dating is very similar. You must be able to roll with the punches and move forward. You really need to develop some thick skin when it comes to women. Here's a great example of what I mean.

Several years back, a few buddies and I were in New Orleans for a week-long stay on Bourbon Street. One evening, I was sitting in a bar with a buddy as he struck up a conversation with two ladies sitting behind us. It turns out they were a mother and daughter out for a drink together. (You pigs, I know you're having mother/daughter fantasies right now. That personally has never crossed my mind…)

Mom was the friendlier of the two. (and actually pretty hot, too) We learned the daughter was getting divorced, and mom was trying to get her out of the house (ahhhh, what a nice mom, trying to get her daughter laid!) My friend is one of the best pick-up artists I've ever seen and he was working them hard. However, after about an hour, the mother and daughter said their goodbyes and stood up to leave.

My buddy is so good that he didn't even bat an eye. Before both women had taken more than a few steps toward the door, my buddy was already scanning the room for a new target. He quickly acquired a "radar lock" on two new girls sitting on the opposite side of a nearby table. My buddy turned to face these new women and held out his hand as he said, *"Hi, my name is John. It's really nice to meet you. What are you drinking?"*

It worked like a charm and the new girls eagerly began talking with us. And oh yeah, you should have seen the looks on the faces of the mother and daughter as they walked away looking at John already working some new potential female targets—priceless!

This is what I meant by getting comfortable with rejection, and online dating provides the perfect venue to gain this experience. In the beginning, I struck out over and over with women I spoke with online. But after a few weeks, I began to get the hang of "chick lingo." A few more weeks and I was going on dates.

Some worked out very well (and I mean *very* well), while others sucked. But I must stress that each of these dates allowed me to learn something new about women and what I wanted in a relationship. Again, every bad date was simply like test driving another car that I discovered I didn't want to buy.

You also get to view a lot of women online before you even choose to talk with one. When you go out to bars/clubs to meet women, you have no idea who you're talking with. For all you know the girl may be a wanted axe murderer from Oklahoma. You don't know what she does for a living, what she likes to do with her spare time, whether she has five kids with six dudes, etc.

Online you at least get to see a profile and some pictures to start. Although many women lie in the profile, it's still a good place to start when compared to just meeting someone at a bar.

You may be a sports nut who simply couldn't date a woman who hated watching sports. If you're communicating with a woman online you can be up front and share your "can't-stands and must-haves." And if she gets all pissy because you've got that style of being direct, then you just quickly move to the next ten women until you find one who piques your interest.

Also, a lot of guys leave a marriage with not much more than the shirt on their back and more debt than a small third-world country. Need I say what this does to a guy's dating self esteem? Maybe you don't even have the money to sit in a bar three nights a week.

If you're one of these guys without even a pot to piss in, you really need not worry. Guess what? A LOT of women are out there just looking for a genuine and nice guy. But remember, being a nice guy does not mean "pussy."

If you're so inclined, you can even become a good old fashioned man-whore while remaining a really nice guy. I know it may sound strange, but it's very possible. You can be nice and assertive all at the same time.

I know many of you dating studs are getting a little bored with some of my elementary explanations and recommendations, but many of us "regular guys" need this. (I know I did) Besides, if you're such a stud and think I'm being too simplistic, then why are you getting divorced and reading my book? So there! Shut up and read on…

As I've mentioned, you need to find out what is best for you at this time in your life and go with it. Don't be afraid to try a lot of different things as you feel the need. Remember, we live in a day and age when there's every type of woman out there for every type of guy.

You could even find a woman to put you in a dog collar and lead you around on all fours with a "gimp ball" in your mouth like something out of the 1994 movie *Pulp Fiction*. Hey, it's not my thing, but there's someone for everyone—right?

But in all seriousness, let me take you back to the very important question, *"Would you date you?"* Seriously, look at yourself in the mirror and ask, *"Would I date me?"* And this by no means infers you need to look like Brad Pitt or James Bond to get a date. I'm not simply referring to your looks. God made us the way we are and that's it. I'm speaking more about you as an overall package.

There're actually a lot of things we as men can do to improve our attractiveness to the females of our species. The bottom line is that, women want a man who can take care of himself and has some pride in his appearance.

Now fellas, don't start complaining until you hear me out. As guys, we actually get off pretty easy in the physical appearance department. It's so true that women find us attractive for much different reasons than we find them attractive.

Women want the power, the money, the security, and the internal confidence a man can offer. But the really great thing is that you don't actually need to have all of these things; you need only to portray them through demeanor and non-verbal communication. If you can't dazzle them with brilliance, baffle them with bullshit.

When it comes to dating and being successful with women, it's all about the image. I personally fought playing this game for years, and I really wish I hadn't. Besides, it's not really playing a game so much as it is assuming the proper male/female roles.

As men, we generally look for a nice ass, a great pair of tits, and a pretty face. But for women, if they're just not attractive (or starting to age poorly) there's not a lot they can do about it. But as guys, we can learn to talk to women and portray the strengths and qualities that women want.

One quintessential example of this is Hugh Heffner—the dude is 80 and bedding down with women young enough to be his granddaughters. (what a stud!) Of course, it's because he's rich, but it's also because of what comes along with being rich.

Heffner has the confidence, charisma, and intelligence women want. He's actually not even that good looking, and he certainly doesn't have big manly muscles bulging from his girly frame. But he projects the power and success that women would kill for. Again, the guy is just a great big stud!

Even if you look like *Nacho Libre* (2006 film starring Jack Black), there's a lot you can do to improve your physical appearance. This will improve your underlying charisma that women are really after.

Maybe you let yourself go a bit when you were married. Okay, I'll just say it—maybe you let yourself get fat! Maybe your teeth could use a little bleaching? Maybe you need to take a trip to the dentist and get a broken tooth fixed? Also, how's your breath? (big one)

Do you need a little help in the clothing department? You don't need to wear Versace clothes or some other brand name overpriced rip-off. You just need to make it clear that you care about your appearance.

I'm actually a shorts and flip-flops guy. But I always make sure my flip-flops are new and don't smell of foot funk, my shorts fit well and aren't old and raggedy, and my shirts don't look and smell like they came from the bottom of my dirty hamper. In short, don't try to be someone you're not. Just look good being you!

I'll give you an example. I began dating a very attractive woman just around the time my divorce was final. Actually, the girl was just plain HOT. She was very into designer clothing and accessories. But as I said, I'm a simple guy who likes cargo shorts, T-shirts, and flip-flops.

When we would go away together, she would pack her nice stuff in very expensive luggage, and I would have my stuff in a large R.E.I.

backpack. The key was that I looked clean, pressed, well-groomed, and my backpack was nice and new. (I didn't look like I'd just come off a 10-day expedition to Mt. Hood) Get my point?

Below are some suggestions I hope you pay close attention to. I've spent a lot of time interviewing women about dating, and below is a culmination of the things they have told me.

- Hair:

  The comb-over has been out since the last Apollo Moon Landings of the 1970s. If you're going bald, get a hair transplant or just shave it off. Remember, bald is now in.

- Back Hair:

  Unless you're looking to date an Amazon woman, back hair is one of the biggest no-no's ever. As men age, it's as if we become like shedding trees. Just as leaves fall from a tree, the hair falls off of our head and takes root in our ears and all over our back. It then grows like weeds in all the wrong places. If you've got hair on your back, just get that shit waxed, lasered, or at least shave it. But for God's sake, do something! I actually use this thing called "The Epilady." (Stop laughing!) It's about the size of an electric shaver and has this spring that runs in a circle and pulls out the hair at the roots. (GOD IT HURTS!) But, if we expect women to take care of their "hair issues," we men must do the same.

- Nose and Ear Hair:

  What is it with guys as they get older; do they just not see the weeds emanating from their ears and nostrils? Need I say more? Just trim that shit.

- Other Hairy Places:

  You should also keep the armpit hair under control. There's nothing worse than deodorant balls matted into the curly locks of your hairy pits. You don't need to shave your pits completely—that's going way too far. Just a little trim is perfect. Again, these are simple ways to show the ladies you have pride in yourself. Oh, and don't forget the eyebrows, too!

- Grooming, uhmmm, "down there:"

  For you guys over the age of 40, this means trim your pubic area. The days of guys and girls going down on each other and coming up with a hairball in their throat went out with *Member's Only* jackets, *parachute pants* and the *Love Boat.* (OH THANK GOD!) Most of us don't like a woman with excessive hair down there, and most ladies think the same way. So just grab a pair of clippers and trim your mound frequently. And by the way, I've been told by several women that when a guy trims down there it makes "it" look bigger. (Ha!) Hey, I'll take all the help I can get…

- Weight:

  This is a touchy subject because so many of us are sensitive about our weight. As the years go by, most of us put on a few pounds. I often joke that I have six-pack-abs; they're just well insulated under my gut! (I know, another bad joke.) But seriously, being a few pounds overweight is much different than being morbidly obese. You don't need to be a marathon runner from East Africa, but weight says a lot to women about your self-image. Have you ever seen a woman who is a bit heavy-set, yet she carries herself and dresses in a way that exudes pride and success? That's all I'm saying. Work on dropping a few pounds while continuing to improve your appearance.

- Teeth:

  If you haven't been to the dentist since the days of the Old West and hand-powered drills, you need to go! You'd also be surprised how far some Crest White Strips from Walmart can get you. Chicks all say they look at teeth as a major indicator of personal pride. If you need braces, it's okay to wear them as an adult. (I wore braces from age 23 to 25) If you don't have the money for braces right now, at least start with the white strips. Crooked teeth are not that big of a deal so long as they're not as yellow as your first morning piss hitting a patch of fresh white snow!

- Fingernails:

  Need I say more? Stop biting your nails and keep them clean. It's okay to have the rough hands of a working man, just make sure they're presentable.

- Clothes:

  You don't need to wear designer threads, just look nice and neat. Your clothes shouldn't look (or smell) like you pulled them from the trunk of you car. As I already mentioned, I'm a simple guy—cargo shorts and T-shirts. I just make sure they're new, neat, and clean. I'm not asking too much, am I?

  Also, tighty-whities (white cotton briefs) belong in the 80s memorabilia section of the Smithsonian. If you're a briefs guy, get some colored ones. (again, cheap at Walmart) These are really good at hiding the visible funk caused by sitting all day in "sweaty ball soup." (What? We're all guys here!) The same is true for boxers—get colored ones instead of white.

- Car:

  Most of us don't have the extra cash to run out and buy a new set of wheels. (especially on a divorce budget) At the very least, clean the one you've got. Spend an afternoon with a scrub brush, a shopvac, a buffer, and some wax, along with a little carpet cleaner and some

Armor All. Your car shouldn't look and smell like a combination of fast food and sweaty gym socks!

- Your Pad:

  I personally remember how much it sucked to have a tiny divorce pad. But don't let this stop you from dating and maybe even inviting women over. Believe it or not, I think this actually works to your advantage so long as your place is CLEAN and you take a few extra steps to make it a "cozy love shack."

  Remember, women love the wounded dove scenario. Don't be afraid for them to see you're a little down right now, you just can't appear weak—it's a delicate balance. Look like a proud man who's doing his best with a difficult scenario. Women actually admire that quality. The underdog who exudes an inner strength and the potential to move beyond his difficult circumstances. I'll say it again: it's all about the image…

  Also, just because you may be poor does not mean you must be a dirty loser. As I've said, throughout my career as a police officer I've met hundreds of poor people who were beaming with pride. Their homes may have been small and simple, but you truly felt pride and comfort when entering. Their houses or apartments were very clean and decorated simply, but were still very nice.

  Your date shouldn't have to sit down on your toilet to enjoy the wandering aroma of stale urine. Also, the kitchen shouldn't resemble a science experiment. Don't try and tell your date, *"But we're growing mold on the dishes as a school project for my kids."* Sorry, but that bullshit ain't gonna fly. You think I'm exaggerating, but we all know sloppy guys who'd try and pull some crap like that with a woman!

When I was married, I always thought cleaning the house was an "Act of Congress" because that's how my ex made it appear. She was a cleaning machine that demanded everyone clear out of her way.

When I moved out, I discovered her way was very complex and not for me. I regularly kept up on my little house and it only took me about 30 minutes twice a week to clean the entire pad. You'd be amazed what a quick vacuum and wipe down of the bathroom and kitchen floors can do. (And don't forget the corners and behind the toilet—believe me, women look!)

Go to Walmart (okay, so I like Walmart. Get over it!), buy some nice cheap frames and put up a bunch of pictures of you and your kids. (if you don't have kids, put up pics of you and friends/family) It shows pride in those close to you and says a lot about your values.

Also, get into candles. I know, I know, I'm asking a lot. But I've became a candle junkie and it's got me more mileage with women than anything else. (And guess where you can buy some really cool candles? That's right, Walmat!) Every woman I brought home said they'd never before seen a guy so into candles before. Show them a sensitive but tough demeanor and it will get you major brownie points. Also, if you get scented candles it can really help mask the smell of "guy funk" in your house.

So what do you think? Am I asking too much? I don't really think I am. Again, men get off pretty easy compared to women.

But more important than anything I just described, men must understand it's all about the attitude. Women can literally fall head-over-heals for a guy who portrays a confident and caring demeanor, regardless of his looks.

Women are attracted to a man who makes them feel protected, special, and important. You don't have to be Hefner to make them feel like you are. It's a balancing act between being confident and cocky. In most cases, cocky is bad; however, confident is essential.

An attractive attitude also translates into being innovative in your dating style. For example, say you finally get to a point where you want to take a girl on a nice date. You've already met her for coffee or drinks, and you both want to go out again.

Don't just revert to the same old boring type of date. Do something she'd never expect. Take the girl on a kind of modified picnic. Now stop laughing! I'm serious. This shit really works. Just hear me out! Dating is all about the persona.

I bet every woman has been on a hundred dates to a bar or a restaurant. That's the typical date; go out to dinner and then for drinks and/or a movie. Maybe some dancing thrown-in. Blah, blah, blah... Normal dates run like clockwork. And then, at the end of the night, you're standing on her porch hoping she'll give you a little smooch.

When it's all said and done, you've dropped 100 bucks on a date that just fades into her memory like every other non-eventful date she's ever been on. All the while you're $100 more in debt on your maxed-out credit card because you've got zero cash until payday and your ex is bugging you for shoe money for the kids.

You want to be different and save money? My example is something very unique that I almost guarantee she's probably never experienced.

As I mentioned before, I live in San Diego. We're lucky enough to have some of best weather and outdoor scenery in the country. We've got perfect beaches, coastal cliffs, mountains, deserts, etc. You name it, San Diego's got it. (And no, you can't move here! It's already too crowded!) So here's how one of my innovative dates would go.

I'd call my date and tell her I had everything planned and that it was a surprise. This is a great start. It shows effort on your part and dictates control. (women love the strong guy thing) I'd then take the doors off my Jeep. (again, you don't need a fancy car)

On the way to pick up the girl, I'd grab some Subway sandwiches or some type of take-out. I'd also have a cooler with some rum and Coke. If I were really on the ball, I'd already know her favorite drink and have it packed in the cooler. But if not, rum and Coke is usually a safe bet. So by then, I'm into the date $12 for food and about $20 for booze and soda. ($32 total)

I'd pick up the girl and she'd immediately zero-in on my Jeep with no doors. They'd almost always say (in that silly and giddy chick voice), *"I've never ridden in a car with no doors."* See, I'm standing out from other guys and didn't even need to buy a new car to do it!

I'd then hand her a warm blanket so she can feel the cool evening air on her face while being wrapped up nice and cozy. I always kept a stocking cap handy just in case her ears got cold, too. (Sensitive and caring. Are you following me?)

If it was a warm night, I'd take her to the cliffs overlooking the ocean. Need I say more about a picnic with an ocean view at sunset? But, if it is a bit cold by the coast, I'd divert to an alternate L.Z. (Landing Zone!) in the warmer inland hills. After a short drive up a dirt road to the top of a hill overlooking a lake, we'd come to the perfectly prearranged spot to watch the sunset and enjoy our feast. The dirt road with no doors really gets a woman's adrenaline flowing.

I guarantee most women haven't done a lot of 4x4ing. Even if it's a really easy dirt road that doesn't require 4-wheel drive, she might not know that. There's no doubt she'll be looking at you as the big strong man because you took her on a 1/4–mile dirt road you could have concurred effortlessly in a beat-up 1990 Nissan Sentra. (again, she doesn't need to know this)

I'd break out a blanket or some folding chairs and proceed to wine and dine her in a way she'll never forget. And once again, do I need to remind you how little this date cost? Also, the folding chairs with the built-in foot rests are only three dollars more at my favorite store.

Another good cheap date is to take a woman kayaking. I have a few plastic kayaks that were relatively cheap. I think I paid about 600 bucks for each for them. They don't need gas and require no maintenance. (also a good thing for the divorce budget)

Now don't be a macho dumb ass and plan to conquer the Grand Canyon Rapids on a first date. This is a romantic event. The key is to act soft, sensitive, and funny, all the while making her feel safe and secure. I know it's a game, but you gotta play it.

I'd get the girl seated on the kayak, give her a quick lesson, and then begin a short paddle. We'd usually end up at one of two places, a bar along the waterfront or at a bayside concert. In San Diego, we have several bars that line the bay shore.

It's a given she's probably never paddled a kayak, let alone paddled to a bar and had a few drinks. Not to mention, you can't get arrested for drunk driving on a paddle craft in California. (I've checked) We also have a few bayside concert venues where you can hear the music perfectly if you anchor right next door. You then get to listen to a free concert while you feed her Subway sandwiches and poor booze from your designer Walmart cooler. She'll think you're a dating God and will never forget the event.

I could go on, but there are a million ways you can take out a woman and not spend a lot of money. But if you have the money and enjoy taking a woman to a nice restaurant, a concert, a romantic weekend away, etc., that's great, too. There's not some steadfast rule saying you can only spend $40 or $50 on a date—you can spend as much as you want. I just don't want you to think money is the end-all in dating.

Spending less on a date is not only for those of us on a divorce budget, I also believe it has a greater place when speaking of "quality" verses "quantity." In the case of dating, it's often the quality of the date rather than quantity (the amount) you spend.

I completed and published this book in 2009, and who will ever forget the recession of this year? Money is super tight for so many people, but this doesn't mean you must stop living life because you may have lost your $100,000 job and now you're working for half that.

I once took a woman camping. It wasn't some long and drawn out expedition to into the deepest rain forest of the Congo. We simply loaded up my Jeep, took off the doors, and headed out to one of my favorite spots in the desert about an hour-and-a-half away. This particular location is amazing; it's a desert canyon that looks just like something out of an *Indiana Jones* adventure. Two hundred foot high walls of water-carved sandstone line the narrow canyon for miles. Small caves dot the cracks and crevasses.

This was her first camping trip ever, so I kept it simple—just one night. I could tell she had a blast. I borrowed a cheap army cot from a friend so she wouldn't have to sleep on the ground. (as I say over-and-over—sensitive and attentive) I think I spent about $40 on gas, and she helped with the food, but only because she really wanted to. In the end, the entire thing cost us both less than probably $80, and it was a *Great* 36-hour getaway.

I don't know about where you live, but in San Diego, one night in a decent hotel room (along with drinks, meals, and extras) will set you back at least 300 bucks. I'm not saying that's not fun—I love a night away at a waterfront hotel sipping margaritas by the pool and looking at my attractive date sunning on a lounge chair. If you've got the money and want to pay for a night or two away, then go for it. There's absolutely nothing wrong with treating yourself and a nice lady to something cool like that.

I simply go on and on with innovative and alternative dating ideas because so many of us don't have that kind of money. Many of us are left financially struggling for years following divorce. But the quality of your life, and of your dating life, doesn't need to suffer. As corny as it sounds, put some thought and effort into dating and women may view you as the strong and resilient Phoenix rising from the ashes of your divorce.

It's just the same as spending time with your kids. You don't need to spend a lot of money. Just give of your true self. Anyone with half a brain can see when you're trying to buy them. So if you do take a woman on a date that costs a lot, just make sure it's not all about the money. The cost should enhance the date, but the interpersonal connection is the real measure of success.

The key is to be different, just not too different. Renting a tandem bicycle and riding along the boardwalk while stopping at a few bars is perfect. Taking a woman on an extreme downhill mountain biking trail where she'll probably eat shit and hurt herself is going too far. Get the picture? A little excitement is good, but too much is bad—always remember balance!

And if you're interested in taking serious steps at becoming a true "pick-up artist," you've got to read, The Game, by Neil Strauss. This book is a work of art. Straus wrote it after years of actual experience and research. Strauss became involved with some real honest-to-God pick-up artists, and he tells all in this masterpiece. Read it and you'll be amazed!

Straus offers so much insight into the interactions between males and females, along with how and why we form attractions for one another. As you read Strauss' book, you'll truly understand how and why women are attracted to a man's attitude much more than his looks. The book's a bit long, but it's really a fun read.

I really challenge you to take the time an effort to understand dating and, more importantly, what women want. Oh yes, I said it. I brought up the age old question, *"What do women want?"* How many times have you and your friends asked this question to each other? The good news is that it's not an elusive answer to a mystical question.

Understanding women is really about understanding their mindset and thought process rather than finding a single answer to this complicated question. Again, I remind you of the need to become a student of your divorce.

Another great book to help men and women understand each other is It's a Guy Thing: An Owner's Manual for Women by David Deida. Deida actually wrote the book as a guide for women to better understand men. I found it to be just as helpful for men trying to understand women. In short, it's simply the perfect book for men and women to understand each other.

Deida spends a great deal of time dissecting the "masculine" and "feminine" aspects of both men and women. He guides us through their differences, their strengths, their weaknesses, and how men and women have both masculine and feminine aspects to their personalities. (Sorry fellas, but you've got some chick in you!)

Deida writes:

> *"The feminine is the ocean, and the masculine is a boat on the ocean. The masculine navigates from one point to another. It takes the ocean currents, the wind and the shifting tides into account in order to reach its destination. The strength of the feminine could crush the masculine at any time. But with skill, the boat can joyfully ride with the ocean's power and achieve a goal. The ocean is all motion, all energy, but doesn't go anywhere specific [that's so true. Women are all over the place! Ha!]. The boat can*

> *be devoured by the ocean, but it can also move with the currents toward a specific place, whereas the ocean flows in many directions at once.*
>
> *The immensity of the feminine energy coupled with the direction of masculine vision result in fullness and balance. Yet the unpredictable and sheer power of the feminine energy is daunting to a man who is weak in his vision. That's why some men say about women, 'Can't live without them, can't live with them.' To many men, women are the most attractive thing in the world, like a deep blue ocean glistening in the sun. And women are also the most frightening and dangerous, especially when a man feels weak."*

Wow, now that's some really deep shit. But the more I think about it, it's so true. And we never really take the time to understand women—just as women don't do the same. Most men simply say stuff like, *"I'm not reading any pussy shit like that! I'm a fuckin' man, for God's sake,"* all while groping their balls trying to look tough!

Well guess what, dumb ass? That's probably one of the main reasons divorce rates are so high. I fully admit that my lack of understanding easily contributed to my divorce.

Again, I'm not asking you to attend poetry readings, join Oprah's Book Club, or watch *The View*. You don't need to become an expert in *The Modern Feminist Movement* and spend hours at the bookstore sipping foo-foo coffee drinks.

It can be as easy as buying Deida's book and keeping it next to your potty. Come on, this is a guy book. Most of us spend at least 20 minutes each day (or more) on the toilet. Hell, sometimes I'm in there twice a day.

So put down the *Playboy* and make divorce-related materials your bathroom reading. I know, I know, you only read *Playboy* for the interesting articles. But maybe if you took some time to understand women, you could eventually date a chick as hot as a Playmate. (rather than simply drooling over one in a magazine—seriously)

However, in spite of having things pretty easy, guys continue to be lazy. I hear guys complain a lot about how their girl doesn't want to have sex or give them a blowjob. Dude, what have these guys done to make their girl want to blow them?

Are you a sloppy and lazy bastard who goes to work, comes home, and doesn't lift a finger to help with the kids, the house, the bills, etc.? I'm not saying you need to become a little sissy while your girlfriend/wife sits on her ass and gets facials eating Bonbons. Just take care of business and you'll have more of a leg to stand on with women.

I remember when all this dating crap finally began to click for me. It was a culmination of so many things. Most importantly, I began to feel and exude a confidence I never before had in my life. I gained control of my life and it felt so good.

I used to mock friends who would say, *"You can't put a price on freedom."* I thought it was such a cheesy statement. But it's now one of the most amazing statements I've ever heard.

I have no "need" for a woman in my life. I'd "like" a woman in my life, but only if she's strong, independent, and complements my life. Never again will I accept a woman being a drain or stress on my life. (and I will never again be a drain on a woman, either) Of course, there are tough times that we must accept in any relationship, but disrespectful communication, nagging, and/or constant complaining or demeaning talk with a motherly tone will never again be part of my life.

I will also never again chase a woman. This is something I wish I'd have learned years ago, but it's never too late! You see, when a woman brushes you off or plays obvious games with you, just move on to the next one. Being a wounded dove with a strong heart is great, but appearing weak is a death sentence in the dating world. In short, don't get pussy blinded and act needy.

Think of "Bruce the Shark" from *Finding Nemo*. All of you fellas with kids have seen *Finding Nemo*, so don't act like you haven't. Remember when Marlin and Dory get brought to the meeting of the sharks who are pledging to stop eating fish? *"Fish are our friends, not food!"* That's the scene I'm talking about.

A few minutes into the scene, Dory bumps her head and a little bit of blood floats through the water right into Bruce's nose. Bruce the Shark gets the smell of blood and he goes nuts. The other sharks have to hold him back as he relentlessly attempts to eat the fish while screaming, *"Come on! Just a bite mate! Just a little nibble!"*

You can't ever appear to go nuts like this over a woman. Bruce was clearly out of his mind as he was blinded by his obsession to eat those fish. I know this is a stupid example, but you can never appear to "lose control" over a woman. I don't care if you think you may have a shot at bedding down with Pamela Anderson.

If she's being weird or treating you funny, it's time to put your foot down. As I said, you don't have to be a dick about it, just assert your rights to be treated fairly. Now of course you may have to go home and play with yourself, but you'll at least have saved your dignity.

Another caution: if you let yourself go too nuts over a woman, you risk alienating your good buddies. As you begin dating, make sure you don't become a weenie and ditch your friends every time a new chick-a-dee wanders onto your farm.

Your true buddies were usually in your life before most women, and they'll almost always be there afterwards. They may object a little to your new love; however, give them a chance to adjust.

Maybe you and your buddies used to hangout a lot and now you're suddenly gone. Maybe you never missed a baseball game, a Sunday dirt bike ride, a weekly poker game, a monthly fishing trip, etc. Yet now your buddies may have to make room for your new love—it can be tough.

I remember one of my good friends used to drool over this little hottie he worked with. However, he was married and not the cheating kind. For years, we listened to him ramble about his little fantasy girl. It was just like listening to the Charlie Brown parents: *"Wha-wha-wha, wha-wha, wha-wha-wha-wha!"* But finally, the time was right after my buddy got divorced, and he began dating this particular hot chick.

At first, I found myself getting a little pissed. He was dodging my calls, not going kayaking, and skipping overnight man camping trips to our favorite desert spots where we drank hard liquor from the bottle and enjoyed getting dirty and smelly—true man trips! But finally, I took a step back and realized my good buddy was just enjoying something he had missed for over 10 years.

My pal suddenly had a hot chick on his arm that screwed his brains out all the time. I saw my good friend happy, and I learned to become happy for him. After a few months passed, and the newness wore off, my good pal drifted back into our circle of friends. We gladly welcomed him back. (but not before giving him a pair of fake balls as a joke. Ha.)

There's also another important lesson here. Make sure you never ignore the serious advice from your good friends about a hot new squeeze. Never forget that your friends are your friends because you guys click and think a lot alike. True buddies are hard to come by. If a good friend shares some serious concerns about a new girl (like maybe she seems to be coming onto him when you're not around), don't just brush it off and accuse your friend of being jealous.

It's also very important you don't ever tell your friends to act differently just because you want to paint a certain picture around a new girl. Although it can be very tempting to do whatever is necessary to keep a hot new squeeze on your arm (and in your bed), it only causes problems when you go out of your way to project a false image of yourself and your friends.

I remember one time when my roommate was going to do something stupid around my new girlfriend. I can't remember exactly what it was, but I'm certain it was some immature guy thing. He suddenly looked at me and caught himself as he said, *"Oh, I better not do that around her."* I abruptly snapped at my friend and virtually ordered him to be himself 100% of the time around my new girl. I stressed how I wanted my new girl to see all of us for who we really are.

Now this doesn't mean you should have "ass-busting contests" or play drinking games to see who pukes first. There're some things that should forever remain banished to "guy time." Simply use some tact. Be respectful while remaining the real you.

If a particular girl has a fundamental problem with you or your good pals, it's a strong possibility she needs to go, no matter how hot she is. It's just really tragic that so many men ignore the advice of good friends about a new girl.

In the end, dating and understanding women may take a while. Don't expect to run out and find all the answers. As strange as it sounds, you should enjoy dating and not having the answers. It will take time to truly become enlightened from your divorce experience. There are so many lessons to be learned that it's impossible to transition overnight. As I've said, you must feel the hurt, live the process, and experience the journey.

When the time is right and you truly least expect it, you never know what joys life will bring. Don't try to be such a control freak when it comes to dating. I once heard a quote that best summarizes the idea of dating, *"If you want to make God laugh, tell him your plans."*

The point being, you just need to be honest and true with yourself while pushing forward. Don't look to a woman for your identity—that's a must. Be you and be strong, and you'll start to see things coming together.

When I first started dating after my divorce, I remember having a conversation with female friend, Monica. She had been happily married for many years, but she told me that she was a little envious of me.

I asked her why and she said, *"Dating can just be so much fun. I'm so happy I'm married and my life is great, but there's something about dating that's just a blast. The going new places, meeting new people, doing outlandish stuff—it's so exciting. I'd never trade my marriage for it, but I sure have some fond memories. Just enjoy your time being single. Before you know it you'll have found your true Mrs. Right and you'll never date again."*

What Monica said made a lot of sense. Dating can be so much fun, so long as you keep everything in perspective. Don't ever get "pussy blinded." Relationships must have the balance of one's heart and one's head.

Thinking with too much heart (too much emotion) can cause unrealistic expectations that could never last. Using too much of your head (your logical side) can easily destroy the emotional aspects of any relationship.

I know this all sounds like a bunch of book writing bullshit, but it's really very true. Stop and think about it. Enjoy the process of self-discovery. Embrace not knowing where the road will take you. Just start by having faith that things will get better. The proof is in the millions of men who've gone before you.

It's now your chance to find a woman who fits with the man you're becoming. As you know, one of my biggest problems was that I wed at the cherry age of 24. Even though I had a good job and was very responsible, I was like most men in that I hadn't reached a state of emotional maturity necessary for a successful marriage.

As I entered my early thirties, I found myself trapped by the image that my wife had developed of me as a very young (and somewhat immature) man. I wanted to break out to the next level. I constantly used to say that I wanted a "reset button" for my marriage.

Well guess what? We all now have our "reset button." We get to meet a woman (or women) and let them see us for who we've become. You get to choose a completely new pattern with women. Maybe you were like me and got with your ex too young. Maybe you never got a chance to "sew your oats." If so, this is your chance. Go out and have fun. I highly recommend it! As I stated before, there's an entire science to this dating stuff, so you don't have to reinvent the wheel!

Hopefully you'll learn enough to make your next serious relationship really work. Always think back to your unhealthy marriage and remember this now is your chance to do it right. Things may not always happen as fast as you'd like, but that's part of the new journey—the quest to find a wonderful and healthy life.

The most important thing is to make sure you're not trying to be someone you're not. If you're not ready to assert yourself and find your Ms. Right, then just go out and take some "test drives." Practice with women, and learn about yourself and how to be in a healthy relationship.

In the end, dating is about trial and error. You cannot have thin skin and expect to be successful. I know it is contradictory to tell you to be tough about something that's supposed to be emotional.

The key is to be tough when it comes to standing for what you want. Don't settle for something less than you desire and deserve. If you're going to be successful in a serious romantic relationship, you're going to have to put forth effort and work hard. However, with the right woman, your efforts will be appreciated and returned.

CHAPTER 12

AFTER THE JOURNEY: YOUR NEW LIFE

So here you are. Your journey is over and you're wondering, *"What's next?"* The title of this book is so important for me because it's a constant reminder that the experience of divorce has a beginning, and it will certainly have an end. The question now is what to do after your divorce is over. In short, you'll begin a new journey as it relates to your former marriage, especially if you have children or any other circumstances causing frequent contact with your ex. If you won't be seeing much of your ex, this chapter may not be as important to you.

Now that I'm truly finished with my journey, I actually don't mind having a regular and friendly relationship with my ex. Actually, interaction with her is often a gentle nudge making sure I never forget the mistakes I made and that I will continue to improve many aspects of my life.

Post-divorce positive interactions with my ex are also somewhat of a vindication for me. As I've said before, I was not the best husband in the world and I made many mistakes. I also allowed things to go on between my ex and myself that I will never again let happen in any future relationship. I was not proud of the way my ex viewed me when we were married. However, in our post-divorce relationship, I get to be a good parenting partner with her. I get to do the right things when it comes to my son.

I get to ensure he sees his dad treating his mother with respect even though we're divorced. Each day of my post-divorce journey, I gain more pride about how I've handled myself and how I continue to improve.

I know this may sound a bit odd, but I hope you see my point. I hope you can find the same peace. As I detailed in "Going Into Battle, The Ex Wars," you don't need to carry hate or behave poorly toward your ex just because you're divorced. Even if you don't have children, you still may run into your ex from time to time.

There's no reason for either of you to be rude or have hatred for the other. Of course, you cannot control how your ex treats you. She may be the "C-word" and treat you horribly. If that's the case, you have no choice but to move beyond her hatred. Just think, *"Thank God I'm no longer married to her,"* and ensure you don't make the same mistakes by selecting a similar woman in the future.

Also, don't expect the end of your divorce journey to be some grand event. I remember the day my divorce was final. Because my process was relatively smooth and amicable from a legal standpoint, we never had to participate in mediation or go to a court hearing. (I know. I'm a lucky bastard!)

I simply received a large manila envelope in the mail about a week before the date my divorce was set to be final. Inside was the typical legal document displaying the left side numbering that increased from top to bottom.

I poured myself a drink (a good old rum and Coke) and perused the 38-page Marriage Settlement Agreement, taking special note of the Judge's signature and the effective date. I actually didn't read it too thoroughly. I'd already studied it meticulously five or six times during the past eight months while my ex and I went back and forth trying to agree on specific verbiage. Therefore, having an almost photographic recollection of the document's wording, I concentrated more on my feelings associated with passing the checkered flag of divorce.

I remember feeling very ironic about getting these documents in the mail. I say ironic because I felt almost the same as I had the day after my wedding, ten years prior. On that day, I remember swimming in the resort's pool looking at my shiny new wedding band while glancing at my new bride sunning on a lounge chair. The odd thing was that I didn't feel a damn bit different than I had 24-hours prior, before the wedding ceremony. And I felt exactly the same as I perused the divorce paperwork. Getting my divorce paperwork turned out to be nothing more than a briefly awkward moment in an otherwise uneventful day.

In either case (the day after my wedding or the day I received my final divorce paperwork), there were no trumpets, no fireworks, no dropping to my knees from the power of an Evangelical healer smacking me on the forehead—nothing. Both events were simply another day in my life.

At that moment I truly began to understand we are the keepers of our own happiness. You, and you alone, dictate how you feel based on the thoughts you process through your head. I'll try to elaborate without getting really far out and sounding like some motivational speaker with bleached-white veneer teeth.

The fact that these two very important days in my life (the day after my wedding and the day of my divorce) were actually not that impactful speaks volumes to me about the concept of marriage and divorce. The day after my wedding was no biggie because we'd lived together for two years prior. Our relationship had already been established, and the only difference was a couple of rings, a name change, and some different titles used during introductions. Sure, I felt a bit more committed (or trapped, whichever you want to call it), but it wasn't the kind of different I thought I would feel.

The same was true for the day my divorce was final. For months, I'd repeatedly pictured the final day in my head. I anticipated I would feel like an LA gangster mourning the loss of a "fallen homie." You've seen the movies—a guy holding a 40oz bottle of Old English. One sip for me, and one sip poured out on the ground for "ma dead homeboy!"

Strangely enough, when the big day finally came, the emotional drama lasted all of about five minutes until I realized, *"This is stupid! It's finally over and I'm not gonna waste one more second on the self-pity train!"*

I shoved the paperwork back into the envelope, folded it shut, and filed it in the closet with all the other crap I'll probably never look at except for during an IRS audit. So that was it—the big grand finale of my 10-year marriage and I didn't feel a single bit different. To this day, only one thing stands out in my mind. I remember asking myself, *"Where do I go from here?"*

As I've said, most of my post divorce concerns centered on my son and the parental relationship with my ex. We had stopped arguing months before. Long gone were the hurt and hostilities of divorce.

It's actually kind of funny now as I look back at some of our stupid shouting matches during the peak of our divorce.

However, just because you may be at a good place with your ex, don't expect to never get a bit nostalgic or feel a little strange when you see her. This doesn't indicate you want to get back together with her. You're not a weirdo because you sporadically feel something when you see your ex.

You were married to this woman. At some point you planed to spend the rest of your life with her. If you had children with her, she'll play one of the most important roles in the rest of your life. You'll constantly cross paths when dropping off and picking up the kids, at little league games, birthday parties, school performances, your kids' future weddings, the births of your grandchildren, etc. Yup, she'll be there every step of the way.

My therapist once used this example for me:

> *"...You'll be at your son's high school graduation. It'll be a beautiful day and you'll be quite happy standing with your new wife—the one true love of your life—and you'll look over at your ex, the mother of your son, and you'll feel kind of weird. You'll probably feel a bit nostalgic about all of the experiences with her and raising a son together even though you were divorced, and it may even bring a tear to your eye. But in the end you'll look at this woman standing next to you—the one you're really supposed to be with—and feel like it all worked out..."*

I think my therapist is right on. I believe in my heart that I'm not meant to be with my ex, and I'm a much happier and emotionally healthy person because of it. However, this by no means frees me from ever experiencing weird feelings and/or being a little nostalgic when around my ex.

Ivan had been divorced for about two years when he told me the following story about an encounter he had with his ex:

> At the time of this incident, Ivan had been separated/divorced for just under a year. Ivan had a particularly

difficult time emotionally with his divorce. This specific incident involved an event at Ivan's son's school. His son was in 4th grade and performing in a school theatrical production. Ivan's son had a great voice and was one of the star singers. Ivan was excited to watch his son; however, Ivan was also somewhat apprehensive because this was the first event his ex was bringing her new man to.

The uncomfortable feeling actually caught Ivan off guard. His divorce had been final about a month prior, and he felt like he was doing really well with everything. In fact, Ivan was feeling downright good about his life. He had truly turned the divorce page. However, a few days prior, Ivan began feeling a bit agitated and irritable. It wasn't anything big, it was just this little subconscious feeling pecking at him. Ivan caught himself thinking more and more about his boy's upcoming performance—a relatively insignificant event.

After all, how many of us give much thought to our kids' school performances? We usually rush there from work, clap for our kids, and go home, never giving the event a second thought. In retrospect, Ivan thinks he was most worried about the possibility of being affected by seeing his ex with a new guy and how everyone was going to react. Even though everyone involved seemed to be in a good place emotionally, he had a really uncomfortable feeling.

Ivan arrived at the event about ten minutes before show time. He made his way to the auditorium via his son's classroom to "hi." Ivan then stood along the back wall of the auditorium looking slowly for his ex.

Ivan spotted her and the new guy sitting together right next to his former neighbors. This couple lived in the same housing development as Ivan and his ex when they had been married. They had three kids, one of whom was a little boy the same age as Ivan's son. The boys had been friends since they were about two. Ivan and his ex had socialized with the couple on numerous occasions, swam in their pool, and even taken joint family vacations.

Rather than joining the *Happy Couples Club*, Ivan tried to play it cool. The seats were full, so Ivan stood in the back with the stature of a gentleman, leaving the last remaining seats for the little old ladies—at least that was Ivan's persona. Believe it or not, it actually worked for Ivan for about ten minutes. He even felt like a tough guy gentleman by standing up. (On a side note, most divorced men I've interviewed have taught me the true power of imagination and perspective.) But unfortunately, Ivan's plan was foiled by the "evil ex." (Okay, so I added the evil ex part just for the story.)

Ivan's cell phone rang, and it was his ex. In her most excited voice, she told Ivan to look down, at which time he saw her waving from the. *"We're saving a seat for you, Ivan!"* Luckily for Ivan, the show was just starting. He had the perfect excuse. Ivan told his ex, *"I'll just stand up here. I don't want to walk down there during the show."* She seemed fine with that and Ivan hung up.

Ivan stayed for the first half of the show to watch his son perform. The entire time, Ivan was trying to enjoy seeing his son, but his mind was drifting to the other things. He kept thinking about how weird it was to be in the situation. Just a year before, when Ivan was still married, he sat in that very same theater with his ex

> and watched their son perform. Funny how a person's life can change in just a year.
>
> At the show's intermission, Ivan walked down to where his ex and her boyfriend were sitting. Everyone was very cordial, and Ivan sat and chatted for a minute. Ivan's ex was her usual smart-ass self and made some wisecrack remarks at Ivan's expense. Ivan just maintained, shrugged off the comments, and said his goodbyes.
>
> Ivan walked away continuing to feel a strange funk about the situation. He got in his car and called me about the situation. Ivan was upset at himself for letting the situation bother him. He felt comfortable that his divorce was over and thought things like this shouldn't affect him. I reminded Ivan that just because the divorce was final didn't mean he'd never again feel anything regarding his ex.

I share Ivan's story because it's about a situation many of us can (or already have) experienced. Situations that may be relatively common and insignificant could be what provoke certain emotions that may, at times, be confusing and difficult.

I don't know what you'll endure. I wish I could tell you. Hell, I can't even begin to speculate on all the situations involving my ex that will roll my way. I've actually got a good friend whose ex remarried and took his three small kids to a new town about six hours away. His ex was such a bitch that she even made the kids call her new husband "dad." Man, that's some bullshit!

The court paperwork also specified that my friend was only allowed one phone call per week with his kids, which was on Monday nights. Sometimes he'd call and the ex would say the kids were already sleeping and hang up. I can't think of anything worse than someone keeping my son from me.

I also feel really bad for guys who took in a child (or children) from one of their ex's previous relationships or marriages. I've got a few friends in that boat. They were real stand-up guys who took in their ex's kids and formed a real bond of love. Then, after their divorce, the ex gave the guy no parental rights—what a tragedy. And these guys don't have a leg to stand on in court. They were forced to sever ties with children with whom they had bonded as a parental figure.

There's a good book called Tea Cut Daddy, by LC Cloud, which is about this very topic. The author was a guy who became involved with a woman who had a young daughter from a previous relationship. The guy just fell in love with this little girl and became a real father figure for her.

The couple married several years later; however, the guy caught his new bride cheating just several months into the marriage. As part of the divorce, this woman prevented the guy from any further contact with her daughter. The guy was so distraught, he wrote a book about his experience with the little girl and called it Tea Cup Daddy.

I'm not trying to freak you out with this story. I pray things will be as easy for you as they've been for me. However, I know this is not going to be the case for so many of you. Just know you're not alone. There are guys out there who've endured it all. You're certainly not the first, or the last, no matter what your situation.

There are an infinite amount of variables that could affect you and your life after the journey through divorce. I'm sure you've already figured out that those of you without kids have it really easy. You don't have to deal with things like splitting of holidays, complicated birthday parties, and joint school functions.

Speaking of holidays, I've got some suggestions that have really helped me. Basically, you don't need to hold your holiday celebrations on the actual holiday. I first saw this work when I was a pre-teen. My mom comes from a family of six kids. As time progressed and more of her siblings married and had families of their own, it became a major pain in the ass to get everyone together on holidays. It was always dramatic trying to arrange the schedules of six siblings, their spouses, and the increasing number of grandkids. So, we began having family celebrations the weekend before or after a particular holiday.

For example, if Christmas fell on a Tuesday, we'd have a huge get-together the Saturday before, which was December 22. It worked extremely well. This new plan turned out to be much better than when we tried to hold the family functions on the actual holiday because everyone could come. To this day, these pre-holiday celebrations are some of my best childhood memories about visiting family and playing with my many cousins.

This system has also worked well for me since getting divorced. For example, the first Easter following my divorce, my son woke up at my ex's house. I admit it was a bit weird, but I was able to make it work out quite well. I bought my son a few toys and called him early on Easter morning. I asked him how the Easter Bunny knew to bring him toys to both his mom's house and my house.

He got so excited over the phone. Rather than feeling weird and sad about spending his first Easter without his mom and dad together, he was fixated on the fact that the Easter Bunny had brought him presents at both homes. When I saw him later he had such a glow on his face from the excitement. He stood looking amazed at his pile of presents in my living room.

And back to the Christmas example. Here's something that really helped in my post-divorce life. After my divorce was final, I eventually did meet a woman I wanted to seriously date. She had a little girl about two years younger than my son, and my son and her daughter quickly became inseparable. It was actually very cute to watch them bond. Within several months, they were referring to each other as brother and sister.

But a year later, when Christmas came around, it was a challenge trying to arrange schedules with both of our exes. It wasn't a confrontational situation; it was simply the reality faced by divorced parents—shared holidays.

I subsequently took from the lessons learned by my mom's side of the family and their aforementioned holiday celebrations. My girlfriend and I chose the Saturday before each Christmas as our own little family celebration. I know it sounds unorthodox, but open your mind and follow me for a minute.

Does it really matter if you celebrate Christmas (or any other holiday for that matter) on the exact day? I discovered that it really doesn't. Here's how it worked for us.

About two weeks before Christmas, I would pretend to be Santa as I disguised my voice and made a phone call to the kids when they were together. Most of the time, I would just step out and call from my cell phone, and the kids never once noticed I was gone for those few minutes. I'd simply place a handkerchief over the telephone and disguise my voice so it sounded like I was far away. (obviously calling from the North Pole! Ha!) It always worked like a charm.

My girlfriend would answer the phone and immediately summon the kids because Santa was calling to talk with them! Acting as Santa, I'd tell both kids that I'd make a "special trip" just for them on the Friday night before Christmas so they could open their presents together. You should have seen their faces; they had smiles hanging from ear-to-ear and were bouncing off the walls with excitement.

This tradition of celebrating Christmas the Friday night or Saturday morning before December 25th will become the norm in my new family. Everyone really loved it—my girlfriend, our kids, and even our exes. My ex-wife and my girlfriend's ex-husband were obviously happy because they got to have the kids on the real Christmas Eve and Christmas morning. It was also very healthy for the kids because they were no longer forced to split their Christmas days.

And a nice little side benefit was that my girlfriend and I made it our own tradition to leave and go somewhere alone on the actual Christmas Eve and Christmas Day. It was great because there were no crowds.

In the end, our kids basically got two Christmas morning celebrations. And especially important is the fact that they'll always have memories of Christmas mornings together. It makes no difference to them that it's not the actual Christmas Day. In fact, it makes the kids feel more special because they get two trips from Santa while most kids only get one.

This example is exactly what I mean when I speak of thinking outside the box. Be creative in your post-divorce life. It's because of innovative thinking like this that I'm living a far better life out of the ashes of my divorce.

To this day, it can literally bring tears to my eyes when I think about my journey and what it has done for my life. I close this book just over two years from that initial day when I moved out into my little one-bedroom divorce pad. I'll never forget that day as long as I live.

As I approach the end of this book, I cannot end it without sharing one final story. It's about a child's birthday party I attended. The kid belonged to my good buddy, Dean. Dean had been divorced for about three years at the time and had two children—a boy, 9, and a girl, 4. This party was for his 9-year-old.

Dean and his ex got along well, so they decided to have a joint birthday party. I actually commend their actions as a divorced couple. Dean's ex-wife, Lisa, had gotten remarried about six months prior. Dean got along pretty well with Lisa's new husband. I met him at the party and he seemed like a good dude.

Dean also had a serious girlfriend he'd been dating for about 18 months. The entire situation was really one of those perfect images of both new families coming together for the good of the children—a truly elevated perspective.

The party was at Dean's house. He'd spent some time and money fixing up his house for the event. A few other buddies and I actually helped Dean with some trips to the dump and a few minor home repairs. His house actually looked really nice.

They ordered a "jumpy" and hired a clown. The party was in the typical boy theme of *Star Wars*. They gave out cheap plastic light sabers to all the kids. By the way, don't ever throw a party full of boys amped up on candy and cake a then give them a bunch of plastic sticks. I think most adults at the party got wacked several times as they crossed the paths of Padwan Jedi deep in battle.

It really was a nice party. Dean's son was so excited the entire day leading up to the party that Dean almost had to give him Benadryl to calm him down before the guests arrived. (I know none of us fathers have ever done anything like that to calm a wild child!)

As for the weather, the day couldn't have been more perfect. It was April and about 80 degrees with a slight breeze. The grass was a deep green and the sky a bright blue. Everyone arrived at about 1:00 p.m.

From the start, each and every kid has a blast. One kid even got a bloody lip from a wayward light saber, and another threw up from bouncing so much in the jumpy. Hey, what's a party without blood and puke, even when it's a little kid's party!

So, there I was, standing with Dean as we perused the crowd. Dean began telling me how he felt a bit nostalgic watching everyone interacting. It was a bit odd to see his ex-wife and her new husband sitting with Dean's buddies and family members. Everyone was drinking, telling jokes, and laughing in the backyard. It was interesting to see my friend ponder the situation in such deep thought. Remember, we as men are far from the cavemen society likes to portray us as.

Everything was going really well for the first few hours; that is, until one of Dean's busybody family members made some inappropriate comments to his girlfriend. To this day, I'll never understand why some people feel it necessary to be bitchy and stir the drama pot. Dean later relayed to me that the conversation had unfolded something like this:

Family Member:	*"So how long have you and Dean been dating?"*
Girlfriend:	*"About 18 months."*
Family Member:	*"Well, do you think that's enough time for you to have moved in?* [Dean's girlfriend had actually moved in with him a few months prior.] *That's not good for the kids, and it's certainly not seen well in the eyes of God."*
Girlfriend:	*"I don't know why you're asking me about something that's none of your business. I think you should talk with Dean about this if you have problems with our decision."*
Family Member:	*"Okay"* [in a very sarcastic tone].

Dean's girlfriend walked away after being devastated by the conversation. As you can imagine, she had put forth a lot of time, effort, and money into the party. She and Dean were already on edge. They were apprehensive about bringing together everyone for the first time.

Dean and his girlfriend had also prided themselves on the way they initially eased his kids into their new relationship. (she didn't have any kids at the time) I personally witnessed Dean have numerous conversations with people about how to properly blend a family. He also read several books and researched the topic thoroughly.

Dean's girlfriend did her best to brush off the comments and enjoy the party, but even I could tell she was affected. There were a few other minor little difficulties. However, besides that brief confrontation, the party was a great hit. The kids had a blast, the adults had a blast, and with one exception, everyone got along great.

I share this story because it's a great example of how outside influences can really affect your post-divorce life. Dean, his girlfriend, his ex-wife, and her new husband all tried to do what was best for the kids. They worked together and acted like true adults. However, one big mouth had to try to get in the way.

Simply because your journey through divorce may be over, it doesn't mean your life is free of confrontation and relationship problems. It may not even be a problem between you and your ex. Think outside the box as you ponder what curve balls might possibly be thrown your way.

In the end, divorce has made me so much stronger than I ever imagined possible. Although I never served in the military, I think I now understand the concepts of military training. The first phase of Military Basic Training involves the instructors literally beating down the recruits. They degrade the trainees to their absolute weakest point. They want them to see just how far down they can go, to push the young men and women to the very bottom of their physical, mental, and emotional limits.

But then the instructors begin building them back up. They make the recruits part of a team, a brotherhood, and a tradition of excellence. Young men and women gain strength from those low moments and learn they have true intestinal fortitude to overcome tragedy and pain. But before they gain this amazing strength, they have no choice but to endure the pain.

I think the parallels between military training and divorce are very apparent. From "Face it, You're Gonna be a Bastard" to "After The Journey: Your New Life," divorce has been the single most inspirational experience of my life. It took me from my lowest point ever to a total and complete rebirth of my very soul. I know it sounds melodramatic, but it's ever so true. Divorce is a very melodramatic experience.

The Thesaurus lists the following words as synonyms of "melodramatic:"

- Historic
- Overdramatic

- Overemotional
- Over the top
- Exaggerated
- Sensational
- Theatrical

My divorce was all of these words and more. So I guess "melodramatic" is most appropriate. Remember, just because your journey may be over, don't ever forget your personal experience. Your divorce should forever be a part of you, so please don't fight the memories.

Here's one final movie analogy to stress my closing points. It's a bit lengthy, but I hope you'll read it with an open mind. There's a very important moral at the end of the story.

The clip comes from the film *Uncommon Valor*. If you've never seen the movie, I highly recommend it. It's a great story about courage, commitment, and friendship. Put this movie on your list for those depressed days when you're cuddling with the cat and a box of Kleenex.

The film takes place in 1982 and stars Gene Hackman as a Korean War veteran whose son went Missing In Action (MIA) in Vietnam ten years prior. It's painfully clear that Hackman is a man obsessed with not knowing what happened to his son.

Early in the movie, Hackman discovers information that his son and several other Americans may still be alive and held as POWs in Vietnam. Hackman quickly develops a plan for a secret mercenary mission to rescue his son and the others.

Hackman forms his team with five veterans from his son's former unit in Vietnam. Each of these five men had since left the service and assimilated into civilian life. However, the film does a great job of portraying how each man remains haunted by memories of the war. Hackman uses these horrific memories to persuade each man into joining his rescue mission. Once the team is assembled, Hackman has the men brought to a secret training facility to prepare for their mission.

One night, after a long day of intense training, the men bed down on Army cots inside of primitive wooden barracks. Suddenly, in the middle of the night, one of the men (played by Fred Ward) wakes from a bad dream. Ward is sweating profusely and breathing heavily as he wraps himself in a woolen military blanket. He then walks out of the barracks and sits down in the middle a nearby open field.

The camera pans to Hackman standing on the small wooden porch of the barracks. Another man, "Woolsey," is also standing on the porch and he begins talking with Hackman as they stare at Ward sitting in the field about a 100 yards away. Woolsey tells Hackman about the one incident in Vietnam that caused Ward's reoccurring nightmares:

> *"One day he [Ward] went into a tunnel by himself. It was pitch black inside and he got startled by two people. He knifed 'em up quick—killed 'em deader than shit. The tunnel then collapsed and he's trapped down there with these two dead bodies. He lights a match and discovers he's killed a woman and her kid. He's then stuck with their dead bodies lying over him while he waits for us to dig him out."*

Hackman then begins walking through the field toward Ward, stopping several feet behind where Ward is seated. The stage is set for one old soldier to try to console another.

Hackman initiates the conversation by softly telling Ward, *"You know, I couldn't sleep for years after Korea. The ground was so frozen we couldn't even bury our dead. All we could do was lash their bodies to the sides of our tanks. They would just stare back at you—those dead frozen faces."*

Fighting back the tears, Ward asked Hackman, *"Did the memories ever go away?"*

Hackman assertively replies, *"No, they never did. But eventually I learned to make friends with those dead frozen faces."*

It was clear that Hackman was telling Ward to make friends with the faces of the dead woman and her son he had killed.

I draw a striking comparison between this scene and the experience of divorce. You should look at your divorce memories much like these men remember their experiences from war. I know my divorce will never leave my memory. Although I don't dwell on it daily, there are so many times when a song, a certain smell, a particular time of year, or just looking into my son's eyes will bring back strong memories of the experience.

But because I don't want to ever repeat the mistakes I made, I'm actually thankful for these memories. I look at them as a gift. As strange as it may sound, my divorce experience has shaped me into a far better man, father, friend, lover, son, and brother than would have ever been possible had I remained married. Therefore, I consider these painful memories some of my best friends ever.

In closing, your journey may be over, but your life goes on. It's now up to you—and only you—to write the rest of your story…

Finish the Journey; A Man's Guide through Divorce

Bibliography / Reference Materials

This Bibliography is slightly more detailed than many others you may have seen. As I mentioned early in this book, I'm but an average man who became obsessed with my divorce and building a better life from the experience. All of the information I've learned—and now share with you—came from the true experts in various fields. Below is a detailed list of all my sources, along with a brief explanation of how each reference may best aid you in your individual quest for self-discovery and personal growth.

It is important to stress that, many of the comments listed under each resource are my own observations and details about how I personally believe each work may assist divorcing men. These comments do not reflect the views of my publisher and/or any organization directly related to each individual source. As always, my recommendations are subjective in nature. I strongly encourage each of my readers to independently explore these selected readings to form their own opinion of the source.

You may also notice my heavy reliance on online sources/references. This is in keeping with my goal of providing information that is easily accessible to all men. However, I must stress that online sources should always be verified by more official and/or a published reference—especially when the information is being used for legal advice.

Printed Resources

Bradley Berry, Dawn. *The Divorce Sourcebook* (McGraw-Hill Companies, 2006)

Comments: (Divorce; Separation; Legal) Borders.com describes this book as, "In The Divorce Sourcebook, Dawn Bradley Berry, a research attorney and legal consultant, explains everything you need to know to protect yourself and your family, and she supplements her expert advice with real-life stories of divorce, including that of her own." I personally found the book to be rather long (and sometimes a bit dry), but it definitely provides a lot of insight into divorce—especially the legal aspects.

Byrne, Rhonda. *The Secret* (New York, NY: Simon & Schuster, 2006)

Comments: (Self-Help; Self-Improvement) I really enjoyed this book on CD. It has many contributors who share the "The Secret" of success in every aspect of life. (physical, mental, emotional, spiritual, financial, relationships, etc.) You'll begin to understand the hidden and untapped power that's within you. This revelation can often bring joy to every aspect of your life. This is a great book so long as you're open to the metaphysical and spiritual side of life.

Clapp, Genevieve. *Divorce and New Beginnings* (New York, NY: Wiley, John & Sons, Incorporated, 2000)

Comments: (Self-Help; Divorce Guidance) Regarding this book, Borders website reads: *"The first edition of Divorce and New Beginnings helped countless men and women emerge from ruptured relationships and build new lives. Enriched with new insights uncovered by researchers and in the author's work with over 2,000 families, this sensitive guidebook provides a wealth of proven coping skills to help you weather the difficult times and eventually build new beginnings— for yourself and, if you have them, your children."* This book is filled with some great guidance—especially when it comes to helping your parent your children through divorce.

Cloud, L.C. *Teacup Daddy* (New York: iUniverse, 2006)

Comments: (A Novel) Based on the story of a man who married a woman with a child—a little girl. He became the girl's loving father, only to lose her in a divorce. (not many states recognize the rights of step-parents following divorce) A sad but inspirational read about the true love of a modern-day father.

Crenshaw, Theresa. *The Alchemy of Love and Lust* (New York, NY: Simon & Schuster, 1997)

Comments: (Psychology; Sex; Relationships) This is definitely an interesting and well-written book. One critique indicated, "*Written by a renowned sex therapist, The Alchemy of Love and Lust unmasks the hidden agendas of our hormones through the different sexual stages. Going beyond testosterone and estrogen, Dr. Crenshaw explores the potent influences of many different hormones and gives substance to the age-old idea of chemistry between the sexes, making for an enticing mix of romance and sex."*

DeAngelo, David. *Double Your Dating* (an online book. I downloaded the 2006 version) http://www.doubleyourdating.com/

Comments: I thoroughly enjoyed DeAngelo's direct and informative writing style. He offers a wealth of insight into meeting women, navigating the complexities dating, and enjoying an overall success with women. DeAngelo also offers several other e-books, along with many articles and on-line bits of information. A must for any man who is anxious about re-entering the dating world, or simply wanting to add more ammunition to their dating arsenal.

Deida, David. *It's a Guy Thing; An Owner's Manual for Women* (Deerfield Beach, Fl: Health Communications, Inc, 1997)

Comments: (Relationships; Self-Help; Psychology) An enjoyable read that details many of the differences between men and women, along with how to find common ground in a relationship. The book is actually written as a guide for women to better understand. But I found the book to be very beneficial to help men and women understand each other.

Handley, Robert. *Anxiety and Panic Attacks, Their Causes and Cure* (Ballantine Books, 1985)

Comments: (Self-Help; Psychology) This is one of my favorite books for those who are suffering form excessive anxiety—or even worse, panic attacks. Handley speaks from the experience of having personally suffered from an extreme form of anxiety, known as "Agoraphobia." His book is easy to follow and provides a great system to overcome worry and fear.

Katie, Byron. *Loving What Is.* (New York: Three Rivers Press, 2002)

Comments: (Self-Help; Inspirational) I believe this book to be one of the best "self-help" books available. I prefer authors who've lived a certain experience and can now share their own individual journey to personal success. Katie's story is amazing and inspirational, and she shares her knowledge in an easy-to-follow work that can provide true life-changing information.

Kubler-Ross, Elisabeth. *On Death and Dying* (New York, NY: Simon & Schuster, 1969)

Comments: (Self-Help; Grief; Inspirational) Although this book is known primarily as a guide to help people confront the death of a loved one, and/or one's own terminal illness, it is also a great resource for anyone facing a life-altering-event—such as a divorce. It is a great book to help us comprehend a process for dealing with grief.

Orman, Suzy. *The Courage to be Rich*: *Creating a Life of Material and Spiritual Abundance* (East Rutherford, NJ: Penguin Group (USA) Incorporated, 1999)

Comments: (Financial Advice; Self-Help) Orman's website describes the book as: *"Practical, spiritual and above all soundly financial, The Courage to Be Rich addresses the rites of passage we all must face—marriage, divorce, death, spending (and overspending), and taking control of our financial tomorrow's today. The Courage to Be Rich shows you how to find the clarity, conviction and courage to meet the obstacles and opportunities of a lifetime."* I wholeheartedly concur with this quote and highly recommend the book.

Rose-Kingma, Daphnie. *Coming Apart: Why Relationships End and How to Live Through the Ending of Yours* (Newburyport, MA: Red Wheel/Weiser, 2000)

Comments: (Self-Help; Self-Improvement) This has become one of my favorite books regarding the emotional suffering caused by divorce. It provides soothing words and guidance that brings the reader to a higher level of understanding. I highly recommend this book.

Straus, Neil. *The Game, Penetrating the Secret Society of Pickup Artists* (New York, NY: Regan Books, 2005)

Comments: One of the best dating reads, ever! Neil Strauss tells the true story of his years penetrating the secret society of male pickup artists. The information contained is truly amazing. It's no wonder the book has the cover and appearance of a bible. If you want to learn tried, true, and unwavering techniques to pick-up women, read The Game!

Washak, Richard Dr. *Divorce Poison, Protecting the Parent-Child Bond from a Vindictive Ex* (New York, NY: HarperCollins Publishers, 2003)

Comments: (Psychology; Family; Divorce; Separation) If you have children, I consider this book to be a must. Even if you and your ex have a cordial relationship, this book still provides you with many of the warning signs of future problems that could develop between you, your ex, and possibly your children. Although the book is a bit long—and at times somewhat dry—I've found the information it provides to be essential.

Wylie, Philip. *Generation of Vipers* (New York, NY: Holt, Rinehart & Winston, 1955)

Comments: (Social Sciences) Borders Books writes: "*Perhaps the most vitriolic attack ever launched on the American way of living—from politicians to professors to businessmen to Mom to sexual mores to religion.*" I personally found this a fascinating read about evolving cultural norms and how family history affects personal development.

Online Resources

Alllaw.com.

http://www.alllaw.com

Comments: Links to resources, information, and links about the legal aspects of divorce. Cited specifically for their online child support calculators.

Center for Divorce Mediation and Training.

http://www.divorcemediation.com/index.cfm

Comments: Provides links, resources and information about many aspects of divorce mediation.

Depression.com.

www.depression.com

Comments: Details links and resource for those suffering from varying levels of depression.

Divorce Info.com.

http://www.divorceinfo.com/

Comments: Provides links, resources and information about divorce mediation.

Divorce Magazine.com.

http://www.divorcemag.com

Comments: Provides many resources, information, and links about the legal aspects of divorce.

Divorce Rate.com.

http://www.divorcerate.com

Comments: A good site for statistical data and links to the most current divorce resources—such as finding an attorney, obtaining emotional support, various divorce trends, etc.

Find Law.com.
http://family.findlaw.com
Comments: Provides links, resources and information about many aspects of divorce. Specifically quoted regarding family law and mediation.

Geocities.com.
www.geocities.com/beyond_stretched/**holmes**.htm
Comments: A link to an online version of the 1967 Holmes & Rahe Life Changes Scale.

Helpguide.org, A Trusted Non-Profit Resource.
http://www.helpguide.org
Comments: An informative website with links to all types of self-help resources; to include abuse and addictions, ADD/ADHD, anxiety, biopolar disorder, depression, eating disorders, grief and loss, stress and trauma, etc. I specifically quoted information about the fear response "Fight or Flight."

Mayo Clinic.com.
http://www.mayoclinic.com
Comments: A search engine and links to hundreds of physical, mental, and emotional conditions.

National Institute of Mental Health.
http://www.nimh.nih.gov/index.shtml
Comments: Provides links and resource for those suffering from varying levels of medical conditions.

Pristiq.com.
http://www.pristiq.com/
Comments: This is the official website of the antidepressant medication Pristiq. It contains information and resources about depression and its treatment.

San Diego County Superior Court.
http://www.sdcourt.ca.gov/portal/page?_pageid=55,1524349&_dad=portal&schema=PORTAL
Comments: Used to obtain information about child support—contains an online child support calculator.

United States Department of Veteran's Affairs.
www.mentalhealth.va.gov/MENTALHEALTH/ptsd/Help.asp
Comments: Used to obtain detailed information of regarding Post Traumatic Stress Disorder.

Us Department of Health and Human Services.
http://www.hhs.gov/ocr/privacy/index.html
Comments: Specifically cited regarding the Health Insurance Portability and Accountability Act of 1996 (HIPAA) Privacy Rule.

Women's Health.com:
http://www.womenshealth.com/home
Comments: Quoted for statistical data regarding sexually transmitted diseases.

Printed in the United States
By Baker & Taylor Publisher Services

Printed in the United States
by Baker & Taylor Publisher Services